STEPS
IN
COMPOSITION

STEPS
IN
COMPOSITION

LYNN QUITMAN TROYKA

JERROLD NUDELMAN

Queensborough Community College
of the City University of New York

PRENTICE-HALL, INC., ENGLEWOOD CLIFFS, NEW JERSEY

31103

© 1970 by Lynn Quitman Troyka and Jerrold Nudelman.

PRENTICE-HALL INTERNATIONAL, INC., *London*
PRENTICE-HALL OF AUSTRALIA, PTY. LTD., *Sydney*
PRENTICE-HALL OF CANADA, LTD., *Toronto*
PRENTICE-HALL OF INDIA PRIVATE LTD., *New Delhi*
PRENTICE-HALL OF JAPAN, INC., *Tokyo*

TO OUR STUDENTS, WHO GAVE US
THE MOTIVATION TO START THIS BOOK;

TO DAVID TROYKA, WHO GAVE US
THE DETERMINATION TO FINISH IT.

PREFACE

Composition is not a dead subject. It is as lively as the latest rock music and as contemporary as manned space exploration. In this book the major basic skills of grammar, rhetoric, vocabulary, and spelling are put into a framework of current, controversial issues which reflect the vitality of modern living.

Some students say, "I never liked to write because I had nothing to say." With this in mind, we center each of the twelve chapters around a different major issue of today's world. Topics range from computer dating to drug addiction, from student protest to poverty. Each chapter opens with *Springboards to Thinking*, which may include photographs, cartoons, a questionnaire, song lyrics, and art works. All of these are designed to stimulate the student's thinking on the particular topic. This section is followed by an appropriate essay written by such authors as Martin Luther King, Max Shulman, and Margaret Mead. The accompanying *Reading Survey* encourages the student to explore the issue further as he checks his skill in reading and understanding main ideas, major details, inference, and opinions.

The next section of each chapter gives the student the opportunity to build and enrich his *vocabulary*. A special feature is that the vocabulary words presented are clustered around the major issue being discussed in the chapter. The student will be able to learn and practice, for example, the vocabulary of social change, the vocabulary of civil rights, and the vocabulary of apathy. The definitions given are simple and functional, and the exercises are designed to confirm the learning. Each chapter also includes a section on *spelling*, which can help the student to gain strength both in the spelling of troublesome "Demons" and in the mastery of useful spelling rules and patterns. So that the practice will be entertaining as well as useful, many of the spelling exercises are modeled after the puzzles and brain teasers that most students enjoy doing. Another special feature is that the vocabulary and spelling words are repeated throughout the book, providing a hidden form of reinforcement.

At the heart of each chapter is a section that presents one or two *grammatical or rhetorical steps* to writing a successful composition. The key steps discussed are: how to write an effective topic sentence; how to develop a paragraph fully and in a logical order; how to write mature, rich sentences rather than sentence fragments, comma splices, and run-ons; how to insure correct verb and pronoun agreement; how to apply paragraph principles to the writing of an expository essay—with special attention given to its introduction and conclusion; how to avoid being illogical; how to use punctuation correctly; how to write a unified essay; how to use the right word; how to use parallelism and other techniques of sentence logic effectively; and, finally, how to write three of the most frequently assigned types of expository essays: explaining a process, constructing a definition, and arguing an opinion.

Complicated grammatical terminology and minor rules are avoided in favor of simple, direct explanations that divide the major rules into uncomplicated steps which will not overwhelm the student. So that he can immediately try out the skill presented, short participatory sections called *You Do This* are generously sprinkled throughout the explanations. Always, the student is an active part of the learning process. The longer exercises which follow the explanations may require the student to complete, rewrite, or create a sentence of his own; but he is never asked merely to put a check mark next to the correct answer. Through new types of exercises which are participatory, what a student learns and practices can be more easily transferred to what he writes when he is faced with a blank piece of paper. The *Refresher*, the last exercise in each chapter, gives the student a chance to practice skills learned in previous chapters so that he can continue to use and polish his skills as he goes along.

The last section of each chapter, *Springboards to Writing*, invites the student to use his newly learned skills by writing an essay on the major issue presented in the chapter. A comprehensive list of suggested topics is given. In addition, if he prefers, the student can explore the full range of his reactions to the *Springboards to Thinking* section and the essay of the chapter.

Although each of the twelve chapters follows this same structured plan, it is possible to rearrange the sequence or skip certain sections to suit personal needs and preferences. A further individualized feature of this book is that the student may transfer the pages of the text to a binder and, in addition, can use looseleaf paper of a matching size for his notes, his individual spelling or vocabulary lists and, if desirable, his daily journal. Such a procedure would further implement the participatory nature of the text.

In designing this book we have kept in mind that ideas must matter to a student before he will write well. Therefore, this book attempts to make issues relevant, expression imperative, and mechanics a means to an end.

New York, 1970   *Lynn Quitman Troyka*

                                                      Jerrold Nudelman

ACKNOWLEDGMENTS

Our project is due in no small part to our many friends and colleagues who were generous with their advice. We especially thank:

Dean George Alterman, of Queensborough Community College of the City University of New York, who first encouraged our attempt;

Jim Krueger, who was always ready to give us his time and the benefit of his experience;

Gary Wolfe, Carol Reilly, and Rita Kaye Schwartz, whose fine artistic skills added vitality to this project;

William H. Oliver, English Editor, and Mrs. Robb Heinemann, Production Editor, who were tactful and enthusiastic in their editorial reinforcement of our purpose.

CHAPTER **one**

CHAPTER **two**

CHAPTER **seven**

CHAPTER **eight**

CHAPTER **nine**

CHAPTER **ten**

STEPS
IN
COMPOSITION

DATE FINDER
BY COMPUTER

Just fill in the questions given, send $5, and you'll receive the names of five people who are matched to you scientifically—by computer!

1. age _____   4. sex _____

2. height _____   5. hair color _____

3. weight _____

    Answer using numbers: (1) often (2) sometimes (3) seldom (4) never

DO YOU

6. Watch television _____   9. smoke _____

7. read books _____   10. read newspapers _____

8. drink _____

QUALITIES:

11. The qualities I look for in a date are (check as many as apply)
- [ ] loyalty [ ] intelligence [ ] mystery [ ] generosity
- [ ] money [ ] sex [ ] humor [ ] honesty

12. I feel most comfortable with people who are (check as many as apply)
- [ ] optimistic [ ] pessimistic [ ] suave [ ] religious
- [ ] artistic [ ] dogmatic [ ] articulate [ ] athletic

13. Most people think that I am (check as many as apply)
- [ ] a swinger [ ] fickle [ ] shy [ ] harsh
- [ ] an atheist [ ] an agnostic [ ] intellectual [ ] frugal
- [ ] strong [ ] sexy [ ] tactful [ ] gullible
- [ ] delicate [ ] brave [ ] a werewolf [ ] a wench
- [ ] compatible [ ] a gourmet [ ] a romanticist [ ] conformistic

OPINIONS:

14. Would you rather: [ ] dance [ ] read [ ] go to the movies
15. The age group I prefer to date is: [ ] my age [ ] somewhat older [ ] younger [ ] much older
16. I feel that premarital sex is alright: [ ] yes [ ] no [ ] it depends
17. Dutch dating is alright: [ ] always [ ] occasionally [ ] never
18. My dreams are: [ ] to be rich [ ] to be happy [ ] to be popular [ ] to be famous [ ] to be artistic [ ] to be loved
19. I am willing to date someone: [ ] of another religion
    [ ] from another city
    [ ] of another race
    [ ] from another country
20. I consider myself: [ ] attractive [ ] average [ ] somewhat homely [ ] exciting [ ] quiet [ ] awkward [ ] stable [ ] nervous [ ] unhappy

FIND YOUR IDEAL MATE
or
MEET YOUR IDEAL DATE

one

SPRINGBOARDS TO THINKING

For informal, not written, response . . . to stimulate your thinking

1. Fill in the sample questionnaire shown. Try to be as honest as possible. If you would prefer that no one see your answers, use your own private code or list your answers on a separate piece of paper.
2. What do you think of the questions that are asked? Did any questions confuse you? . . . embarrass you? . . . annoy you?
3. For any of these questions, did you think of answers which were not covered by the choices given? Does the filled-in questionnaire represent a complete picture of you? What else might have been asked which would help describe you—and others—better?
4. Does the use of a computer to arrange "matches" seem like a good idea to you? Do you think tests like this are reliable? Do you think that people should be required by law to take tests like this before they are allowed to get married?
5. Some people are horrified at the idea of using a computer for date matching. What do you think might be the basis for the worry? Do you think that there are any dangers for mankind in the use of computers for such things as finding a date? Why or why not?

Boy . . . Girl . . . Computer

GENE SHALIT

(1) Out of computers, faster than the eye can blink, fly letters stacked with names of college guys and girls—taped, scanned, checked, and matched. Into the mails speed the compatible pairs, into P.O. boxes at schools across the land. Eager boys grab their phones . . anxious coeds wait in dorms . . . a thousand burrrrrrrings jar the air . . . snow-job conversations start, and yesses are exchanged: A nationwild dating spree is on. Thousands of boys and girls who've never met plan weekends together, for now that punch-card dating's here, can flings be far behind? And oh, it's so right, baby. The Great God Computer has sent the word. Fate. Destiny. Go-go-go. Call it dating, call it mating, it flashed out of the minds of Jeff Tarr and Vaughn Morrill, Harvard undergraduates who plotted Operation Match, the dig-it dating system that ties up college couples with magnetic tape. The match mystique is here: In just nine months, some 100,000 collegians paid more than $300,000 to Match (and to its MIT foe, Contact) for the names of at least five compatible dates. Does it work? Nikos Tsinikas, a Yale senior, spent a New Haven weekend with his computer-Matched date, Nancy Schreiber, an English major at Smith. Result, as long date's journey brightened into night: a bull's-eye for cupid's computer.

(2) "How come you're still single? Don't you know any nice computers?"

(3) Perhaps no mother has yet said that to her daughter, but don't bet it won't happen, because Big Matchmaker is watching you. From Boston to Berkeley, computer dates are sweeping the campus, replacing old-fashioned boy-meets-girl devices; punch bowls are out, punch cards are in.

(4) The boys who put data in dating are Jeff Tarr and Vaughn Morrill, Harvard undergraduates. At school last winter, they and several other juniors—long on ingenuity but short on ingenues—devised a computer process to match boys with girls of similar characteristics. They formed a corporation (Morrill soon sold out to Tarr), called the scheme Operation Match, flooded nearby schools with personality questionnaires to be filled out, and waited for the response.

(5) They didn't wait long: 8,000 answer sheets piled in, each accompanied by the three-dollar fee. Of every 100 applicants, 52 were girls. Clearly, the lads weren't the only lonely collegians in New England. As dates were made, much of the loneliness vanished, for many found that their dates were indeed compatible. Through a complex system of two-way matching, the computer does not pair a boy with his "ideal" girl

unless he is also the girl's "ideal" boy. Students were so enthusiastic about this cross-check that they not only answered the 135 questions (Examples: *Is extensive sexual activity* [in] *preparation for marriage, part of "growing up?" Do you believe in a God who answers prayer?*), they even added comments and special instructions. *Yale*: "Please do not fold, bend, or spindle my date." *Vassar*: "Where, O where is Superman?" *Dartmouth*: "No dogs please! Have mercy!" *Harvard*: "Have you any buxom blondes who like poetry?" *Mount Holyoke*: "None of those dancing bears from Amherst." *Williams*: "This is the greatest excuse for calling up a strange girl that I've ever heard." *Sarah Lawrence*: "Help!"

(6) Elated, Tarr rented a middling-capacity computer for $100 an hour ("I couldn't swing the million to buy it"), fed in the coded punch cards ("When guys said we sent them some hot numbers, they meant it literally"), and sped the names of computer-picked dates to students all over New England. By summer, Operation Match was attracting applications from coast to coast, the staff had grown to a dozen, and Tarr had tied up with Data Network, a Wall St. firm that provided working capital and technical assistance.

(7) In just nine months, some 90,000 applications had been received, $270,000 grossed and the road to romance strewn with guys, girls, and gaffes.

(8) A Vassarite who was sent the names of other girls demanded $20 for defamation of character. A Radcliffe senior, getting into the spirit of things, telephoned a girl on her list and said cheerfully, "I hear you're my ideal date." At Stanford, a coed was matched with her roommate's fiancé. Girls get brothers. Couples going steady apply, just for reassurance. When a Pembroke College freshman was paired with her former boyfriend, she began seeing him again. "Maybe the computer knows something that I don't know," she said.

(9) Not everyone gets what he expects. For some, there is an embarrassment of witches, but others find agreeable surprises. A Northwestern University junior reported: "The girl you sent me didn't have much upstairs, but what a staircase!"

(10) Match, now graduated to an IBM 7094, guarantees five names to each applicant, but occasionally, a response sets cupid aquiver. Amy Fiedler, 18, blue-eyed, blonde Vassar sophomore, got 112 names. There wasn't time to date them all before the semester ended, so many called her at her home in New York. "We had the horrors here for a couple of weeks," her mother says laughingly. "One boy applied under two different names, and he showed up at our home twice!"

(11) Tarr acknowledges that there are goofs, but he remains carefree. "You can't get hung up about every complaint," says Tarr. "You've got to look at it existentially."

(12) Jeff, 5′ 7″, likes girls, dates often. "If there's some chick I'm dying to go out with," he says, "I can drop her a note in my capacity as president of Match and say, *Dear Joan, You have been selected by a highly*

personal process called Random Sampling to be interviewed extensively by myself.... and Tarr breaks into ingratiating laughter.

(13) "Some romanticists complain that we're too commercial," he says. "But we're not trying to take the love out of love; we're just trying to make it more efficient. We supply everything but the spark."

(14) Actually, computer dating supplies more. According to Dr. Benson R. Snyder, MIT's chief psychiatrist, it acts as a method that society condones for introducing a girl and a boy. "A boy knows that the girl has expressed her willingness to date by the act of joining. I think that's one of the most important things that it provides. It reduces the anxiety of the blind date; you know that the girl wants to go out with someone roughly like you."

(15) "However," warns Dr. Snyder, "if this is taken too seriously, and it becomes institutionalized, it could be seen as a pressure for a safe, conformistic approach. In all relationships, there is a need for the unexpected; even that which is a little anxiety-laden."

(16) With all the joys and ploys of computer dating, social life at sexually segregated schools in the Ivy League remains plenty anxiety-laden. At noncoed schools like Yale and Dartmouth, students lead lives of social isolation. Many are consumed by plans for weekend dates. "We try to pack a whole week into Friday and Saturday night," says a Princeton sophomore. "If we don't make out—if we don't sleep with the girl—the whole thing's a colossal failure."

(17) Comments a distinguished New York psychoanalyst: "Ivy League students are forced to behave like monk-scholars. When they're freed on weekends, they seek emotional release. Almost all college boys are psychological adolescents, with an overpowering need for companionship, and they cannot be expected to live in seclusion. It's no surprise that sexual relations are more and more common among college-aged boys and girls."

(18) "All-boy colleges create a climate for fantasy," says Carter Wiseman, a Yale sophomore. "Girls become unreal beings, so on the weekend, you try to force the reality to fit into the fantasy you've created, and it *won't work!*"

(19) "Getting dates down here for the weekend is a terrible waste of time," says John de Forest of Yale. "Hotel acccommodations for the girl, expenses, arrangements...trying to find a girl in the first place. That's why Match is here to stay. I approve of it as a way to meet people, although I have no faith in the questionnaire's ability to match compatible people. The machine has no way of telling whether or not the girl has pazazz!"

(20) But, Wiseman insists, "The odds of getting along with a girl are better if she's been screened by a computer. Say you're interested in Renaissance art, and the machine gives you a chick who's interested in Renaissance art, you've got a basis to build on. You can't just go up to some girl on the street and say, 'Hello, do you like Botticelli?'"

4

(21) "In midwinter, it's tough to meet a girl a couple of hundred miles away on any pretext whatever," says a snowbound Dartmouth senior. "Match is a great icebreaker: the girl will at least talk to you if you call."

(22) Even before boys telephone their matches, most girls have a line on them through Ivy-vine sources—tipsters at boys' schools and upper-class girls who've dated extensively. Lists are passed through the dorms, where girls pencil comments next to familiar names: *cool; hang up when he calls; swings; fink.*

(23) "What troubles me about all this computer jazz," says a sophomore at Connecticut College, "is my feeling that boys don't level when they fill in their questionnaires. I was honest with mine, but I wonder if some guys fill out theirs to see if they can get a first-nighter."

(24) "Boys want one kind of a girl to date, but someone quite different to marry," says a Mount Holyoke senior. "Guys are just out for a good time, but I don't know any girl who goes on a date without marriage crossing her mind. When college kids are together, the girl thinks: *'I wonder what it would be like to be married to this fellow?'* and the boy thinks, *'I wonder what it would be like to sleep with this girl?'* "

(25) "I don't see how the questionnaire can possibly result in compatible matches," says Ellen Robinson of Connecticut. "Guys don't care about attitudes and interests. They all want a blonde with a great figure. But if you must fill out a questionnaire, I think the one from Contact is better."

(26) She gets no argument from David DeWan, 22, the MIT graduate student who owns Contact, Match's principal rival in New England. "The Match questionnaire is unbeatable for national distribution," he says. "But in the Northeast, I can use a vocabulary that will be more effective than it would be in the Midwest. Phrases like *verbal fluency* and *aesthetic appreciation* sell far better at schools like Princeton and Harvard."

(27) DeWan, a brilliant math and engineering student, does not have an organization as sprawling or yeasty as Tarr's. In fact, he has no organization at all. A frugal man, he runs deep in the black: He has no full-time employees. His office is a room in his grandparents' home, near Cambridge. He uses a Honeywell 200 computer at three o'clock in the morning, when the rental is low. In one distribution of questionnaires, he drew 11,000 responses at four dollars each.

(28) DeWan has been going steady with a girl at Wellesley, so when he organized Contact, they put themselves to the test. Sure enough, the computer matched them. But the computer also matched her with an Amherst boy, who won her away. "It was very sad," says DeWan, "but it proved my system works. It found her a more compatible guy."

(29) "I think that's a riot," says Dr. Snyder, who invited DeWan to discuss the computer project at a meeting of the MIT psychiatric staff. "I was a little bit appalled by its *1984* overtones, but was much less concerned after we talked. Contact provides students with a chance to get over the initial hurdle of knowing that they're not going to be immediately rejected. At their age, it's often difficult to make the kind of small talk

5

that's so important at the initial stages of a relationship. My guess is that computer-matched people are more able to explore comfortably their interests. I think it's a useful social mechanism, but it would be misused if boys used it merely to make a connection for a sexual good time."

(30) "I don't know that Match and Contact can really work," gainsays Dr. Morris S. Davis, astronomer and director of the Yale Computer Center. "Until body chemistry can be inputed into the computer to simulate the actual reactions of two persons, I have my doubts concerning the efficacy of the method."

(31) Dr. Snyder agrees that the computer can't predict compatibility. "But it's not just chemistry," he insists. "It's because you can't program something as complicated as the whole cluster of feelings and associations that surround a boy's notion of what a girl ought to be. What a computer *can* do is increase the probability of a satisfactory relationship by removing incompatible persons."

(32) To test this theory, Christopher Walker, a senior at Yale, organized a dance for 200 college boys and girls, who were selected at random, matched by computer and tested before and after the dance. They spent time with their matches, then with dates they "picked up" during the dance's designated free period. Preliminary findings: Most had most fun with their "pickups." "If it turns out that way," says Walker, a psychology student who is a great admirer of Match, "it will be because a dance is a one-night stand, where the only thing that counts is physical attraction."

(33) Not everyone has faith in computers. At the University of Wisconsin, two enterprising graduate students, Glenn Weisfeld and Michael Rappaport, have a service called SECS—Scientific Evaluation of Compatibility Service. They offer a short questionnaire, charge one dollar, provide one date, and somehow, it works. Says Weisfeld, "We had our proudest moment when we were congratulated for makings SECS a four-letter word."

(34) Just the same, Tarr feels the future belongs to the computer. He's working on campus installations of hundreds of special typewriters, all linked to a centralized "mother computer." A boy, typing his requirements, will receive in seconds the name of a compatible girl on his campus who's free that night. Tarr is also organizing a travel service. On deck: a transatlantic cruise by an ocean liner packed with compatible couples. (Rejected name: *Ship of Fools*. Scene: night. The deck awash with moonlight. In the shadows, a boy sings, "Come To Me, My Correlated Baby." Below decks, in the salon, a girl murmurs, "How do I love thee? Let me count the punch cards.")

(35) Tarr already has outposts in New York, Chicago, Los Angeles, will soon go international, providing students summer dates all over Europe.

(36) Since collegians must fulfill each other's requirements, the questionnaire is designed to produce the profile of the applicant and the profile of the applicant's ideal date. Boys have discovered that there is more

to getting the girl of their daydreams than ordering a blonde, intelligent, wealthy, sexually experienced wench. They must also try to guess what kind of boy such a girl would request, then describe themselves to conform to her data. The future suggests itself: A boy answers the questions artfully. A girl does too. The computer whirs. They receive each other's name. Breathlessly, they make a date. They meet. They stop short. There they are: Plain Jane, and So-So-Sol. Two liars. But they are, after all, exactly alike, and they have been matched. It is the computer's moment of triumph.

READING SURVEY

1. Main Idea
What is the central theme of the essay?

2. Major Details
(a) Why do some psychiatrists express worry over the idea of computer-selected matches?
(b) Is it financially profitable to finance a computer dating service?
(c) According to the author of this essay, boys often have different expectations than girls do when on a date. What are they?

3. Inference
(a) Read paragraph thirteen again. Do you think that this explanation is logical? Now read paragraph thirty-one again. Do you think that this explanation is logical? Is there any difference between the two explanations? Explain.
(b) Read the last paragraph of the essay again. Is a touch of sadness intended? Why or why not?

4. Opinion
(a) Do you think that computer matching might lead to people not only fooling themselves, but also fooling others? Do most people prefer to live with what is real—reality—or with what is pretended—fantasy? Explain.
(b) Do you think that matching by computer could lead people to mistrust their judgments about others?

VOCABULARY BUILDING

Lesson Two: Words about People, Part I

I There are many words which describe people and their characteristics. Some of them appear in this essay:

compatible	(paragraph 1)
romanticist	(13)
conformistic	(15)
aesthetic	(26)
frugal	(27)
wench	(36)

If you get along well with people, you are *compatible* with others.

If you imagine things to be full of emotional adventure and hidden romance, you are a *romanticist*.

If you prefer, without question, to frequently adjust your ideas and behavior to fit in with a group of people, you are *conformistic*.

If you are artistic or if you appreciate beauty, you are an *aesthetic* person.

If you prefer not to spend money, you are *frugal*.

If you are a young woman of the servant—prostitute type, you are a *wench*.

EXERCISE 1A: Fill in the blank with the type of person.

1. He hates to part with any money. He is _____.

2. He loves to see beautiful paintings. He has an _____ appreciation of things.

3. He is easy to get along with; he is _____ with his friends.

4. She is quite a dish, that _____.

5. She loves to dream about romance and adventure. She is a _____

_____.

6. He likes to go along with the crowd. He is _____.

A SPECIAL NOTE: Can you think of someone, male or female, young or old, who fits each of the above descriptions? If so, associate that person with the word—it will help you to remember each word.

Name: _____ *Date:* _____

II Here are a few more words about people. These words do not appear in this essay, but they are convenient to use when discussing and writing about people.

egoist   demagogue   obsequious   pompous

If you always think of yourself first and see yourself as the center of all things, you are an *egoist*.

If you encourage discontent in society for the sole purpose of advancing yourself politically, you are a *demagogue*.

If you are overeager to please to the point of being sickeningly polite and servile, you are *obsequious*.

If you always act like a snob and think yourself superior, you are *pompous*.

EXERCISE 1B: Which type of person says each of these things?

1. "You're the best teacher I have ever had. You're good looking too. How would you like me to erase the board for you?"   _____

2. "Why don't you pay more attention to me? I can do it just as well as you can. Watch me!"   _____

3. "Everyone is enslaved in our society. Only I can break your bondage."   _____

4. "Listen you, I'm a movie star and I'm too busy to have time for someone like you."   _____

Lesson Two: Words about People, Part II

As you look around, you will notice many different types of people. Some you will dislike, while others you will like very much. Thinking about people is often easier when you know more words to describe their characteristics. Here are some words which appear on the computer dating form which you saw at the beginning of this chapter:

optimistic	**articulate**	**gourmet**	**gullible**
suave	**fickle**	**intellectual**	**werewolf**
dogmatic	**agnostic**	**tactful**	

He says that the glass is half full, not half empty because he always looks at the bright side; he is *optimistic*.

That man is very "smooth" with the ladies. He is *suave*.

That man is *dogmatic* when he insists on his point of view.

Because he is *articulate*, he speaks clearly and can always find the right words.

He is being *fickle* when his tastes change suddenly and quickly.

Only an *agnostic* feels that it is impossible to know if there is a God.

As a *gourmet* he enjoys good food which is prepared with delicate and artful tastes.

He enjoys *intellectual* activities of the mind.

In considering the other person and trying not to hurt anyone's feelings, he is being *tactful*.

He will believe anything you say because he is so *gullible*.

He is a *werewolf* because he is like a mythical man who, when the moon is full, turns into a monster wolf that likes to chase women.

EXERCISE 1C: Fill in the blank with the type of person.

1. He is very considerate in the way he says or does things. He is _____.

2. He is an overgrown, unpleasant beast with women. He is a _____.

3. He always sees the happy side of things. He is _____.

4. He believes the story that the moon is made of green cheese. He is _____.

5. He speaks very well. He is _____.

6. He knows how to handle women with style and ease. He is _____.

EXERCISE 1D: Which type of person says each of these?

1. "The sauce is so unusual and delicious."   _____

2. "I like to read and learn whenever I can."   _____

3. "Although people debate that question, I insist that there is only one correct point of view."   _____

4. "I'm really not sure whether God exists."   _____

5. "Last week I liked Joan. Yesterday I liked Shirley. But today I like Virginia."   _____

Name: _____ *Date:* _____

SPELLING

Lesson One: Spelling Demons

These commonly used words are frequently misspelled. You should give some special attention to the Spelling Demons in this and every chapter. The Demons listed below are taken from "Boy . . . Girl . . . Computer."

actually	congratulate	familiar	preparation
adolescent	create	fantasy	psychology
basis	difficult	guarantee	similar
brilliant	eager	interest	sophomore
characteristic	efficient	lonely	surprise
commercial	expense	personal	theory

Lesson Two: Methods to Improve Your Spelling

Although there are no particular rules to help you learn the Demons, there are some helpful techniques for memorizing these words and any others that you find troublesome. Read each of these technique suggestions and then try each one out for yourself. Become skilled through practice at using the techniques which you favor. You will benefit greatly.

A. KEEP AN INDIVIDUAL SPELLING LIST: Use the last page of a school notebook for your spelling list. Each time that you misspell a word add it to the list. Go back over these words in your spare time; it may be during lunch in the cafeteria or on the bus in the morning. The point is to make your word study a habit. After you have about fifteen words on your list, look at the types of errors which you always make. Most people make certain kinds of spelling mistakes, and you can probably diagnose your particular kind: it can be double letters, or vowels (using an *i* for an *e* and vice versa), or vowel combinations, or confusion of *v* and *f*. If a clear pattern of kinds of mistakes is not obvious, ask your instructor to take a look. Sometimes another observer can see trends that you might miss.

B. ENLARGE THE TROUBLE SPOT: If you forget the "d" in "knowledge," then enlarge the "d" when you write the word on your spelling list. Do the same with the "c" in "conscious" as a reminder of your trouble spot.
knowleDge   consCious

C. USE THE DICTIONARY: When you write, keep a dictionary nearby so so that you can quickly look up any problem words that you may want to use. It is important to find the correct spelling of a word *before* you actually write it; each time that you write a word incorrectly you re-

11

inforce the misspelling in your mind. Some students complain, "I need to know how to spell the word in order to find it in the dictionary. So what's the use?" You usually have a fairly good idea of how to spell the problem word; the confusion is centered in just one or two syllables—not the whole word. Thus, the search is not that difficult. When you find the word, it will be separated into syllables, making it easy for you to see clearly the part that was causing you trouble. After having looked up a word often enough, you will find that you have learned to spell it and do not need to look it up again.

D. LEARN THE PROPER PRONUNCIATION: Many words are misspelled because they are pronounced incorrectly. If you omit letters from words —such as quan*t*ity and proba*b*ly—when you say them, you are sure to do the same when you write them. If you add an "e" to "athletic" and "disastrous" when you speak, you will add the "e" when you write. Pronouncing "children" as "childern" will lead to writing it the same way. When you are not sure of how a word is pronounced, listen to it carefully whenever you hear it. Check the pronunciation in the dictionary or ask someone you can trust if you are still not crystal clear on the pronunciation of certain words.

E. DIVIDE THE WORD INTO SEPARATE PARTS: Identify compound words, roots, suffixes, and prefixes. Then divide the word into smaller parts that are easier to spell. For example, "knowledge" could be divided into "know" and "ledge." "Considerably" can be divided into "consider" and "ably."

F. USE FLASHCARDS: Instead of using a spelling list, you may prefer to use the flashcard method. Write the troublesome word—in large letters —on one side of a 3″ × 5″ index card. Concentrate on the word for a few minutes, and then turn the card over. When you can visualize the word on the blank side of the card, you have mastered it. As an alternate method, use one side of an index card for the word and the other side for its definition. When you want to study the word, first read the definition; then spell the word that goes with it, and turn the card over to check your spelling.

G. USE MEMORY TRICKS: Sometimes it is helpful to use little memory tricks to learn a word. To memorize "business" you might remember that bu*sin*ess is no sin. You would surely remember to put the "w" in "knowledge" if you realize that a person with knowledge must kno*w* a great deal. To memorize "stationery" remember that pap*er* is sta-tion*er*y and that you st*a*nd still when you are station*a*ry.

EXERCISE 1E: In each of the following Demons, circle the letter or letters that are likely to cause you trouble. Then recopy the word in the space provided, enlarging the trouble spot so that it stands out as a reminder.

1. sophomore _____   3. guarantee _____

2. congratulate _____   4. theory _____

Each of the following Demons contains another word in its spelling. Using this new word and the original Demon, compose a sentence that will help you to associate the two.

Example: dil*emma*   Emma is in a dilemma.

1. personal _____

2. surprise _____

3. adolescent _____

4. familiar _____

With the aid of a dictionary, divide these Demons into syllables.

1. interest _____   4. similar _____

2. preparation _____   5. characteristic _____

3. psychology _____   6. commercial _____

Six of the demons have double letters in them. Write them here and either circle or enlarge any letter(s) that seem to be difficult.

1. _____   4. _____

2. _____   5. _____

3. _____   6. _____

Name: _____ Date: _____

EXERCISE 1F: Unscramble the ten sets of jumbled letters to form the missing words in each sentence. If necessary, check your spellings with the list of Demons in this chapter.

1. LATINRILB   Intellectuals have great respect for ＿＿＿＿＿＿＿ thinkers.

2. GAREE   Many college students are ＿＿＿＿＿＿ to conform because they want to be part of the group.

3. YTNASAF   Walt Disney, a true romanticist with a great imagination, was the father of ＿＿＿＿＿＿＿＿.

4. NEXSEEP   Frugal Freddie is always worried about the ＿＿＿＿ ＿＿＿＿＿＿＿＿ of things.

5. SIBSA   The ＿＿＿＿＿＿＿ of a good diplomat is his ability to be tactful.

6. YENLOL   Because they are snobs, pompous people are often ＿＿＿＿＿＿＿＿.

7. LCAYLUTA   "Wench" is ＿＿＿＿＿＿＿ an old-fashioned word that is sometimes used to add a light tone to writing.

8. CEFNITEFI   John Kennedy will always be remembered as an articulate speaker and an ＿＿＿＿＿＿＿ administrator.

9. FLUDITFIC   Joe is so gullible that he finds it ＿＿＿＿＿＿＿ to recognize a lie when he hears one.

10. ERTACE   An aesthetic person may not be an artist himself, but he has a keen appreciation of what others ＿＿＿＿＿＿＿.

Name: ＿＿＿＿＿＿＿＿＿ Date: ＿＿＿＿＿＿＿

THE TOPIC SENTENCE

You will be writing many paragraphs and essays in college—both for your English classes and for your other subjects. Here are a few basic guides for writing. Follow them exactly and your writing will be clearer and more sensible than ever before.

(a) *One topic to a paragraph*: Always put only one main idea into a paragraph. In this way your points will stand out more clearly and your paragraph will have unity.

(b) *Start with a topic sentence*: Always begin each paragraph with a sentence that tells what the paragraph will be about. This sentence is called a *topic* sentence. It serves as an introduction to the paragraph. It reveals the topic of the paragraph. It tells the reader what to expect next in the paragraph.

A SPECIAL HINT: If you skim your eye through the essay, the reading of the topic sentences should provide a brief summary of the essay.

Here is an example of a paragraph that starts with a topic sentence and that contains only one main idea:

To call a girl and tell her that you have learned her number from a computer could be embarrassing. How might you put it? Could you say, "Univac sent me" or "I was having the most interesting conversation with a computer the other day when your name came up"? Neither approach sounds very casual.

☞ YOU DO THIS:

1. Underline the topic sentence.
2. Is there more than one main idea in the paragraph?

Here is another example of a paragraph. As you read it check to see if the two basic guides are followed:

A school football game is a good place to make new friends. Everyone who is there has the same interest in mind—to watch the game and to share with others the pleasure of rooting for the home team. This unifying spirit breaks down barriers between strangers. The noisy excitement makes it easy to talk and laugh with someone you have never met before. As you are watching the game, perhaps you prefer the beefy two-hundred pound tackle who blocks the other team every time, while the lovely creature seated to your left prefers the agile quarterback who passes the ball with bullet-like speed. A disagreement like that just might take a long time to argue—long enough, in fact, to get acquainted.

15

☞ YOU DO THIS:

1. Underline the topic sentence.
2. What is the main idea in the paragraph?
3. Is there anything in this paragraph which is not part of that main idea?

EXERCISE 1G: For each topic given below, write a topic sentence.

(a) Dating: _____

(b) Food: _____

(c) People: _____

(d) Cars: _____

(e) Outer Space: _____

A SPECIAL NOTE ABOUT TOPIC SENTENCES: The topic sentence limits and controls what you can discuss in the paragraph. For example, look at this topic sentence:

To call a girl and tell her that you have learned her number from a computer could be embarrassing.

In the paragraph which follows such a sentence, you can discuss only the *embarrassing* aspects of computer introductions. You cannot, in this paragraph at least, discuss the excitement of meeting strangers or the horror you experience when you think about the dehumanization of modern life. Each of these topics would need a separate paragraph.

☞ YOU DO THIS:

1. Write two things which come to your mind about football games.

(a) _____

(b) _____

Name: _____ Date: _____

2. Now look at the following topic sentence:

A school football game is a good place to make new friends.

Can the two things which you just wrote down be included in a paragraph that starts with such a topic sentence? (Remember: the topic sentence *limits and controls* what you can discuss in the paragraph.)

Can (a)? yes _____   no _____

Can (b)? yes _____   no _____

It will help you to remember that when you write a topic sentence, it must limit and control what follows. If a topic sentence is too general, the paragraph might go off in many directions at once. For example:

poor topic sentence (too general)	John F. Kennedy was one of the greatest men of all time.
better topic sentence (limits and controls)	One of the things that made President John F. Kennedy great was his concern for the poor people of the world.

☞ YOU DO THIS:

1. List two things that you might put into a paragraph which follows the better topic sentence above.

   _____

   _____

2. Could the following be put into a paragraph using the better topic sentence?

   Yes   *No*

   _____ _____ (a) food stamp program in West Virginia

   _____ _____ (b) visit to city of Berlin

   _____ _____ (c) summit conference with the Russians

   _____ _____ (d) the Peace Corps idea

Name: _____ Date: _____

EXERCISE 1H ESSAY ANALYSIS: Answer these questions about the essay "Boy . . . Girl . . . Computer."

1. What is the topic sentence of the fourth paragraph?

    _____

2. Is there anything in paragraph four which does not belong? Answer this question by remembering that the topic sentence must limit and control what is said in the paragraph. _____

3. What is the topic sentence of the fifth paragraph?

    _____

4. Is there anything in paragraph five which does not belong? _____
5. What is the topic sentence of paragraph thirty-four?

    _____

6. Is there anything in paragraph thirty-four which does not belong?

    _____

Name: _____ *Date:* _____

EXERCISE 1I: Revise each of the following topic sentences so that the main idea will limit and control the paragraph that will follow.

1. In recent years there have been many wonderful advances in science.

_____

_____

2. A college education has become very important in today's world.

_____

_____

3. Martin Luther King was one of the greatest men of all time.

_____

_____

4. Computers have many uses.

_____

_____

5. California borders on the Pacific Ocean.

_____

_____

EXERCISE 1J: Look back at the topics which you used in Exercise 1G and the topic sentences that you wrote for that exercise. Does each sentence limit and control the topic? If so, recopy it; if not, revise it. Use separate paper.

Name: _____ Date: _____

PARAGRAPH DEVELOPMENT: PART I

After you have (1) decided what topic to discuss in your paragraph and (2) written your topic sentence, you must write the rest of the paragraph. Here are a few basic guides which will help you to complete your paragraph properly.

(3) *Be careful not to repeat the topic sentence in other words*: It is dangerously easy to fall into the trap of repeating your topic sentence over and over again. The same idea repeated in new words is not paragraph *development*. The key is to DEVELOP your topic sentence.

(4) *Decide on your method of development first*: There are many ways to develop your main point. Some of the easiest are:

    (a) facts
    (b) examples
    (c) incident, anecdote, or story

Any of these will help you put the "meat on the bones" of your topic sentence. (Additional methods of development are presented in the next chapter.)

(a) Here is an example of a paragraph developed with *facts*:

The questions asked on a computerized dating service questionnaire vary from company to company. Of the five companies which are the most popular these days, three ask fifty questions or more, while the other two ask only about thirty questions. As for types of questions, it is intriguing to see that one of the longer questionnaires has devoted twenty-three questions to moral and sexual standards, while one of the shorter forms has assigned only two questions to that topic. All five questionnaires ask at least ten questions about educational background and cultural interest.

HINT: *facts* usually include numbers, statistics, or other things which can be proved.

☞ YOU DO THIS:

1. Underline the topic sentence.
2. Is there more than one main idea in the paragraph?
3. In your own words state two of the facts used to develop the paragraph.

EXERCISE 1K: Choose one of these topic sentences and develop it into a paragraph using *facts*.

1. This college has a varied curriculum.

2. I've lost touch with a great many of my high school friends.

3. While attending college, I spend most of my time studying.

(b) Here is an example of a paragraph developed with *examples*:

Different people like to spend their leisure time in different ways. Some like to watch a sporting event while others prefer to play ball or go skating. Some people like to dance to the gyrating rhythms of popular music, while others enjoy nothing as much as an excellent orchestra performance. Some people like to go to big parties, while others choose to spend their free time with a few close friends. When it comes to leisure time, there seem to be almost as many preferences as there are people.

☞ YOU DO THIS:

1. Underline the topic sentence.
2. Is there more than one main idea in the paragraph?
3. In your own words state two of the examples used to develop this paragraph.

EXERCISE 1L: Choose one of these topic sentences and develop it into a paragraph using *examples*.

1. There are many different types of people in my city.

2. This has been a year of significant news events.

3. Fads in dress are completely unpredictable.

(c) Here is an example of a paragraph developed with an *incident, anecdote, or story*:

I used to think that computers could never make a mistake, but now I know better. Once a friend of mine, who was an excellent student, was expecting a report of her final grades earned at the end of eleventh grade. Final grades were particularly important that semester because these would be the grades seen by college admission departments. When her report came she found that she had received three "D's" and two "C's." She was horrified and very upset. But as is typical of human nature, after a few hours she began to accept what had happened. Soon she began to recall some of the errors she might have made on her tests. Then, three days later, she received in the mail this notice printed in the squared letter type of computers:

DEAR STUDENT:
DUE TO AN ERROR IN OUR COMPUTER, ONE NAME WAS SKIPPED IN THE LISTING. NEVERTHELESS, THAT PERSON'S GRADES IN THREE OF THE FIVE SUBJECTS WERE LISTED. AS A RESULT, ALL REPORTS OF GRADES WERE THROWN OFF SEQUENCE. YOUR CORRECT GRADES APPEAR BELOW. WE ARE SORRY FOR ANY INCONVENIENCE THIS HAS CAUSED YOU.
HISTORY A   PHYSICS B   ENGLISH B   SPANISH A   MATH A

21

☞ **YOU DO THIS:**

1. Underline the topic sentence.
2. Is there more than one main idea in this paragraph?
3. In your own words explain why the incident supports the topic sentence.

EXERCISE 1M: Choose one of these topic sentences and develop it into a paragraph using an *incident*.

1. A car in the hands of a bad driver can be dangerous.

2. Once while on a date I found myself in a very embarrassing situation.

3. Some people have no manners at all.

EXERCISE 1N ESSAY ANALYSIS: Answer these questions about the essay "Boy ... Girl ... Computer."

1. Is paragraph five developed with facts, examples, or an incident?

   _____

2. Is paragraph eight developed with facts, examples, or an incident?

   _____

3. Is paragraph thirty-two developed with facts, examples, or an incident? _____

   dent? _____

4. What combination of methods is used to develop paragraph thirty-four? _____

   four? _____

EXERCISE 10: Using the three types of paragraph development, write the following essay on your own paper. Choose one of the four topics given.

The Pressures of Being . . . A Teenager
                        . . . A College student
                        . . . A Parent
                        . . . A Consumer

   I. Introduction
  II. One Pressure (you select)
 III. Another Pressure (you select)
 IV. A Third Pressure (you select)
  V. Conclusion.

BE SURE THAT YOU: . . . begin each paragraph with a topic sentence.
     . . . decide how you will develop each paragraph. (Try out a few different ways until you can select the one that seems best.)
     If you have difficulty with your introduction and conclusion, you might want to look ahead to Chapter Six.

EXERCISE 1P REFRESHER: On separate paper, rewrite the following paragraph. Remove any material which is not part of the main idea stated in the topic sentence that begins the paragraph and add facts, examples, or incidents to develop the paragraph more fully.

A computer can do a wonderful job of analyzing technical data, but it cannot deal with those magical elements that create a romance between two people. Hundreds of workers can be replaced by a few computers that do the same job more efficiently and in much less time. The electronic brain can juggle statistics such as age, height, weight, and income. It can even digest information concerning personality traits, interests, and moral standards. However, when it comes to a date we each have personal preferences that cannot be programmed. In addition, many people tend to lie when they fill out a computer questionnaire. Although it is certainly a great technological achievement, the computer will never become a successful matchmaker.

SPRINGBOARDS TO WRITING

1. As a result of filling in the computer dating questionnaire, reading the essay, or answering the questions at the beginning of this chapter, you might have some thoughts about the central theme—computerized dating. (Look back at those pages to refresh your memory.) For help in planning such an essay, refer to the guide which follows.

GUIDE FOR PLANNING AN ESSAY

(a) select one topic which interests you and . . .

(b) create a title for the essay. Be sure that the title is not too broad or too narrow as you . . .

(c) write topic sentences which indicate your major points (and which limit and control what you say). These topic sentences should be seen as an outline of your essay which will help you judge your title and your plan . . . so that you can

(d) adjust and revise your title and/or topic sentences as necessary . . . and

(e) develop each paragraph so that you have a complete essay.

2. Here are some topics which have not been directly mentioned in the questions asked so far in this chapter. Perhaps one of them would be an interesting springboard for you:

(a) An Ideal Mate

(b) An Ideal Date

(c) First Impressions Are Often (Never) Correct

(d) Modern Living Is Becoming Less Human Daily

(e) The Case for (against) a Federal Data Computer Center

Courtesy Wide World Photos.

NEGROES
FOR SALE.

I will sell by Public Auction, on Tuesday of next Court, being the 29th of November, *Eight Valuable Family Servants*, consisting of one Negro Man, a first-rate field hand, one No. 1 Boy, 17 years o' age, a trusty house servant, one excellent Cook, one House-Maid, and one Seamstress. The balance are under 12 years of age. They are sold for no fault, but in consequence of my going to reside North. Also a quantity of Household and Kitchen Furniture, Stable Lot, &c. Terms accommodating, and made known on day of sale.

Jacob August.
P. J. TURNBULL, *Auctioneer.*
Warrenton, October 28, 1859.

Printed at the *News* office, Warrenton, North Carolina.

Courtesy Chicago Historical Society Library.

SPRINGBOARDS TO THINKING

For informal, not written, response . . . to stimulate your thinking

1. Read the sale poster completely. What are all the items it lists? What words are used to interest and attract the buyer?
2. In addition to the fact that this poster advertises the sale of human beings, is there anything else about its contents that you find jolting? In general, how does this poster make you feel?
3. The photograph was taken at a large civil rights rally, the March on Washington in 1963, one hundred years after the Emancipation Proclamation. According to the signs held by the people, what are the problems which exist for the Negro in America today?
4. More than one hundred years after the Emancipation Proclamation, are the Negroes in America "free"? Why do many people feel that physical bondage is only one type of slavery?
5. When a new law is made, is it always obeyed? What do you think is the difference between "the letter of the law" and "the spirit of the law"?

Bull Connor's Birmingham

MARTIN LUTHER KING, JR.

(1) If you had visited Birmingham before the third of April in the one-hundredth-anniversary year of the Negro's emancipation, you might have come to a startling conclusion. You might have concluded that here was a city which had been trapped for decades in a Rip Van Winkle slumber; a city whose fathers had apparently never heard of Abraham Lincoln, Thomas Jefferson, the Bill of Rights, the Preamble to the Constitution, the Thirteenth, Fourteenth, and Fifteenth Amendments, or the 1954 decision of the United States Supreme Court outlawing segregation in the public schools.

(2) If your powers of imagination were great enough to enable you to place yourself in the position of a Negro baby born and brought up to physical maturity in Birmingham, you would have pictured your life in the following manner:

(3) You would be born in a jim-crow hospital to parents who probably lived in a ghetto. You would attend a jim-crow school. It is not really true that the city fathers had never heard of the Supreme Court's school-desegregation order. They had heard of it and, since its passage, had consistently expressed their defiance, typified by the prediction of one official that blood would run in the streets before desegregation would be permitted to come to Birmingham.

(4) You would spend your childhood playing mainly in the streets because the "colored" parks were abysmally inadequate. When a federal court order banned park segregation, you would find that Birmingham closed down its parks and gave up its baseball team rather than integrate them.

(5) If you went shopping with your mother or father, you would trudge along as they purchased at every counter, except one, in the large or small stores. If you were hungry or thirsty you would have to forget about it until you got back to the Negro section of town, for in your city it was a violation of the law to serve food to Negroes at the same counter with whites.

(6) If your family attended church, you would go to a Negro church. If you wanted to visit a church attended by white people, you would not be welcome. For although your white fellow citizens would insist that they were Christians, they practiced segregation as rigidly in the house of God as they did in the theatre.

(7) If you loved music and yearned to hear the Metropolitan Opera on its tour of the South, you could not enjoy this privilege. Nor could your white fellow music-lovers; for the Metropolitan had discontinued scheduling Birmingham on its national tours after it had adopted a policy of not performing before segregated audiences.

(8) If you wanted to contribute to and be a part of the work of the National Association for the Advancement of Colored People, you would not be able to join a local branch. In the State of Alabama, segregationist authorities had been successful in enjoining the N.A.A.C.P. from performing its civil-rights work by declaring it a "foreign corporation" and rendering its activities illegal.

(9) If you wanted a job in this city—one of the greatest iron-and-steel-producing centers in the nation—you had better settle on doing menial work as a porter or laborer. If you were fortunate enough to get a job, you could expect that promotions to a better status or more pay would come, not to you, but to a white employee regardless of your comparative talents. On your job, you would eat in a separate place and use a water fountain and lavatory labeled "colored" in conformity to citywide ordinances.

(10) If you believed your history books and thought of America as a country whose governing officials—whether city, state, or nation—are selected by the governed, you would be swiftly disillusioned when you tried to exercise your right to register and vote. You would be confronted with every conceivable obstacle to taking that most important walk a Negro American can take today—the walk to the ballot box. Of the 80,000 voters in Birmingham, prior to January, 1963, only 10,000 were Negroes. Your race, constituting two-fifths of the city's population, would make up one-eighth of its voting strength.

(11) You would be living in a city where brutality directed against Negroes was an unquestioned and unchallenged reality. One of the city commissioners, a member of the body that ruled municipal affairs, would be Eugene "Bull" Connor, a racist who prided himself on knowing how to handle the Negro and "keep him in his place." As Commissioner of Public Safety, Bull Connor, entrenched for many years in a key position in the Birmingham power structure, displayed as much contempt for the rights of the Negro as he did defiance for the authority of the federal government.

(12) You would have found a general atmosphere of violence and brutality in Birmingham. Local racists have intimidated, mobbed, and even killed Negroes with impunity. One of the more vivid and recent examples of the terror of Birmingham was the castration of a Negro man, whose mutilated body had been abandoned on a lonely road. No Negro home was protected from bombings and burnings. From the year 1957

through January of 1963, while Birmingham was still claiming that its Negroes were "satisfied," seventeen unsolved bombings of Negro churches and homes of civil-rights leaders had occurred.

(13) Negroes were not the only persons who suffered because of Bull Connor's rule. It was Birmingham's Safety Commissioner who, in 1961, arrested the manager of a local bus station when the latter sought to obey the law of the land by serving Negroes. Although a federal district judge condemned Connor in strong terms for this action and released the victim, the fact remained that in Birmingham, early in 1963, no places of public accommodation were integrated except the bus station, the train station, and the airport.

(14) In Bull Connor's Birmingham, you would be a resident of a city where a United States senator, visiting to deliver a speech, had been arrested because he walked through a door marked "Colored."

(15) In Connor's Birmingham, the silent password was fear. It was a fear not only on the part of the black oppressed, but also in the hearts of white oppressors. Guilt was a part of their fear. There was also the dread of change, that all too prevalent fear which hounds those whose attitudes have been hardened by the long winter of reaction. Many were apprehensive of social ostracism. Certainly Birmingham had its white moderates who disapproved of Bull Connor's tactics. Certainly Birmingham had its decent white citizens who privately deplored the maltreatment of Negroes. But they remained publicly silent. It was a silence born of fear —fear of social, political, and economic reprisals. The ultimate tragedy of Birmingham was not the brutality of the bad people but the silence of the good people.

(16) In Birmingham, you would be living in a community where the white man's long-lived tyranny had cowed your people, led them to abandon hope, and developed in them a false sense of inferiority. You would be living in a city where the representatives of economic and political power refused to even discuss social justice with the leaders of your people.

(17) You would be living in the largest city of a police state, presided over by a governor—George Wallace—whose inauguration vow had been a pledge of "segregation now, segregation tomorrow, segregation forever!" You would be living, in fact, in the most segregated city in America.

READING SURVEY

1. Main Idea

What is the central theme of this essay?

2. Major Details

(a) List three examples of discrimination against Negroes in Birmingham, Alabama.

(b) Who was Bull Connor? What type of atmosphere did he create in Birmingham?

(c) In Birmingham, why was the silent password *fear?*

3. Inference

(a) Read paragraph one again. What do you think has happened since April 3, 1963?

(b) Read paragraph fourteen again. What is the significance of the senator's arrest?

4. Opinion

(a) Would most of the problems in Birmingham have been eliminated if all adults had been allowed to vote?

(b) If you were a Negro who had to bring up your children in a place like Birmingham, how would you have managed to help your child grow up free and happy—without crippling fear or destructive hate?

VOCABULARY BUILDING

Lesson One: The Vocabulary of Civil Rights

As the civil-rights movement becomes increasingly important, words that describe the movement come into prominence. Some of them appear in Dr. King's essay:

emancipation	(paragraph 1)
segregation	(1)
jim-crow	(3)
ghetto	(3)
desegregation	(3)
integrate	(4)
brutality	(11)
racist	(11)
oppressed	(15)
ostracism	(15)

The setting free of a people is called their *emancipation.*

The separation of one group of people from another group of people is called *segregation.*

The name of a Negro song-and-dance act in the nineteenth century, today *jim-crow* is a term which stands for the insult and the segregation of the Negro.

A *ghetto* is an area of a city which is set aside for only one type or group of people.

The mixing of different groups of people who were formerly segregated is called *desegregation.*

To combine people, qualities, or ideas in order to form a perfect whole is to *integrate.*

Cruelty and physical violence against another person is called *brutality.*

A person who believes that all other races are inferior to his own and, therefore, should be separated from society is a *racist.*

A person who is enslaved and must suffer many burdens is *oppressed,* and the people who cause this *oppression* are called *oppressors.*

To cast out a person from a group is called *ostracism.*

EXERCISE 2A: Fill in the blanks with the correct word.

1. The decree which set the slaves free is called the _____

   _____ Proclamation.

2. I hate all other races. I am a _____.

3. I want to unite with all other people to form a harmonious society.

   I believe that we should _____ our society.

4. He certainly suffers many burdens. He is really _____.

5. I do not want to sit near any of those people. I believe in _____

   _____.

6. Because it is the only one that Negro children can attend, it is called

   a _____ school.

7. I will ignore him completely. Soon he will know that my acts of

   _____ have cast him out of the group.

8. I believe that the schools should no longer separate minority groups

   from the rest of society. I am in favor of _____.

9. Some people think that physical violence and cruelty is the only way

   to do things. They believe that _____ works.

10. I prefer that those people live in their own section of the city. I think

    that they belong in a _____.

Name: _____ Date: _____

Lesson Two: Negative Words

There are many words which suggest a negative attitude, action, or state of being. Some of them appear in Dr. King's essay:

defiance	(paragraph 3)	**intimidate**	(12)
abysmally	(4)	**mutilated**	(12)
inadequate	(4)	**apprehensive**	(15)
violation	(5)	**deplore**	(15)

angry refusal . . . . defiance
hopelessly bad . . . . abysmally
not good enough . . . . inadequate
the breaking of a law . . . . . . violation
to scare and make timid . . . . . intimidate
scarred and wounded . . . . . . mutilated
frightened and anxious . . . . . apprehensive
to hate and feel disgust for . . . deplore

EXERCISE 2B: Fill in the blanks with the correct word.

1. His hand was _____ as a result of his car accident.

2. His _____ was obvious from his face, his tone of voice, and the way he held his head.

3. He was very _____ about walking down that dark street.

4. I feel _____ for the task. I just know I will not do a good enough job.

5. I have failed _____ and I know it from the complete mess I have made of things.

6. I _____ deeds like that because they are cruel and horrible.

7. You _____ me when you try to scare me into doing that.

8. It is a _____ of everything that is right and proper if I go along with what you are doing.

34

SPELLING

Lesson One: Spelling Demons

Here are some more words that are frequently misspelled. Using the helpful techniques given in Chapter One, be sure to learn these new Demons, which are taken from "Bull Connor's Birmingham."

against	comparative	imagination	separate
apparently	condemn	obstacle	since
attitude	consistently	physical	speech
audience	decision	prevalent	strength
authority	disillusioned	privilege	tragedy
certainly	government	schedule	tyranny

Lesson Two: Sound-Alikes

Many of your spelling errors may be caused by a confusion of words which have different spellings but similar pronunciations. Since the confused words sound alike, their pronunciation is no clue to their spelling. Instead you must rely on their meanings if you are to spell them correctly. Below is a list of some of these troublesome Sound-Alikes. They are words that you use frequently in your writing, so be sure to learn to spell them correctly.

1. *capital* (chief, major, leading city, money)
    Albany is the capital of New York.
    Joe invested all his capital.
    capitol (only the building)
    We met on the steps of the Capitol in Washington.

2. *hear* (listen)
    We could not hear the radio because of the interference.
    here (in this place)
    The boys will wait here for their friends.

3. *its* (belongs to it)
    The dog could not wag its tail.
    it's (it is)
    It's the best of all possible worlds.

4. *passed* (went by)
    I passed your home on the way to school.
    past (a former time)
    If we are not careful, the past will catch up with us.

5. *peace*   (the absence of war and strife)

   The United Nations hopes to bring peace to the world.

   piece   (a portion of)

   Have a piece of cake with your coffee.

6. *principal*   (most important, chief person, or the original amount of a loan)

   What is the principal idea of this essay?

   Mr. Denn is the school principal.

   Joe paid the interest and fifty dollars on the principal.

   principle   (a basic doctrine or rule)

   The many principles of physics are difficult to learn.

7. *then*   (at that time)

   We went to an early movie, and then we went home.

   than   (used to compare unequal things)

   His speech was much longer than mine

8. *their*   (belonging to them)

   It is their privilege to vote against the amendment.

   there   (at that place)

   There is the oldest schoolhouse in America.

   they're   (they are)

   They're the best audience one could hope for.

9. *to*   (toward or part of the infinitive)

   Joe gave his schedule to me.

   They like to condemn all his decisions.

   too   (also, more than enough)

   Mike likes Greek tragedy too.

   Jack was much too dogmatic.

   two   (the number 2)

   We consulted two authorities.

10. *weather*   (the state of the atmosphere)

    The weather was fine for a trip to the lake.

    whether   (in case; if; indicating alternatives)

    Lynn could not decide whether to stay home or go out.

11. *who's*   (who is)

    Who's against the new French government?

    whose   (belongs to whom)

    Whose children are they?

12. *your*   (belonging to you)

    It is your decision to make.

    you're   (you are)

    You're the last obstacle to my happiness.

A SPECIAL NOTE: Memory tricks are especially helpful for learning these Sound-Alikes:

Remember that you *hear* with your *ear*.
We waited *here* and not *there*.
The princi*pal* is my *pal* and the *chief* person in a school.
The princip*le* is a ru*le*.
The capit*ol* has a *dome*.
The w*ea*ther was cl*ea*r.
He ate a *pie*ce of *pie*.

EXERCISE 2C: Underline the correct word from the set of words in parentheses.

The (*weather, whether*) was perfect for a trip (*to, too, two*) Washington, D.C. Our former high school (*principal, principle*), (*who's, whose*) father was a United States senator, had been invited by our college to be our guide. He (*passed, past*) out guide books during the bus trip. Upon reaching Washington, we went (*to, too, two*) the White House first. (*Their, There, They're*) we met Frank Parks, (*who's, whose*) the (*piece, peace*) candidate in the next election. (*Than, Then*) we visited the (*Capital, Capitol*) building, the seat of our democratic (*principals, principles*). (*Hear, Here*) we were lucky enough to (*hear, here*) speeches given by (*to, too, two*) (*passed, past*) ambassadors. (*Their, There, They're*) in (*their, there, they're*) seventies but are (*to, too, two*) energetic to retire. Next on the agenda was the Lincoln Memorial, one of the (*principal, principle*) tourist attractions in the city. With (*its, it's*) many tall columns, (*its, it's*) more impressive (*than, then*) the Washington Memorial, which we saw (*to, too, two*). As it got late, we had (*to, too, two*) decide (*weather, whether*) to travel to Mount Vernon or Arlington. I munched on a (*peace, piece*) of candy as the bus headed home. (*Your, You're*) not a true American until you have seen (*your, you're*) nation's (*capital, capitol*).

Name: _____ Date: _____

EXERCISE 2D: Fill in the blanks with any missing letters.

1. The sp____ch is s____duled for tomorrow.

2. We must always sep____rate the imag____ation from the reality.

3. The gover____ment must have the stren____th to overcome the tyra____y of the masses.

4. *Macbeth* is cert____nly Shakespeare's best tra____y.

5. The at____tude of the aud____nce is important to the performer.

6. Public auth____rity will always condem____ ph____cal violence.

7. Sin____e the Garden of Eden, man has always made the important de____sions.

8. It is his pr____lege to consist____ntly speak out aga____nst his enemy.

Name: _____ Date: _____

PARAGRAPH DEVELOPMENT: PART II

In Chapter One you learned three methods of developing your topic sentence into a full paragraph—facts, examples, and incidents. There are other methods which can also help you to emphasize and "drive home" your main point. Two of these are:

   (a) Definition
   (b) Comparison and contrast

Decide on your method of development before you begin to write. You may develop a paragraph using just one of the methods, or you may use any combination of methods. It is up to you to decide the best way to stress and prove your topic sentence.

   (a) Here is an example of a paragraph developed with a *definition*:

When we speak of the born teacher, we do not mean the pompous intellectual who is interested only in displaying his vast knowledge. No, the born teacher does not have to be a world authority on Shakespearean tragedy or governmental tyranny. Rather he must have the conscious desire to awaken the curiosity and imagination of his students. Minds must be encouraged to formulate personal opinions and to create new concepts. But most of all, the born teacher gives his students the desire to touch and taste all that life has to offer, for that is the road to a true education.

☞ YOU DO THIS:

1. Underline the topic sentence.
2. Is there more than one main idea in the paragraph?
3. In your own words state the definition of a born teacher as given in the paragraph.

EXERCISE 2E: Choose one of these topic sentences and develop it into a paragraph using a *definition*.

1. Before talking about freedom, we should define what it is.
2. No two people have exactly the same idea of a good date.
3. The ideal parent would have to possess an extraordinary set of qualities.

(b) Here is an example of a paragraph developed through *comparison and contrast*:

At first glance, Birmingham and New York might seem to be completely unalike in their handling of racial situations. While the Negro child in Birmingham has to attend a jim-crow school, his New York counterpart is assigned to his district school. Because many Birmingham businessmen behave like racists, the most intelligent Southern Negro usually has to settle for work as a porter or laborer. New York City has a Human Rights Commission which tries to prevent such job discrimination. The Birmingham Negro is apprehensive about voting because he is sure to be intimidated on his way to the polling place. In contrast, the League of Women Voters carries on an advertising campaign to encourage voter registration in New York. Yet in spite of these apparent differences, Birmingham and New York have one deplorable similarity: the Negroes of both cities live in ramshackle, rat-infested ghettos.

☞ YOU DO THIS:

1. Underline the topic sentence.
2. Is there more than one main idea in the paragraph?
3. In your own words state three of the comparisons and contrasts used to develop the paragraph.

EXERCISE 2F: Choose one of these topic sentences and develop it into a paragraph using *comparison and contrast*.

1. Negro freedom in America has (has not) improved in the last ten years.
2. Football is (is not) a much better sport to watch than baseball.
3. Popular music has changed in the last few years.

EXERCISE 2G   ESSAY ANALYSIS: Answer these questions about the essay "Bull Connor's Birmingham."

1. Paragraphs three through ten are the development of paragraph two. Is the development done by facts, examples, incidents, definition, or

    comparison and contrast? _____
2. What is the topic sentence of paragraph twelve?

    _____

    How is paragraph twelve developed? _____
3. Paragraph fifteen is developed with a combination of definition and comparison and contrast. What two groups are being compared?

    _____

    What is being defined? _____
4. Paragraphs sixteen and seventeen, taken together, are developed by

    what method—incident or definition? _____

EXERCISE 2H: Using three different types of paragraph development, write the following essay. Choose one of these three topics.

Things to Consider in . . . Selecting a career
                      . . . Choosing a spouse
                      . . . Selecting a car

   I. Introduction.
  II. One Consideration (you select)
 III. Another Consideration (you select)
 IV. A Third Consideration (you select)
  V. Conclusion

BE SURE THAT YOU: . . . begin each paragraph with a topic sentence.
                      . . . decide how you will develop each paragraph. (Try out a few different ways until you can select the one that seems best.)
                      If you have difficulty with your introduction and conclusion, you might want to look ahead to Chapter Six.

Name: _____ Date: _____

ORDERING OF DETAILS IN A PARAGRAPH

Now that you know the five basic methods of paragraph development, it will help you to plan the details of your chosen method of development. Before haphazardly throwing information into a paragraph, decide on a plan for the order and arrangement of your details. The three basic, and most useful, arrangements are:

(a) Details arranged by order of importance

(b) Details arranged by order of time

(c) Details arranged by order of location

The order you select should depend on the topic of the paragraph and the kinds of details that it will be necessary to use. The ordering of details in any of these three ways will improve the clarity and effectiveness of your writing.

(a) *Details arranged by order of importance*: Just as an orchestra begins quietly and builds to the climactic crash of the cymbals, so you may build your paragraph the same way with the least important details first and the most important last. Notice how it is done in this paragraph:

The Governor's recently televised speech certainly contained some interesting points. He began by announcing that the Capitol would soon be renovated at a cost of two million dollars. Then he revealed a plan to enlarge the state park system by adding two public recreation areas, a newly created beach, and a huge zoo. Immediately after this news, we were told that government spending had declined slightly in the last year. As a result, state taxes would be lowered as of the first of the year. Although the Governor wanted to leave us in happy spirits, he ended his address by stating that he would not run for re-election.

HINT: You may choose to give your most important details first and the least important last, but the opposite order is generally more effective.

EXERCISE 2I: Use order of importance to fill in the details for the following topic sentence.

I was the first one to arrive at the scene of the car accident.

(1) _____

(2) _____

(3) _____

(4) _____

(5) _____

(6) _____

EXERCISE 2J: Choose one of these topic sentences and develop it into a paragraph that uses details arranged according to *order of importance.*

1. Athletics hold many benefits for the average person.

2. Improvement in Negro freedom is needed in many areas.

3. A part-time job should be a requirement for all teenagers.

(b) *Details arranged by order of time*: If you are telling how something is made, how a game is played, or how a system developed, you should use the order of happening, often called chronological order. You will be telling the sequence of events in the order of their occurrence. Notice how it is done in this paragraph:

To study for an examination, first find a quiet room where you will not be disturbed. Be sure that you have adequate lighting, a comfortable chair, and a great deal of desk space. After you have gathered together a few pens and pencils, some scrap paper, your class notes and texts, you are ready to begin studying. Read through your notes completely, so that you can get a total picture of the course and so that you can pick out the major points that need to be studied. Then concentrate on one topic at a time, using a pen and scrap paper to recopy important names and dates. Finally, read your text books to fill in any gaps in your notes and to reinforce what you have already studied. When you have finished, pray that the test will be easy!

43

EXERCISE 2K: Use chronological order to fill in the details for the following topic sentence.

It was one of those "I should have stayed in bed" days.

(1) _____

(2) _____

(3) _____

(4) _____

(5) _____

(6) _____

EXERCISE 2L: Choose one of these topic sentences and develop it into a paragraph using details arranged according to *order of time*.

1. Getting ready for school in the morning is a ritual for me.

2. It is easy to make a _____.

3. Registration at my school is a most hectic process.

(c) *Details arranged by order of location*: When you describe a place or wish to take your reader from one place to another, you must do it in an orderly fashion so that the reader can picture the scene in his mind. You would use order of location to describe such things as a college campus, or your room, or even something as small as a penny. In each instance, you should give the position of one thing in relation to something you have already described. For example:

She had been born in a small town, and her block looked like many others in countless small towns across the nation. The oak trees were bent in all directions; some were arched over the cracked sidewalks, while others leaned out toward the narrow, tar-patched road. A row of two-family houses, each one like the others, stood back from the street in the shadows of the trees. Serving as a driveway, a thin ribbon of cement ran along the side of each house and passed an open back porch, which faced a dilapidated, two-car garage. To the left of this wooden structure, one invariably found some sort of a flower garden and perhaps a few fruit trees. The surrounding yard was mottled with crab apples, waiting to be crushed underfoot by children.

Name: _____ Date: _____

EXERCISE 2M: Use order of location to fill in the details for the following topic sentence.

Surprisingly, a dime can be an interesting object to examine.

(1) _____

(2) _____

(3) _____

(4) _____

(5) _____

(6) _____

EXERCISE 2N: Choose one of these topic sentences and develop it into a paragraph using details arranged according to *order of location*.

1. Often a typical ghetto street reflects the despair of the people who live there.

2. My bedroom should be declared a national disaster area.

3. My school campus is made up of quite a variety of buildings.

EXERCISE 2O   ESSAY ANALYSIS: Answer these questions about the the essay "Bull Connor's Birmingham."

1. Are the details in paragraph nine arranged in order of importance, time, or location? _____

2. What other arrangement of details could have been used in paragraph nine? _____

   Would it be as effective? Why? _____

   _____

Name: _____ Date: _____

EXERCISE 2P REFRESHER: On separate paper rewrite the following paragraph. Remove any material which is not part of the main idea stated in the topic sentence that begins the paragraph and add facts, examples, incidents, definitions, or comparisons and contrasts to develop the paragraph more fully.

We will not have complete racial equality until our system of education is changed. Because a child spends a major portion of his formative years in school, education has a great influence on the young mind. Only the home environment has a greater influence. Parents should remember this fact as they carry out their daily activities; children tend to copy the behavior of their elders. As it now exists, the learning process reinforces discrimination. Our children must be taught to communicate with and to respect all races. In contrast to the present situation, the educational system of the future should also create a harmony between peoples which will bring a lasting peace to our nation.

SPRINGBOARDS TO WRITING

1. As a result of looking at the sale poster and photograph, reading the essay, or answering the questions which follow each, you might have some thoughts about the central theme—civil rights. (Look back at those pages to refresh your memory.) For help in planning such an essay, refer to the Guide for Planning an Essay, which appears in Springboards to Writing, Chapter One, page 25.

2. Here are some topics which have not been directly mentioned in the questions asked so far. Perhaps one of them could be a writing spring-board for you:

   (a) You are suddenly of another race or color. Write about: A Typical Day in My Life.

   (b) A plan for achieving racial harmony in this country.

   (c) The psychological effects of prejudice on both the oppressed and the oppressors.

   (d) Using Dr. King or another great American, comment on the old saying:
   A tree can best be measured after it falls.

   (e) Have fair housing and labor laws done anything to improve the life of the Negro in America?

   (f) Have the busing of school children, the parental control of schools, and the study of Negro heroes done anything to eliminate "jim-crow" school practices?

   (g) Many extremist groups have suggested the establishment of a separate Negro state. What do you think of such an idea?

   (h) My experiences as a member of a minority group.

   (i) Minorities in America.

Just having you to love, dear,

Each day the whole year through

Has made my way a happy one,

And brought me skies of blue,

And on a day like this, dear,

All other things above

I'm thankful for the joys I've known

Just Having You To Love

Courtesy Hallmark Cards, Inc.

Condition Red  (As recorded by the Goodees/Hip)   DON DAVIS   FRED BRIGGS

Condition red, don't you come over tonight
Cause mommy and daddy don't approve of you
*   and me getting too tight*
Why doesn't he get a haircut
Why doesn't he shave
You know he used to be such a nice lookin' fellow
Before he grew that awful beard
That's why my mommy and daddy
*   keep saying to me*
And everytime they down you boy
I try to make them see,
That though your hair is long
And your mind is in the sky
For me you're the right guy.

Condition red, baby please stay away
Cause I don't know what mommy and
*   daddy might say*
It's gonna be hard for us to keep on

Lovin' this way but I gotta keep seein' you
Boy, no matter what they say
No matter how they down you boy
And say you're not my kind
I'm gonna love you honey till the end of time
I guess we'll have to meet down at the corner
*   from now on*
That look in your eye
Where you goin'
Can I go with you, take me with you
Don't go away mad
Please come back, can't you see I just don't
*   care what they say*
Take me with you, cause my love for you
*   is so strong*
Hey there's a car
Watch out for the car
Condition red, I'll never see you again
Condition red, condition red.

© Copyright 1968 by East-Memphis Music Corp. and Groovesville Pub. Co.

48

three

SPRINGBOARDS TO THINKING

For informal, not written, response . . . to stimulate your thinking

1. The Valentine card pictured here is typical of the ones used a century ago. What is "old-fashioned" about

    . . . its design?
    . . . its message?
    . . . its sentiment?

2. Judging from the card, would you describe the love sentiments in those days as "polite, with each person staying in his proper place" or as "open, with each person on equal terms with everyone else"? Explain.

3. Read the lyrics to the song. What is the story? Is there anything surprising about the ending? What was the year this song was written?

4. The so-called "generation gap" is a sub-theme of this song. What did the girl and her parents disagree about? In your experience, what other things contribute to the generation gap?

5. What might be the advantages of the "old-fashioned" love relationship? Which type of relationship—that shown by the Valentine card or that shown by the song—appeals to you the most? Why?

The New Case for Chastity

DR. ERNEST GORDON

(1) Out of many years' experience in counseling college-age young people, I am convinced that there is emerging a powerful case, perhaps a *new* case, for chastity. Simply put, it is this: Sexual freedom, under the so-called "New Morality," should be regarded by today's youth as a challenge to their freedom of choice. And freedom of choice, in the area of sex as elsewhere, involves the demand to choose for oneself, influenced by neither old-fogy fears nor hipster pressures, the course that will contribute to the richest and fullest life.

(2) I know that the presumption of our time is that the "new morality" is simply a synonym for "no morality." But that presumption may well be wrong. Among college students today, I find increasing recognition—and resentment—that their freedom of choice in moral action is being pushed around quite as much by libertarian "Thou shalts" as their parents' was by "Thou shalt nots."

(3) There's no denying that the pressures toward loose conduct are strong. Ours is a society drenched in sex. Illicit sexual relations, graphically portrayed, are a large part of many contemporary books and movies. Provocative sex symbols underlie much advertising. Education in the physiology of sex and open discussion between the sexes have done away, in the minds of this generation at least, with the anxieties inherited from a neo-puritanical tradition, and new and easier methods of contraception have diminished the fear of unwanted pregnancies. In view of all this, why be pure?

(4) It isn't easy to answer this question. The old morality, based on centuries of human experience, has a good case. But it no longer convinces our young people. The authoritarian morality of "Thou shalt not" is out. And so is the practical argument, "Nice girls don't do it, because they will be in trouble if they do."

(5) This situation baffles the older generation. If young people reject the old arguments for morality, they must be rejecting morality itself. Not necessarily. The encouraging fact is that young people are actually free to be *more* moral. Many are seeing that the "new" in the "new morality" is the freedom to choose chastity rather than have it thrust upon them by fears or pressures.

(6) Among college youth today I sense an increasing scorn, tinged with pity, for those of their members who plunge into promiscuity to express their "freedom." Again and again I hear, "Poor kid, she (or he) is so insecure." Such remarks recognize that sexual promiscuity, far from

being a sign of self-confidence and social poise, is actually an earmark of anxiety and fear. The Don Juan who flits from woman to woman is attempting to convince others, but mostly himself, of his masculinity. And so it is with the girl who, afraid of being unpopular, prostitutes her body in a vain attempt to correct her anxiety. In the process, her insecurity is intensified, her reputation is destroyed, her prospects for sexual satisfaction are decreased.

(7) I was delighted to hear recently of a lovely, well-integrated girl who said to her mother, "Don't worry about me. I'm a nonconformist. I intend to remain a virgin until I marry." This remark stamped her as one mature enough to respect her own body and to preserve its purity for the man she loves, or will come to love. She is the confident person—the girl with a future instead of a girl with a past.

(8) I am convinced that the prevailing attitude of most young people today is not a rejection of all moral standards but an honest search for those that are higher and more meaningful—and therefore more permanent—than the old ones based on fear. They *want* standards, and the questions they ask, no matter how flippantly, reveal the seriousness of their search.

(9) Under the old morality, many young people believed that they could show their individuality only by being unchaste, because it was difficult to distinguish between those whose chastity was based on fear and those for whom it was a matter of choice. Under the "new morality," chastity is more of a freedom than a restriction. Thus, a young person can remain chaste and still show his individuality. With this new freedom, however, comes a responsibility to be informed. Many fallacies have emerged which may mislead young people. For example, there is the often-heard, "Everybody's doing it, aren't they? Why shouldn't I?"

(10) It takes little effort to explode that flimsy cliché. The Kinsey report found that 58 percent of college-bound males had had no sexual experience, and 80 percent of unmarried women in the 16-to-20-year-old class were virgins. More recent surveys of both sexes reveal scant change in these figures. To students making this weak point I simply say, "It would be more accurate to say everybody's *talking* about it."

(11) Another fallacy voiced by advocates of premarital sex is what Dr. Evelyn Duvall calls the "try before you buy" argument. This advances the notion that sexual compatibility, so important in marriage, can only be determined by "giving it a whirl" before marriage. Dr. Duvall, a recognized authority on sex and family-life problems, cites in her book *Why Wait Till Marriage?* a study made by the American Institute of Family Relations which concludes: "The previous sexual experience of a woman is no help to her in making a good sexual adjustment in marriage."

(12) But perhaps the trickiest device, used by seducers since time began, is the "test of love" theory. Again and again I'm asked, "But isn't sexual intercourse itself the true test of love? Surely it can't be wrong if those

51

who enjoy it love one another!" In reply, I contend that the experience of being in love is far greater than a "rub" and a "tickle," to borrow from one of Dylan Thomas's poems.

(13) For those truly in love, erotic love is transcended by a much deeper love—that of self-giving, of seeking the highest good for the other. This love elevates physical passion to the level of genuine concern for the beloved. As one young man said not long ago, "My fiancée and I discussed having sexual relations, and decided we'd rather not. I love her too much to have that relationship a furtive one."

(14) When young unmarrieds in complete earnestness ask, "With all the risks removed from premarital sex, what have I got to lose?" I have to remind them that, while some obvious risks have disappeared, sex remains complex and precarious. Outside a loving marriage, it may be more damaging than rewarding.

(15) This was tragically illustrated to me one day recently when I arrived at my office to find an undergraduate, obviously deeply disturbed, awaiting me. As he fumbled for words, I thought I would shock him into coherent speech. "Have you killed someone?" I asked.

(16) "Yes, I have," he shuddered, lowering his face into his hands. I had to guess quickly what his confession meant, so I asked, "Have you been involved in an abortion?"

(17) Nodding, he burst out with his story—an all too common one. For two years he had been sleeping regularly with his girlfriend. They had used contraceptives, but something had gone wrong. This did not worry the young couple unduly, for their friends had told them where to get an abortion for $600. When the illegal operation was over, the girl broke down completely. What had been an easy solution to an embarrassing problem suddenly became a tragedy. She felt that she was responsible for destroying a life.

(18) Equally shattered, the boy demanded, "What right have we to go on living?" I was able to show him that they did have a right by indicating some of the ways they could live out their forgiveness. The first thing he determined to do was to marry the girl and to protect her from her fears. The second was to tell his friends and acquaintances of their experience so that they, too, would learn from it. Almost too late, this couple realized that time-tested standards existed to protect, not inhibit, their personal freedom.

(19) But the argument based on "What have I got to lose?" contains other risks. Not the least of these is the loss of one's self-respect, without which life becomes empty, often leading to self-hatred. Indeed, near the top of a list of the costs of unchastity is a very much lowered self-esteem —yet the power to love another rests on the ability to respect oneself.

(20) Whatever may be modern youth's attitudes, real or pretended, toward sexual "freedom," one thing that most of them want is a relationship that is sincere and permanent. This is where chastity comes in. Chas-

tity does not mean a denial of sexuality; on the contrary, it implies its fulfillment. The sexual act itself is simply an organic one, a biological function, it has little significance outside a personal relationship. A prostitute, for example, is interested only in money. The man who uses her is interested only in pleasure. Neither of them is interested in the other. If there is any relationship at all, it cannot be classified as anything more personal than a relationship between a man and a glass of beer.

(21) The word chastity is derived from the Latin word *castus*, meaning pure. A pure relationship is surely an honest one. When two people are honest with each other, they enter into a relationship which is one of mutual respect, or moral integrity, a relationship in which one moral person will not use another moral person simply as a means of pleasure. Such a relationship needs the support and strength of marriage. For only in an open relationship can a man and woman be free to give themselves honestly to each other without reservation.

(22) What many fail to grasp, at the time their freedom of choice is being exercised, is that depth studies of married couples, such as the one made by the late Prof. Lewis M. Terman of Stanford University, have concluded that "of those men and women who have had premarital sexual intercourse, the more promiscuous they have been premaritally, the less likely they are to be happy maritally." To this Dr. Duvall adds: "Men and women who have been permissive sexually before marriage cannot be expected to change miraculously when they marry."

(23) In my counseling work I have found that many of the marriages which break up are those in which marital integrity is lacking. I remember trying to keep one couple together. Both members had had a series of premarital experiences, and each refused to believe in the sincerity of the other. Each readily accepted the other's guilt but not his own. They were divorced, they have remarried, and they have repeated the experience—and they will continue to do so.

(24) From experience, I am forced to conclude that chastity and monogamy are twins. They stand for the dignity of both the man and the woman. Women are probably more aware of this than men. Recently, I was having a conversation with a lovely middle-aged woman who was commenting on the joys of marriage. One thing she said stays with me. It was a simple phrase: "I'm glad I have this man to love." She did not say " *a* man," but "*this* man."

(25) The center of her love was a particular man with a particular name and personality. The years had not dulled the thrill of loving nor erased the joy of being with her man. Love opened the door of life for her. By it she entered into the life of "*this* man." There is no more satisfying self-expression, for it is centered not upon the self but upon the other.

(26) Thus, the case for chastity rests finally upon the uniquely God-given character and dignity of men and women. It is a good case, and it is original in every generation.

READING SURVEY

1. Main Idea

What is the central theme of this essay?

2. Major Details

(a) How does the author combat . . . the "everybody's doing it" theory?

                . . . the "try before you buy" argument?

                . . . the "test of love" theory?

(b) According to Dr. Gordon, what are the possible psychological effects of premarital sexual relationships?

(c) What makes the author believe that chastity and monogamy are twins?

3. Inference

(a) In the first four paragraphs, what does the author imply about the sexual guidance of the older generation?

(b) Does paragraph nine suggest that Dr. Gordon is for or against sex education?

4. Opinion

(a) Do you agree or disagree with Dr. Gordon's argument? Explain?

(b) Do you think the "New Morality" is a major cause of the so-called "generation gap"?

VOCABULARY BUILDING

Lesson One: Words about Morality: Part I

Morality is discussed when people consider what is right and wrong. People think about right and wrong when it involves behavior toward other people, personal honesty and integrity, and sexual behavior. The degree of a person's morality is often measured by what is taken as the standard to which the larger part of society conforms.

Here are a few words which appear in "The New Case for Chastity" and are useful when discussing morality:

illicit	(paragraph 3)
provocative	(3)
promiscuity	(6)
chaste	(9)
furtive	(13)

A person who does something illegal or forbidden is said to do something that is *illicit*.

A person whose behavior or ideas are stimulating and arousing is said to be *provocative*.

A person accused of loose sexual behavior is often accused of *promiscuity*.

A person who is a virgin is *chaste*.

A person who does something in a sly and hidden way has a *furtive* manner.

EXERCISE 3A: Fill in the blanks with the correct word.

1. Why didn't you tell me? Why did you have to do that in such a thief-

    like and _____ manner?

2. Many people choose to be _____ until they are married.

3. Of course, you realize that what you have done is _____
    because it is against the law.

4. People accuse her of _____ because she be-
    comes sexually involved with every man she meets.

5. When she asked that _____ question, the
    students became very interested in the discussion.

Name: _____ Date: _____

Lesson Two: Words about Morality: Part II

Here are more words which do not appear in the essay but are useful when you talk about morality:

altruistic	**righteous**	**impious**
contemptible	**amoral**	**unscrupulous**
magnanimous	**ethical**	**notorious**

His ideas show that he cares about the welfare of other people. He is *altruistic*.

His ideas are disgusting and make others despise him. His ideas are *contemptible*.

His ideas are full of generosity and show forgiveness towards others. His ideas are *magnanimous*.

His ideas are upright and often religious. He is *righteous*.

His ideas show no concern for what is right. He is *amoral*.

His ideas are very proper and fair. He is honest and moral towards others. He is *ethical*.

His ideas show no respect for anything holy. He is *impious*.

His ideas are dishonest and unprincipled. He likes to exploit people. His ideas are *unscrupulous*.

His ideas are famous for their wickedness. He is *notorious*.

EXERCISE 3B: Who has what attitude toward extreme poverty? Choose from:

altruistic   contemptible   notorious   magnanimous

1. Everyone knows me—I'm widely known for taking advantage of the

    poor. I am _____.

2. As long as it doesn't affect me, let the poor people starve. I am _____

    _____.

3. I forgive you and want to help you make up for your mistakes. I am

    _____.

4. I am concerned about the well-being of all people. I am _____.

Name: _____   Date: _____

EXERCISE 3C: Which word describes him? Choose from:

righteous
amoral
ethical
impious
unscrupulous

1. He likes honesty and hates cheating. _____

2. He laughs at the idea of a God. _____

3. He does not care who he hurts as long as he gets rich. _____

_____

4. He believes that it is Godly to do the right thing. _____

5. He does not care one way or the other about justice. _____

SPELLING

Lesson One: Spelling Demons

Here are some more words that are frequently misspelled. Using the helpful techniques given in Chapter One, be sure to learn these new Demons,
which are taken from "The New Case for Chastity."

acquaintance	meant
argument	methods
challenge	original
completely	particular
determine	permanent
distinguish	practical
embarrassing	realize
enjoy	recognize
experience	significance
genuine	simply
influence	symbol
marriage	therefore

Name: _____ Date: _____

Lesson Two: Spelling Rule—Changing Y to I

Many of the words in Ernest Gordon's essay can be learned easily with the help of this one simple spelling rule.

Words ending in y preceded by a consonant change y to i before suffixes—EXCEPT when the suffix begins with i.

☞ YOU DO THIS:

Add the suffixes indicated to the following words.

	-ed	-ing	-(e)s
classify	_____	_____	_____
destroy	_____	_____	_____
deny	_____	_____	_____

Here are some examples:
anxiety + es = anxie*ties*   satisfy + ing = satisf*ying*
portray + ed = portra*yed*   intensify + ed = intensif*ied*
century + es = centu*ries*   tricky + est = trick*iest*

☞ YOU DO THIS:

Apply the y to i rule to the following words.

fallacy + es = _____   glorify + ed = _____

imply + ing = _____   country + es = _____

deny + al = _____   lovely + est = _____

A SPECIAL NOTE: Here are four words that you see frequently which—if you look at them closely—are exceptions to the above rule.

lay + ed = laid   pay + ed = paid
say + ed = said   day + ly = daily

EXERCISE 3D: Apply the y to i rule to these new words.

1. study + ing = _____

2. accompany + ed = _____

3. colony + es = _____

4. friendly + ness = _____

5. lively + hood = _____

6. bury + es = _____

7. carry + ed = _____

8. industry + es = _____

9. valley + es = _____

10. apply + ing = _____

11. beauty + ful = _____

12. theory + es = _____

13. vary + ous = _____

14. try + es = _____

15. lonely + ness = _____

16. monkey + s = _____

17. family + es = _____

18. marry + ing = _____

19. story+ es = _____

20. controversy + al = _____

Name: _____ Date: _____

EXERCISE 3E: Using the definitions given as clues, fill in this puzzle. If necessary, check your spelling with the list of Demons in this chapter.

Down

1. fully; thoroughly
2. real
3. to discover; find out
4. to summon to a duel
5. importance
6. opposite of temporary
7. the first
8. to affect
9. procedures
10. an emblem; representation

Across

11. intended
12. to see clearly
13. to be caught in a lie is an
   _____ situation
14. easily
15. a dispute
16. to become aware of
17. I know him slightly; he is
   an _____
18. wedlock
19. to obtain pleasure from
20. to identify

Name: _____ Date: _____

THE SENTENCE FRAGMENT

A group of words set off as a sentence must be complete. This is a simple requirement and an easy one to test, but the writing of sentence fragments is a common error for the beginning writer. To avoid writing sentence fragments, you must learn this:

Three-step Test of Sentence Completeness

(a) Find the conjugated verb.
(b) Find the subject.
(c) Look to see if the subject and verb are introduced by a DANGER WORD. (See list on page 64.) If so, the sentence is not a complete thought.

Now each step in this test will be discussed further:

(a) *Fragment caused by a missing conjugated verb*: A VERB expresses action, existence, occurrence, etc. An easy way to identify a word as a verb is to use the slot method. Only verbs will fit properly in the blank space.

Let's _____ something.

The method can be tested with some common verbs

Let's *throw* something.	Let's *smell* something.
Let's *be* something.	Let's *consider* something.
Let's *think* something.	Let's *want* something.

A SPECIAL NOTE: The various forms of the verb *to be* will not fit properly in the blank space of the slot method. Because *to be* is the most often used verb, you should be completely familiar with its many forms: *am, are, is, was, were*, etc.

The verb in a sentence must be complete and conjugated. Notice that there are two ways it is not conjugated:

(1) if it has an *-ing* ending without a helping verb,

Fragment	*Corrected*
Jim studying data processing.	Jim *is* studying data processing.
	OR
	Jim *was* studying data processing.

(2) if it is an infinitive (*to* run, *to* go, *to* do, etc.)

Fragment	*Corrected*
Jim to program a computer.	Jim *is* to program a computer.
	OR
	Jim programs a computer.

61

Each sentence must have a complete conjugated verb. The verb in one sentence cannot be thought of as part of the next sentence; the verb *must actually appear* in the sentence.

John has many varied interests. Such as psychology, philosophy, and politics.

The first statement is a complete sentence; the second is a fragment because it has no verb.

☞ YOU DO THIS:

Draw two lines under the verbs in the following word groups. Then correct any fragments so that they are complete sentences.

1. Ethical people always influence others.

2. Joe to enjoy his summer vacation in Mexico.

3. A notorious criminal with a long list of arrests.

(b) *Fragment caused by a missing subject*: The SUBJECT is the noun or pronoun unit about which something is said. To find the subject of a sentence, first find the complete conjugated verb. Then simply ask, "*Who or what* is doing the action?" For example:

The boy threw the ball.

The verb is *threw*. *Who* or *what* threw? The *boy* threw. Therefore, the boy is the subject of the sentence. In a command the subject is usually not given but it is implied as *you*. For example:

Run for your life! Close the window before it rains!

Who should run? You. Who should close the window? You. Therefore, *you* is the subject of these and most commands. A word group may sometimes be the subject of a sentence:

Going to a movie is great fun.
Whoever can pass the test will be given an "A" as a grade.

To find the subject, you just find the verb and ask the same question: who or what is great fun? *Going to a movie.* Who or what will be given an "A" as a grade? *Whoever can pass the test.* Therefore, a word group is the subject of each sentence.

You may sometimes forget to include the subject of a sentence because you have just used it in the preceding sentence and because it obviously seems to be the subject of the fragment. But you must always remember that the subject *must* be included in each sentence (with the exception of a command).

The trapeze artist was in a precarious situation as he flew through the air. Reached for the swing and finished the stunt.

The first statement is a complete sentence; the second is a fragment because it has no subject. *Who* reached for the swing and finished the stunt? The fragment does not tell us.
To correct this error:

connect the fragment to the preceding sentence

OR

put a subject into the fragment

Examples: The trapeze artist was in a precarious situation as he flew through the air, reached for the swing, and finished the stunt.

He reached for the swing and finished the stunt.

☞ YOU DO THIS:

Draw two lines under the verbs and one line under the subjects in the following word groups. If a subject is missing, put one in to make the fragment into a complete sentence.

1. The stranger cast a furtive glance in my direction.

2. Pocketed the bracelet and left the jewelry store.

(c) *Fragment caused by a* DANGER WORD: If the conjugated verb and its subject are introduced by a DANGER WORD, you do not have a complete sentence; it does not express a complete thought. It is merely a cliff-hanger, because it begins a statement but does not finish it.

Example: If you come home

... what?

The most commonly used DANGER WORDS are:

after	unless		
although (though)	how		
as (if)	when		
because (for)	where	who	whoever
before	while	whom	whomever
if	until	which	what
since	so that	that	whatever

Most of the DANGER WORDS are readily noticed because they come before the expression they affect.

Because Al was too dogmatic to prevent the argument
After Sally asked her most provocative question
Although he was very athletic when he was younger

The introductory DANGER WORD makes each of these a fragment without a complete thought. What happened because Al was too dogmatic? What happened after Sally asked her most provocative question? What happened although he was very athletic when he was younger? The DANGER WORDS suggest that the answers to these questions must be included in the sentences.

The DANGER WORDS which are listed in the box at the right (especially *who, which,* and *that*) frequently appear between the subject and verb.

The man who is embarrassed easily
The vase which is lightly tinged with gold
The advertisement that drew the greatest response

None of these incomplete sentences tells the reader what happened. What will the man who is embarrassed easily do? What about the vase? What about the advertisement? The thought is not complete.

A SPECIAL NOTE: Do not forget about the Danger Words completely. *When used correctly,* they are excellent tools for writing complex sentences. This will be fully illustrated in the next chapter.

To correct the fragment caused by a DANGER WORD:

Attach the fragment to the previous sentence or to the one that follows, whichever is most closely connected in thought to the fragment.

Examples: After Sally asked her most provocative question, the class became much more interesting.

Joe had gotten flabby in his later years, although he was very athletic when he was younger.

OR

Complete the fragment with the necessary words.

The man who is embarrassed easily should stay out of arguments.

A PROOFREADING SUGGESTION: You may find it easier to spot a fragment in your writing if you read your paragraphs from the last sentence to the first sentence. In this way, you disconnect the fragment from the surrounding sentences, which are usually closely linked to the fragment in thought and, therefore, might blend when you read them.

☞ ## YOU DO THIS:

Draw two lines under the verbs, draw one line under the subjects, and circle any DANGER WORDS in the following word groups. Correct the fragments so that they are complete sentences.

1. Hal is really quite an unscrupulous businessman.

2. Although he always pretends to be such a righteous person.

3. A man who could be completely trusted.

EXERCISE 3F: Rewrite any fragments so that they are complete sentences. (Some of the word groups may already be complete.)

1. Although Mark was known as an altruistic man

   _____

2. An opportunity to seek recognition

   _____

3. The teacher who was a gourmet

   _____

4. The scene was carefully described

   _____

Name: _____ Date: _____

5. The dog burying the bone

_____

6. Mr. Nelson, an old acquaintance of mine

_____

7. When Jim realized the significance of the ordinance

_____

8. Embarrassing everyone in the audience

_____

9. If Al behaves abysmally, he will lose our respect

_____

10. A practical experience that everyone should have

_____

11. To avoid being mutilated

_____

12. Simply a case of the contemporary music replacing the old

_____

13. Denying his original statement

_____

14. The washer which was fully guaranteed

_____

15. Before he made another one of his impious remarks

_____

16. Unless they are stopped, racists will always intimidate Negroes

_____

17. The government interested in ethical values

_____

Name: _____ Date: _____

31103

18. Without any knowledge of psychology

_____

19. Whoever asks the most provocative question

_____

20. Being a highly compatible couple with three children

_____

EXERCISE 3G: Each of the following paragraphs contains one fragment. Make it into a complete sentence, rewriting where necessary. Use the space provided.

1. Ernest Gordon's article deals with a very provocative subject. The search for new moral standards by this country's young people. The author denies the existence of widespread promiscuity. Gordon's argument makes one think.

_____

2. Dr. Schweitzer was certainly a rare example of selflessness. His work in Africa showed him to be a truly altruistic man. A man who dedicated his life to combatting disease. The doctor will always be remembered as a symbol of man's greatness.

_____

3. I filled in the questionnaire quickly. Eager to meet some compatible dates. I knew the dates might not work out. But I decided to remain optimistic.

_____

4. Although Dan was a very friendly fellow, he consistently suffered from loneliness. Whenever he made a new acquaintance. he was overly attentive. Apparently, this excessive interest drove people away. Because Dan's obsequious attitude made them feel uncomfortable.

_____

5. Jesse James was quite a notorious outlaw. He used the trickiest and most furtive methods of escape. But, in the end, was caught anyway. That old saying is true: crime does not pay.

_____

Name: _____ Date: _____

6. Mike has demonstrated that a person can be too ethical. As an experiment, he was completely truthful for one week. Then he moved to another city. Leaving behind many angry, disillusioned people.

_____

7. How to program a computer. First, feed the data into the machine. Push the necessary buttons that will make the computer correlate the material. Then, simply read off the answers received.

_____

8. Business efficiency is not what it used to be. Especially during the hot summer months. The heat makes the workers very lazy and irritable. Thus, air conditioning is a good investment.

_____

9. Trying to save a few dollars, Jim bought his car from "Solid Sam, the Used Car Man." In two days' time the car broke down. Solid Sam denied any responsibility. Just what one would expect from an unscrupulous car dealer.

_____

10. It was a touching sight. The children playing gently with the tiny puppy. It was a good opportunity to take some pictures. These satisfying moments would be permanently recorded.

_____

Name: _____ Date: _____

COMMA SPLICES AND RUN-ON SENTENCES

Like the sentence fragments, the comma splice and the run-on sentence are serious errors which can be eliminated with the help of the three-step test of sentence completeness. (See page 61.) Let's use the test on the following sentences:

<u>Mary</u> <u>was</u> fickle. <u>She</u> <u>went</u> steady with three boys in one month.

Both of these sentences are complete because they each have a subject and verb which are not introduced by a DANGER WORD. Now let's examine the same sentences which have undergone one seemingly minor change:

<u>Mary</u> <u>was</u> fickle, <u>she</u> <u>went</u> steady with three boys in one month.

We still have the same complete sentences, but they have now been joined by a comma. Because two complete sentences cannot be joined by just a comma, the above illustration is an error called a comma splice.

Notice how the next set of sentences repeats the mistake:

The <u>man</u> who i̸s̸ unscrupulous <u>will</u> eventually <u>pay</u> for his evil deeds, however, <u>he</u> <u>will</u> <u>have</u> many profitable years until his judgment day.

Although the verb *is* has been cancelled out by a DANGER WORD *who*, there are still two separate subjects and two separate verbs. Thus, we have two distinct sentences that should not be fused with a comma, as the corrected sentences indicate:

The man who is unscrupulous will eventually pay for his evil deeds. However, he will have many profitable years until his judgment day.

Now use the test of sentence completeness to examine the following:

Because J̸o̸e i̸s̸ so ethical, <u>he</u> <u>makes</u> many enemies, <u>people</u> <u>are</u> often <u>offended</u> by the truth.

Although the first possible subject and verb are cancelled out by the DANGER WORD *because*, we are still left with two subject-verb sets. Again we have two sentences which have been spliced together with a comma and need to be separated.

Because Joe is so ethical, he makes many enemies.
People are often offended by the truth.

Compare the previous error to the one made in the next sentences:

Sex education must certainly be a provocative subject it is easy to form a discussion group for such a topic.

Here we also have two separate subject-verb sets in what should be two sentences. But unlike the comma splice, these sentences have been run together without even a comma.

Sex education must certainly be a provocative subject. It is easy to form a discussion group for such a topic.

Now the sentences are written correctly. You should note that the run-on is considered a more serious error than the comma splice because it implies that the writer does not sense a pause between two distinct thoughts.

There are several ways to correct the comma splice and run-on sentence. The method you choose will depend on the content of your sentences. To correct your error you might:

End the first sentence with a period and begin a new sentence with a capital letter.	Examples: The man who is unscrupulous will eventually pay for his evil deeds. However, he will have many profitable years until his judgment day.

OR

Place a semicolon between two sentences if they are closely related in idea. Do *not* begin the second sentence with a capital letter.	Because Joe is so ethical, he makes many enemies; people are often offended by the truth.

OR

If the two sentences are of equal importance, join them with one of these five conjunctions: and, or, nor, but, for. Notice that the conjunction is preceded by a comma.	Sex education must certainly be a provocative subject, for it is easy to form a discussion group for such a topic.

☞ YOU DO THIS:

Draw two lines under the verbs, draw one line under the subjects, and circle any DANGER WORDS in the following word groups. Then correct the comma splice and run-on sentence.

1. Because Al is so tactful, he is sure to get the post as ambassador to Chile, therefore, he will soon be leaving his present job.

2. Sky diving is a sport that everyone should try it is such a thrilling experience.

70

EXERCISE 3H: Write a sentence to follow each of the sentences given below. The punctuation following each sentence below should be a hint of how to start the added sentence.

1. A good imagination is a necessity for a writer;

   _____

2. Everyone deplores violence and brutality,

   _____

3. He sounds like a very fickle person.

   _____

4. Hal looked down the alley in a furtive manner,

   _____

5. Jesse James was one of the most notorious outlaws of the West;

   _____

6. Politicians always seem to be very altruistic,

   _____

7. Computer programmers will never replace matchmakers.

   _____

8. The audience enjoyed the speech considerably;

   _____

9. A demagogue cannot succeed in an enlightened society,

   _____

10. Against a background of poverty and filth stood the mutilated shacks of the Negro ghetto;

    _____

Name: _____ Date: _____

EXERCISE 3I: Identify the comma splices and run-ons and revise them in the spaces provided. Some of the sentences may already be correct as they are.

1. Neither the weather nor your warnings will make me change my mind, I still intend to drive to the country.

   _____

   _____

2. There is one thing I simply must know is Joe as pompous as he seems?

   _____

   _____

3. A little knowledge makes us hunger for more, consequently, we are always growing intellectually.

   _____

   _____

4. The history teacher, together with his students, tried to approximate the height of the Washington Memorial, then they posed for a class picture in front of the monument.

   _____

   _____

5. Please send me some money I am almost broke.

   _____

6. Although I quickly saw the error in Joe's argument, I did not challenge him, he would only become disillusioned.

   _____

   _____

7. An agnostic is not sure if there is a God an atheist, on the other hand, positively denies that there is a God.

   _____

   _____

Name: _____ Date: _____

8. We must integrate our schools and relieve the poverty of the oppressed, thus, we will bring about true racial equality.

_____

_____

9. Although he was annoyed with Mary's dogmatic attitude, the preacher listened quietly, smiled politely, and held in his anger.

_____

_____

10. I have always admired Joe's special qualities, he manages to be both articulate and tactful at the same time.

_____

_____

11. When will social ostracism cease to be a part of our society, I wish I knew.

_____

_____

12. Frank is certainly one of the most amoral people I have ever met, however, Helen more than makes up for her husband's contemptible behavior.

_____

_____

_____

13. The lecturer described the Picasso canvas with its unusual combination of red and purple, the painting is an excellent example of the artist's use of color.

_____

_____

_____

Name: _____ Date: _____

14. If you remain optimistic in the face of the most disastrous situation, you will eventually achieve success attitude is everything.

_____

_____

15. Joe finds it easy to influence others, why can't I?

_____

16. Computerized dating services overlook one very important aspect, when people fill out the computer questionnaire, they tend to lie about their physical appearance and personality traits.

_____

_____

_____

17. Marriage should always be thought of as a permanent relationship, therefore, you should not be hasty in making such a binding decision.

_____

_____

18. John Kennedy did not believe that the government should provide the country's strength rather he thought that the people should provide the government's strength.

_____

_____

_____

19. A moment of recognition can be an embarrassing experience, for example, your boss may praise you for work that was actually done by someone else.

_____

_____

_____

20. Please do not condemn me for my actions I know what I am doing.

_____

Name: _____ Date: _____

1. Correct the fragments, comma splices, and run-ons in these paragraphs, which were taken from a student's theme on sex education in the schools.
2. Answer the additional questions that follow the paragraphs.

As the schools begin sex education programs. They should enlist parental support and involvement. With the parents' help, the educators can proceed with confidence and the parents will not feel left out of such an important learning process. The parents and teachers must learn to trust and understand each other if there is to be full cooperation, moreover, the parents should be involved in group discussions, seminars on human sexuality. Although specially trained teachers would run the program. All kinds of teachers — and even the school nurses — would be encouraged to participate. Sex should not be left for just one class it should be part of any course in biology, literature, sociology, and psychology.

Sex education should be taught in a definite sequence, the preschool education should deal with the growth of plants and animals. In addition to information about puberty and reproduction, elementary schools should deal with problems concerning one's emotions. Such as love, anger, and aggression. Junior high school education should include discussions about dating and the physical relationship between boys and girls, high school sex education should deal with such problems as venereal disease, early marriage, unwanted pregnancies, and abortions. Films, recordings, and guest lecturers would be used to supplement classroom discussions on each school level.

ADDITIONAL QUESTIONS

1. What is the topic sentence of each paragraph?

   Paragraph one: _____

   _____

   _____

   Paragraph two: _____

   _____

   _____

2. Is there more than one main idea in each paragraph?

   Paragraph one: _____

   Paragraph two: _____

3. What order is used to develop the second paragraph?

   _____

Name: _____ Date: _____

SPRINGBOARDS TO WRITING

1. As a result of looking at the Valentine card and song, reading the essay, or answering the questions that follow each, you might have some thoughts about the central theme—premarital teenage relationships. (Look back at those pages to refresh your memory.) For help in planning such an essay, refer to the Guide for Planning an Essay, which appears in Springboards to Writing, Chapter One, on page 25.

2. Here are some topics which have not been directly mentioned in the questions asked so far. Perhaps one of them could be a writing springboard for you:
   (a) The case for (against) the theme of sex in advertisements.
   (b) The case for (against) the theme of sex in plays, movies, or books.
   (c) Abortion should (should not) be legalized.
   (d) What is love?
   (e) The case for (against) sex education in the schools.
   (f) A plan for sex education in the schools.

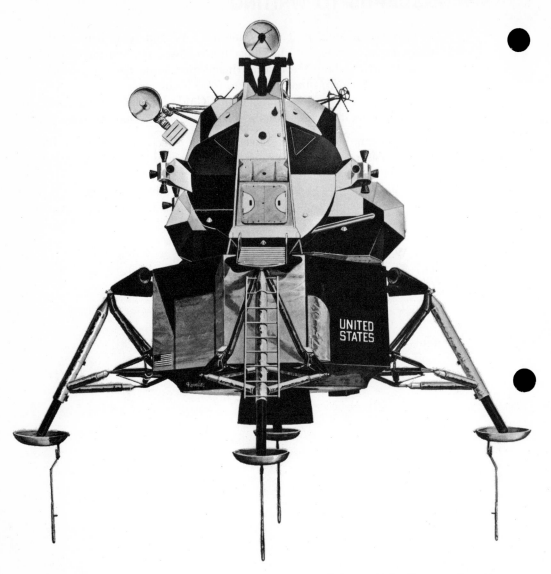

© Courtesy of the Grumman Aerospace Corporation. Artist Craig Kavafes.

CHAPTER four

"Hey, look! Here's a report that says we don't exist."

Cartoon by Joseph Farris. Copyright
1969 Saturday Review, Inc.

SPRINGBOARDS TO THINKING

For informal, not written, response . . . to stimulate your thinking

1. What parts of the United States' Lunar Excursion Module (LEM) make it look human to many who look at it? Do you think you would be startled at the sight of the LEM?

2. Do the beings in the cartoon look friendly? Why or why not? Would you look friendly to them? Why or why not? Would the LEM look friendly to them? Why or why not?

3. Can anything exist if the newspapers report that it does not exist? Why or why not? How can you prove your point of view?

4. Would the sight of a strange looking thing landing on earth frighten you? Why are many concerned people worried about the possibility of unintentional war with beings from outer space?

5. Do science-fiction stories help us prepare ourselves for the sight of unusual looking extraterrestrial beings or machines? Why or why not? How can we be able to convince such "visitors" who do not speak English—or any other earth language—that we are intelligent beings rather than plant life?

Celestial Crockery

J. P. CHAPLIN

I

(1) The time was 1:15 P.M.; the date January 7, 1948; the place, the control tower at Godman Air Force Base outside Louisville, Kentucky. A call had just come in from the Kentucky highway patrol. It seemed that several people in Marysville, a small town some eighty miles from Louisville, were concerned about a strange object they had seen in the sky. Quite naturally the police officers considered celestial problems outside of their jurisdiction and had turned the matter over to the Air Force. But Godman knew of no aircraft, mysterious or otherwise, that had not been accounted for in the vicinity. So Godman, in turn, inquired of Wright-Patterson Field in Ohio. Again, no Kentucky-bound flights had originated from that area.

(2) At 1:35 the highway patrol called again. The strange denizen of the skies had passed to the west of Louisville, and by this time a number of people in two towns had seen it. The spotters were able to report that the mysterious object was circular in shape, some 260–300 feet in diameter, and moving westward at a good clip.

(3) Ten minutes later the control tower personnel at Godman, along with other officers on the base, saw the unidentified object. Several of the airmen peered at it through binoculars, but none was able to hazard an identification.

(4) About 2:30 P.M. four F-51's came within range of the control tower. It was a routine flight of National Guard airmen under the leadership of Captain Thomas F. Mantell, Jr. The tower radioed Mantell and asked him to look into the matter of the still-hovering unidentified object. The captain took two of his wingmen (the third was low on gas) in pursuit of the mysterious visitor. Since none of the pilots could see the object, the tower gave Mantell a bearing. and the airmen began to climb in the direction the tower had suggested.

(5) By the time they reached 10,000 feet, Mantell had taken such a lead on his wingmen they could hardly see him. Shortly afterwards, the Captain called the tower and reported that at last he could see his target. Later there was some disagreement as to just how Mantell described the object, but according to the collective memory of those who were in the tower that day he was supposed to have said the object was "metallic and tremendous in size . . . it appears like the reflection of sunlight on an airplane canopy." A little later he added, "It's bright and climbing away from me."

(6) By now Mantell was at 15,000 feet and without oxygen, since the routine flight had not been planned for an excursion of such high eleva-

tions. When asked for a further report, Mantell replied he was going to 20,000 feet, and if he failed to close in, he would give up the chase.

(7) This was the last anyone heard from Mantell. Neither the tower nor his wingmen could see him, and, after flying around for a while, the wingmen landed long enough to refuel and take on oxygen. They took off again to look for their leader but were unable to find any trace of him. At 3:53 P.M. the tower lost sight of the mysterious object, and a few minutes later word was received that Mantell had crashed and was dead. An eyewitness of the plane's final moments said the pilot acted as if he didn't know where he was going just before the plane went into a power dive towards the ground. The plane, according to the witness, exploded halfway down.

(8) Since this was the sixth month of the first year of the age of flying saucers, wild stories about what had happened at Godman soon found their way into circulation. The plane, according to various reports, was said to have been "disintegrated," "shot full of holes," "magnetized," "made radioactive," and Mantell himself was rumored to have been reduced to primeval elements by his clash with the "flying saucer."

(9) The more prosaic explanation of the accident given out by the Air Force was that Mantell had unwisely ascended to a height where he blacked out from oxygen deficiency, and in the resulting dive his out-of-control plane had lost a wing. The Air Force denied that either the wrecked plane or the body demonstrated any injuries of extraterrestrial origin and concluded the report by suggesting that Mantell had been pursuing the planet Venus. This was the first casualty resulting from an attempted saucer interception.

II

(10) The saucers first visited Earth a little over six months earlier on June 24, 1947, when Kenneth Arnold sighted nine odd-looking craft near Mount Rainier while piloting his private plane from Chehalis to Yakima, Washington. The weather was fine for flying, and he could see saucer-like objects clearly as they dipped in and out of the mountain peaks at terrific speeds, estimated by him to be over a thousand miles an hour. This was the beginning of a ten-year saucer-in-the-skies mania that is still going on, though much diminished in the last few years. It may well be the greatest mass delusion in the history of the planet. It has resulted in thousands of sightings, several deaths, and tens of thousands of wasted man hours spent in tracking down reports of unidentified celestial visitors. During the height of the hysteria, the President and members of Congress were deluged by letters demanding an "explanation." The Air Force came under heavy fire from the Believers who in books and magazine articles repeatedly charged the Pentagon with maintaining a conspiracy of secrecy about the nature and mission of the saucers. Among the Believers, some held that the saucers were secret weapons, some favored the spaceship

theory, and still others were inclined toward the possibility of unauthorized reconnaissance flights originating from the USSR.

(11) It all began as a reaction to the Arnold sighting. Arnold, it has been claimed, never called the saucers "saucers," but described the unidentified craft over Mt. Rainier as "saucer-like." However, the newsmen who wrote up the incident christened them "flying saucers," and this was the name that stuck. Arnold was given a bad time by the newspapers. They reported his sighting with tongue far out in cheek, and Arnold was finally moved to comment on the possibility of future sightings to the effect that "even if it were a ten-story building flying through the air" he would disregard it.

(12) The Air Force's reaction to Arnold's sighting was to send a search party of five P-51's on hunt over the Pacific Northwest, but the searchers found no trace of saucers, and, in view of the negative findings, announced there were insufficient facts to warrant any further investigation. Meanwhile, reports of saucers in the skies were originating as far east as New York and from as far around the world as Australia. However, it was rare for anyone to take the sightings seriously as yet. The New York *Times* on July 6, 1947, came out with a hot weather editorial poking fun at the rash of saucer sightings. Along the same lines, an enterprising reporter asked Andrei Gromyko, who was representing Russia at Lake Success at the time, what he thought of the whole business; the Russian suggested the apparitions might be due to excessive importations of Scotch whiskey into the United States. More to the point, a professor of physiology in Sidney, Australia, had four hundred and fifty students go out and stare at the heavens and report back to him what, if anything, they were able to see. Within ten minutes some had returned with reports of discs in the sky. The professor charged the sightings to the students having seen blood corpuscles coursing across their retinas.

(13) The citizenry in general were quick to react to Arnold's report and apparently took the saucers no more seriously than either the press or foreign commentators. *Life* magazine in its July 23, 1947 issue, published just a month after the Mt. Rainier incident, was able to summarize the situation across the Republic as follows: A rash of things have been seen. A woman in Seattle, Washington, brushed the excitement aside with the blasé statement, "Why they come through our yard all the time."

(14) In Spokane, eight flying washtubs had been sighted. A dietary fanatic in Chicago believed the saucers were hallucinations brought on by bad dietetic practices. He thought the skies would clear if Americans would only eat fifty dandelion blooms every day. Earnest Hooten, the famous Harvard anthropologist, had a different explanation: he believed the saucers were misplaced halos searching for persons who had been killed on the Fourth of July. Not only were saucers reported but chromium hub caps, dimes, teardrops, ice cream cones, and pie plates as well. The sky, it appeared, was becoming a veritable junk shop.

(15) Of course, the hoaxters also got into stride shortly after the initial

reports were published. In Shreveport, Louisiana, an aluminum disc with fake jet-propulsion units crashed into the street, and when a portion of a buzz saw blade struck a church in Grafton, Wisconsin, the edgy priest called the F.B.I.

(16) Such was the state of the skies in July. The New York *Times* had already put it all down to a mass delusion and believed the saucers would soon be consigned to the "limbo" reserved for such human vagaries. But the sightings continued, and in September of 1947, Project "Sign" was initiated by the Air Force to deal with the increasing flow of reports of unidentified airborne objects. At first the project employed only Air Force personnel, but these were soon augmented by astronomers, psychologists, physicians, physicists, meteorologists, and representatives of the dread Federal Bureau of Investigation.

(17) It was early in 1948 that the death of Captain Mantell occurred; but curiously enough, 1948 did not prove to be a good saucer year. The only significant event aside from the Mantell incident occurred during the summer when there was a rash of sightings along the Eastern Seaboard, but these turned out to be released water balloons. Of course there were scattered reports of unidentified flying objects every month. A dossier to the Air Force throughout the year and were duly, but unsuccessfully investigated. [sic]

(18) By the early part of 1949, the Air Force was ready with a report. On the average they had been receiving twelve reports of unidentified flying objects every month. A dossier of two hundred and forty cases had been accumulated by April of 1949, and an analysis revealed that thirty percent were traceable to known phenomena such as meteorites, weather balloons, formations of ducks, and the like. Another thirty percent were probably of conventional origin, and the final forty percent remained a question mark. The big problem was a lack of accurate data; the witnesses had no way of making measurements of the speed, altitude, size, and other characteristics of objects they had seen coursing through the skies. This problem was to continue to plague the analysts for years to come. Meanwhile, on February 11, 1949, Project Sign was dissolved and Project Grudge took its place as the official Air Force agency for investigating flying saucer reports. According to Captain Edward J. Ruppelt in his *Report on Unidentified Flying Objects* the whole policy of the project was to "get rid" of flying saucers. It was, according to the Captain, "the Dark Ages" of the saucers. The Air Force did not believe in saucers but would grudgingly investigate further reports.

(19) In April and May of 1949, two articles by Sidney Shalett appeared in the *Saturday Evening Post*. These accounts represent milestones in the history of the saucers, since they were published with the blessing of the Air Force and were definitely antisaucer in their treatment of the subject. The Believers denounced the articles as following the "party line" of certain "Pentagonians" who, they alleged, were trying to hide the facts of the saucer menace from the American people. After the *Post* articles any-

thing that was subsequently published under the imprimatur of the Air Force was immediately regarded by the Believers as part of a "conspiracy" of silence and misinformation they attributed to the Pentagon.

(20) As spring wore into summer, reports continued to come in. In Seattle, Washington, a woman called the police when she discovered a flaming saucer on her roof. A hammer and sickle and the letters USSR had been crudely painted on the fiery missile. The device, however, turned out to be a homemade affair constructed of plywood; it was definitely *not* of Soviet origin. According to a UP report, some Texans saw flying bananas, saucers and a plate in the sky. This was the nearest thing to an entire airborne dinner reported up to that time. Up in New England, MIT sent up twenty-five research balloons which gave rise to a saucer scare in those conservative latitudes. Some of the New Englanders who had spotted the balloons excitedly reported there were "ghost riders in the sky."

(21) In August, two old flying machines were discovered in a Maryland barn, and the Air Force thought these might be the answer to the saucer craze. The unconventional craft were the inventions of one Jonathan E. Caldwell who had disappeared in 1941, apparently abandoning his brain children to rust and decay. One was a kind of helicopter with a saucer-like body; the other looked more like a large wooden wash tub. The Baltimore *Sun* quoted the Air Force officer who investigated the strange craft to the effect that Caldwell might now be in another part of the country flying workable models of his "saucers" and that this might have resulted in the rash of saucer reports. Needless to say, the elusive inventor never showed up piloting a saucer.

(22) By December, the Air Force was ready with its second report. After spending two years investigating the saucers, the Air Force announced that it was through. All the evidence indicated the air-borne crockery was: [1] misinterpretations of conventional aircraft or celestial phenomena; [2] mass hysteria; [3] hoaxes. Thus ended the second year of the saucers.

(23) In 1950, the Believers came into their own. It all began with an article in *U.S. News and World Report*, asserting the saucers were real. They were, in fact, United States Navy planes, still secret, and more or less saucer-like in general appearance. Henry J. Taylor, a radio network news commentator, seconded the motion that the saucers were top-secret United States inventions and newsmen immediately rushed to President Truman with the story. He denied that the Republic had any such aircraft and in a characteristic Trumanese said he was "just as puzzled as the next fellow."

(24) It was also in the early part of the year that tales of captured "Saucerians" began to circulate. Up to this time one of the most puzzling features of the saucers was the fact that they never seemed to land or crash. Either event would have been most welcome from the Air Force's point of view, since the unprecedented machines could then be studied

84

first hand. However, the Saucerians' lack of cooperation was soon made up for by Earthmen's imagination.

(25) Out in Denver, Colorado, a mysterious "expert" on saucers, identified only as "Dr. Gee," gave a lecture at Denver University in which he stated that three saucers had been captured with thirty-four dead bodies aboard. If the Saucerians had been alive, they would have been from thirty-six to forty inches in height. Evidently the spacemen were more advanced in scientific matters than earthlings, since they had no cavities in their teeth and subsisted on food wafers, one of which put in a gallon of water caused such a plethora of mush that the vessel overflowed.

(26) The saucers themselves were definitely not of earthly origin. The gears were unconventional in design, and there was no evidence of lubricants in the machinery. The metal defied classification, and in one case proved to be so hard that $35,000 worth of diamond drills were spoiled in trying to force an entry. Much was made of the saucers' measurements which always came out to be multiples of nine for all dimensions. The craft had no apparent motive power but it was believed that they operated on a "magnetic principle." Just what was involved was not made clear.

(27) "Dr. Gee," it turned out, was no expert at all but Leo GeBauer, the operator of a radio and television wholesale house in Phoenix, Arizona. Among his many terrestrial activities was the invention of an electronic dowser for locating oil deposits. He and an associate, Silas Newton, a Denver geophysicist, sold the device to a Denver businessman. The latter spent over a quarter of a million dollars on worthless oil land discovered by the "doodlebug." The two were convicted of a swindle when it turned out that the electronic dowser was a jumble of war surplus radio equipment worth approximately $3.50. In view of the circumstances, there seems to be little reason to put much credence in Dr. Gee's report.

(28) In June, another saucer reached the earth. It had been shot down and was found to contain twenty capsules filled with little men. The Saucerians were wrapped in aluminum foil for protection against cosmic rays.

(29) Finally, there was the report of a space ship which had crashed in New Mexico with fifteen spacemen aboard. The latter were unable to talk, but one drew a map of the solar system and pointed to Venus—presumably their point of departure. A wise Earthman thereupon suggested that the Venusians be placed in a pressurized chamber containing carbon dioxide, since that gas abounds on Venus according to astronomical observations.

(30) Understandably, the Air Force made no official comment on these reports. Something of this same skeptical attitude was revealed at a big airshow put on by the Air Force in San Antonio, Texas. It was announced over the loudspeakers that a top secret revelation about flying saucers would be given out as a climax to the affair. The excited spectators buzzed with anticipation, but the "revelation" turned out to be 30,000 paper plates released by planes flying overhead.

85

READING SURVEY

1. Main Idea

What is the central theme of the essay?

2. Major Details

(a) How did the Air Force explain the death of Captain Mantell?

(b) How were the unidentified flying objects christened "flying saucers"?

(c) After its two-year investigation, what were the conclusions of the Air Force concerning flying saucers?

3. Inference

(a) Read paragraph fourteen again. Judging from it—and from the essay's title—what is J. P. Chaplin's attitude towards flying saucers?

(b) Why does the author capitalize the word Believers when he refers to those who consider flying saucers real?

4. Opinion

(a) Do you think that flying saucers exist?

(b) Do you think the government has to "play down" reports of flying saucer sightings?

VOCABULARY BUILDING

Lesson One: The Vocabulary of Space Travel

I When one talks about space travel, there are many words which can be useful. Some of them appear in this essay:

celestial	(title)
elevation	(paragraph 6)
extraterrestrial	(9)
reconnaissance	(10)
propulsion	(15)
astronomical	(29)

Because *celestial* means heavenly,
we understand . . . celestial map
celestial navigation

Because *terrestrial* means earthly,
we understand . . . terrestrial plants
terrestrial transportation
extraterrestrial (nonearthly, celestial)

86

Because the prefix *astro* means star and/or heavens,
we understand . . . astrodome (look through and see stars)
astronaut (traveller of heavens)
astronomy (study of stars)
astronomical (as big as the number of stars)

Because *elevation* means height,
we understand . . . elevator
elevated highway

Because *propulsion* means push,
we understand . . . jet propulsion

Because *reconnaissance* means a survey to gather information,
we understand . . . military reconnaissance
reconnaissance plane (usually a spy plane)

EXERCISE 4A: Choosing from the list to the left below, substitute the one word which has the same meaning as the italicized words in this paragraph.

elevation
terrestrial
reconnaissance
celestial
astronomical
jet propulsion

The *spy* (   ) plane took off under *jet*

drive (   ) to a *height* (   )

of sixty thousand feet. For a navigation check the pilot looked for a few

heavenly (   ) bodies by visual sighting. Although

the mission was to photograph earthly (   )

locations, the pilot's personal interest was in a *huge*

(   ) number of stars in the galaxy.

Name: _____ Date: _____

II Here are a few more words which do not appear in this essay, but which are useful when discussing space travel:

aeronautics	**module**
probe	**rendezvous**
satellite	

First of all, it is important to know that *aeronautics* is the science of flight. Aeronautics combines information about both terrestrial and celestial conditions.

A SPECIAL NOTE: Many of these words were part of our terrestrial vocabulary long before space exploration began.

probe: terrestrial: A dentist *probes* between the teeth to investigate cavities.

    celestial: Before making a large study of something in outer space, scientists send up a preliminary investigation vehicle for a *probe*.

satellite: terrestrial: A country under the rule of, and subordinate to, another is a *satellite* of the ruling country.

    celestial: A body which orbits a larger body is a *satellite*. The moon is the earth's natural *satellite*, while other *satellites*, such as telestar, are man-made.

module: terrestrial: One part of an electric component is a *module*.

    celestial: Any one section of a spaceship is called a *module*: the section which houses the astronauts is called the command *module*; the section which holds most of the equipment is called the service *module*; and the section which leaves the mother ship to land on the moon is called the lunar *module*.

rendezvous: terrestrial: When people plan a meeting, they are planning a *rendezvous*.

    celestial: When space ships or modules are scheduled to meet in outer space, they *rendezvous* in space.

EXERCISE 4B: Choosing from the list to the left below, substitute the one word which has the same meaning as the italicized words in this paragraph.

satellite
probe
rendezvous
aeronautics
module

The specialist in *the science of flight* (   )

recommended that the United States send up a small *orbiting vehicle*

(   ) in order to *investigate* (   )

radiation conditions in outer space. The main *section* (   )

of the satellite would send back scientific information and would also

have a *meeting* (   ) with one of the

telestar satellites.

Lesson Two: The Vocabulary of Increase and Decrease

In our modern world many things go from one opposite extreme to another very quickly. World problems, for example, often decrease; but increase of such problems is equally possible. Many words can be used when discussing the opposites of increase and decrease. A few sets of such words appear in this essay:

decrease
deficiency = lack of
diminish = lessen
insufficient = not enough
disintegrate = break apart

increase
plethora = excess of
augment = enlarge
excessive = too much
unify = bring or put together

EXERCISE 4C: Use this exercise to learn the above words. Fill in the appropriate word from the list above.

1. (a) Some people say that UFO's are able to *break up*

    (   ) approaching planes.
   (b) Perhaps if UFO's do come from another galaxy, it will *bring to-*

    gether (   ) the nations of this planet to meet
    the unknown visitors from outer space.

2. (a) An *excess* (   ) of gadgets on a spaceship
       make it too heavy and complex.

   (b) On the other hand, it can be dangerous if there is a *lack of*

    (   ) safety backup features on a
    spaceship.

3. (a) Some people think that the explanations which the Air Force

    gives about UFO's are *not enough* (   ).

   (b) Other people think that the interest in UFO's is *too much*

    (   ) in view of the incomplete evidence.

4. (a) A man would *enlarge* (   ) his talents as an
       astronaut if he learned aeronautics.

   (b) A man's chance of becoming an astronaut would *lessen*

    (   ) if he suddenly needed eyeglasses.

Name: _____ Date: _____

SPELLING

Lesson One: Spelling Demons

Here are more words that are frequently misspelled. Using the helpful techniques given in Chapter One, you should make it a point to learn these new Demons, which were taken from "Celestial Crockery."

accurate	height
analysis	magazine
answer	mysterious
anticipation	naturally
article	operate
circumstances	originate
cooperation	practice
definitely	representative
describe	reveal
dissolve	tremendous
evidently	various
forty	warrant

Lesson Two: Proofreading

When a friend or teacher points out a misspelled word in your writing, do you sometimes insist, "But I know how to spell that word"? As we search for errors in our writing, we all tend to overlook the easy words and to concentrate on the difficult ones. But this leads to the painful experience of losing credit on a paper because of some careless spelling errors. Thus, one of the most important skills that a writer can learn is to proofread.

When you first learned to read, your eyes concentrated on each word and each letter within that word. But as your reading speed increased, you began to scan the sentences, paying attention only to certain key words. This is a fine technique for reading—but not for *proof*reading. To proofread your writing with success you must slow down your reading speed in order to take in the individual letters of each word. It has been found that the most effective way to do this is to place a ruler or sheet of paper under the line you are proofreading. Your eyes are now forced to move more slowly because they cannot automatically run on to the next line.

With the sheet of paper or ruler placed under the line, begin to examine each word, allowing the tip of your pen or pencil to rest on each syllable as you read it. If necessary, pronounce each word aloud. Most of all, as you proofread do not exceed your vision span. That is, do not exceed the number of letters you are able to identify clearly with a single glance. To determine your vision span, look at the top of the following triangle and then look down, reading the letters on each line *without moving your eyes.* When you can no longer identify all the letters on a line with a single glance, you have reached your limit and have determined your vision span.

```
            e
           e n
          e n h
         e n h s
        e n h s v
       e n h s v k
      e n h s v k b
     e n h s v k b t
    e n h s v k b t m
   e n h s v k b t m l
  e n h s v k b t m l o
```

Most people are able to identify about six letters without moving their eyes. Whatever your span, do not try to exceed it when you are proof-reading your writing. Now read the triangle of words given below. When you reach a group of letters that exceed your vision span, you should divide them into smaller units that you can check more accurately.

```
            I
           a m
          s a d
         w h e n
        b o o k s
       r e v e a l
      v a r i o u s
     p e r s o n a l
    h a r d s h i p s
   c o n c e r n i n g
  i l l u s t r i o u s
 g o v e r n m e n t a l
a c q u a i n t a n c e s
```

These few simple proofreading techniques can probably help you to eliminate about half of your spelling errors. Just remember to place a sheet of paper or a ruler under the line of writing, to use a pen or pencil to mark off the syllables, and not to exceed your vision span.

While this discussion has been limited to proofreading for spelling errors, the methods given are also useful for finding errors in grammar and punctuation. Again, it is a matter of reading slowly and with enough concentration to pick out your errors.

EXERCISE 4D PROOFREADING: Using the techniques given in this chapter, proofread the following paragraph for spelling errors, making any necessary corrections in the space directly above the misspelled word.

Newspaper and magazene readers should be aware of the varous ways in which news is withheld from the public. A recent artical on price fixing in the drug industry will serve as a good example. When high government officials were questioned, they asked the reporter not to reveel the circimstanses surrounding the investigation. Representitives of the drug industry refused to anser the reporter's questions about their business pratices, and paid informers supplied information that was far from acurate. Natrally, this lack of coperation forced the reporter to write an incomplete analisis of the situation.

Name: _____ Date: _____

EXERCISE 4E: Using at least eight of the Spelling Demons listed in this chapter, on separate paper write a brief description of the lunar module that is illustrated on page 78. Be sure to proofread your paragraph for any misspelled words.

EXERCISE 4F: In each of the following Demons, circle the letter or letters that are likely to cause you trouble. Then recopy the word in the space provided, enlarging the trouble spot so that it stands out as a reminder.

1. mysterious _____

2. definitely _____

3. operate _____

4. evidently _____

5. tremendous _____

6. various _____

7. forty _____

8. height _____

9. dissolve _____

10. warrant _____

Name: _____ Date: _____

COORDINATION

When two ideas are mentioned in a sentence, it is good to show their relationship to one another. One way to show relationship of ideas is to put them together using *coordination*. When you coordinate ideas, be sure that both ideas are related and of equal *importance*.

How to Employ Coordination

Example: His heartbeat became fainter, and soon he was dead.

Pattern: | independent sentence | , and | independent sentence |

> the *only* words which can be used here:
> and . . . but . . . for . . . nor . . . or

> sometimes you can leave these out and use the semicolon (;) *only.*

More examples:

She had prayed he would live, but she knew he would die.
She wept very hard, for now she was alone.
She would never forget his face, nor would she forget his warm eyes.
Even months later she would listen for his heavy breathing, or she would expect to hear his frisky bark.
It was time to buy a new one; everyone told her so.

☞ YOU DO THIS:

Practice correct coordination. Does (a) or (b) coordinate better?

1. The rendezvous had been started, _____.
   (a) and the probe cost five million dollars.
   (b) and the module responded well.

2. Their reconnaissance mission was successful, _____.
   (a) and the stars shone brightly.
   (b) and the extraterrestrial beings left for home.

3. You must diminish the air flow, _____.
   (a) for it is warm in here.
   (b) for the amount is excessive.

4. Some people thought he was ethical, _____.
   (a) but he was unscrupulous.
   (b) but he was pompous.

A FEW SMALLER POINTS: There is always a comma between two independent sentences joined by the words: and, but, for, nor, or. Look back and check!

Never coordinate more than two independent sentences because it is considered both bad and dull style. While two ideas may be equally important, three ideas usually have more complicated relationships with one another.

☞ YOU DO THIS:

Write with correct coordination:

1. A sentence about sports: _____

_____

2. A sentence about flying saucers: _____

_____

3. A sentence about computer dating: _____

_____

EXERCISE 4G: Does (a) or (b) coordinate better?

1. He was not a pompous man, _____. (a) nor was he a werewolf.
                                              (b) nor was he an egoist.

2. People were oppressed, _____. (a) and people were compatible.
                                  (b) and people were intimidated.

3. (a) The elevation was correct _____, but the propulsion was insufficient.

   (b) The module was silver

4. She is gullible; _____. (a) he is frugal.
                          (b) he is suave.

5. That is a fallacy, _____. (a) for you are not accurate.
                           (b) for you are an adolescent.

Name: _____ Date: _____

EXERCISE 4H: Make up an appropriate coordinate sentence. Remember that both parts must be related and of equal importance.

1. She was fickle, but _____.

2. The dog had died, and _____.

3. Celestial navigation is easy, for _____

_____.

4. He had aesthetic tastes; _____.

5. Emancipation is not complete, nor _____

_____.

EXERCISE 4I ESSAY ANALYSIS: Find examples of coordination in the essay "Celestial Crockery." Give the first and last word of the entire sentence and the connector used to put the two parts together.

<u>first word</u> . . . <u>connector</u> . . . <u>last word</u>

1. paragraph two: _____ . . . _____ . . . _____

2. paragraph three: _____ . . . _____ . . . _____

3. paragraph five: _____ . . . _____ . . . _____

4. paragraph eleven: _____ . . . _____ . . . _____

5. paragraph twenty: _____ . . . _____ . . . _____

EXERCISE 4J: Using the topics given below, on separate paper write sentences with correct coordination. Use each of the six types of connectors (and, but, for, nor, or, ;) at least once.

1. People
2. Civil Rights
3. Cars
4. Love
5. War
6. Hunger
7. the Peace Corps
8. Happiness
9. Parents
10. Television

Name: _____ Date: _____

☞ **YOU DO THIS:**

Use subordination.

1. A sentence about food: Although _____

   _____.

2. A sentence about civil rights: Before _____

   _____.

3. A sentence about flying saucers: _____

   until _____

   _____.

Once you have learned the pattern of subordination, use it! It can be particularly helpful when you are using too much coordination. Because ideas are usually not of equal rank, arrange them so that the more important idea is in the independent sentence and the less important idea is in the subordinate section.

Coordination: Paul was hurrying, and he cut his finger.
Subordination: Because Paul was hurrying, he cut his finger.

☞ **YOU DO THIS:**

Rewrite these sentences using subordination rather than coordination.
1. She saw two flying saucers, and she reported the sighting to the police.

   _____

   _____

2. That boy's mother was born in Italy, but she speaks English very well.

   _____

   _____

3. He came home, and he remembered that his wallet was still in his locker.

   _____

   _____

Name: _____ *Date:* _____

EXERCISE 4K: Fill in the blank lines. In some sentences you will need an independent sentence while in others you will need a dependent section. Notice that a comma separates the parts.

1. Although she was quite a wench, _____.

2. Unless you stop being furtive, _____.

3. While I have never met an agnostic, _____.

4. _____, jim-crow practices still exist.

5. _____, he is contemptible.

6. _____, the ghetto is crowded.

7. As long as you are willing to wait, _____.

8. _____, few remembered his face.

9. _____, the fire spread rapidly.

10. Before you speak to that extraterrestrial being, _____

_____.

EXERCISE 4L: Fill in a dependent section after the independent sentences given. Notice that no comma separates the parts.

1. Brutality was part of his life _____.

2. Never say hello to an egoist _____.

3. The rendezvous was secret _____.

4. He was ethical _____.

5. Parking there is a violation _____.

EXERCISE 4M: On separate paper, make up a sentence about each topic below. Put the subordinate section before the independent section. Use a comma to separate the parts.

1. Apes	5. Music	8. Chastity
2. Hot Dogs	6. Sports	9. the Sun
3. Heat	7. Space Travel	10. the English Language
4. a Picket Sign		

Name: _____ Date: _____

EXERCISE 4N: Here are sentences which use coordination. While a few are better in this form, most should be changed to subordination. Decide which ones would benefit from a change to subordination and rewrite them accordingly.

1. Paul was extremely busy, but he always had time to listen to our problems.

   _____

   _____

2. The module was tremendous, and the astronauts were comfortable.

   _____

   _____

3. The man was frugal, for he was afraid of dying poor.

   _____

4. The astronauts took excellent pictures of the cloud formations, and then the probe was considered successful.

   _____

   _____

5. She was a wench, but she was smart.

   _____

6. It was time to leave for home, but Tom became apprehensive about what he might find there.

   _____

   _____

7. He searched everywhere, but he could not find his contact lens.

   _____

   _____

Name: _____ Date: _____

8. You can learn how to surf, and you will be thrilled at the experience of riding the waves.

_____

_____

9. She liked him very much, and she never wanted to hurt him.

_____

_____

10. Chicken is delicious, but I like octopus better!

_____

EXERCISE 40 ESSAY ANALYSIS: Look back at the essay "Celestial Crockery" and answer these questions:
Find examples of the first pattern of subordination.
Give the first and last word of the entire sentence.

	first word	. . .	last word

1. paragraph four: _____ . . . _____

2. paragraph eight: _____ . . . _____

3. paragraph twenty: _____ . . . _____
4. What is the pattern sequence in the last sentence of paragraph six?

_____

Find the sentence using coordination and change it to subordination. Then decide which form you think is more effective and tell why.

5. paragraph two: _____

_____

I think _____ coordination _____ subordination is better here because:

_____

6. paragraph twenty-one: _____

_____

I think _____ coordination _____ subordination is better here because:

_____

Name: _____ Date: _____

A SPECIAL CASE OF SUBORDINATION

Subordination that starts with *who* or *which* often works best in the middle of the sentence.

Example: Gary, who is fascinated by aeronautics, is planning to design a new type of spaceship.

Special Case Pattern: | independent, who ～～～～～, sentence. |

More examples:

The Queen Elizabeth, which was docked at Pier 19, sailed on Friday.
Lee Ann, who is always optimistic, was not apprehensive about her finals.

☞ YOU DO THIS:

Fill in an appropriate subordinate section.

1. Mr. Wolfe, who _____ , was ethical.

2. The Golden Gate Bridge, which _____ ,
   is in San Francisco.

A FEW SMALLER POINTS: Use *who* to refer to a person and use *which* to refer to a thing or place.

Note that in the pattern above commas surround the subordinate section. This is because the subordination *adds information about a specific subject*. In the examples above: Gary is a specific man, the Queen Elizabeth is a specific ship, and Lee Ann is a specific woman. Therefore the information given in the subordination is ADDED INFORMATION not basic for identification and you need to ADD COMMAS.

Commas are *not* used to surround the subordinate section when the information is needed for basic identification.

Example: The scientist who is fascinated by aeronautics is going to design a new type of spaceship.

Pattern: | independent who ～～～～～ sentence. |

More examples:

The boat which was docked at Pier 19 sailed on Friday.
The girl who is always optimistic was not apprehensive about her finals.

Name: _____ Date: _____

☞ **YOU DO THIS:**

Fill in an appropriate subordinate section. Are commas needed?

1. The man who _____ is a werewolf.

2. The elevation which _____ is insufficient.

EXERCISE 4P: Fill in an appropriate subordinate section. Surround the section with commas when necessary.

1. David's wife who _____ is an agnostic.

2. The brutality which _____ was horrible.

3. The man who _____ liked to eat octopus.

4. Muriel who _____ is a romanticist.

5. The Emancipation Proclamation which _____ was only the first step needed to free the slaves.

6. The hurricane which _____ caused excessive damage and death.

7. No one who _____ would like to eat octopus.

8. The West End Bowling Association which _____

   _____ awards a trophy both to the best and the worst bowler in town.

9. The President of the United States who _____

   _____ is required by law to be no less than thirty-five years old.

10. The violation which _____ led to a fifteen dollar fine.

Name: _____ *Date:* _____

EXERCISE 4Q REFRESHER: Find and correct any sentence fragments comma splices, and run-ons. Then rework the sentences so that there are at least three samples of subordination and one of coordination.

The Orckins of Zena were puzzled. They were determined to get a closer look. Even with their powerful on-saucer telescope. They could not beleive what they saw. Slowly they steered their saucer closer to the surface of earth. They prepared equipment to take time-spots of all interesting sights. To take home and proudly show their leaders and, of course, their children and grandchildren.

Steering closer to earth, the Orckins saw that it was true. Earth beings were under a spell the god that cast the spell was very odd looking. It looked just like a round, blank time-spot with twelve symbols equally spaced around its edge. Coming out of the center of the time-spot. There were two pointed sticks which moved in slow, measured steps from symbol to symbol.

This god was powerful. He was worn on wrists, hung on walls, and installed on the outside of tall buildings. The earth beings were afraid of their god, they would look at the god frequently. Then they would usually frown and begin to run, or get nervous, or even lie down and hide under a piece of white fabric as if dead.

The Orckins soon steered away from earth, they felt sorry for earth beings. Because their god was so demanding. What had happened to the pure joy of living? How had such a cruel god been able to become so powerful?

SPRINGBOARDS TO WRITING

1. As a result of looking at the sketch of the LEM and the cartoon, reading the essay, or answering the questions that followed each, you might have some thoughts about the central theme—unidentified flying objects. (Look back at those pages to refresh your memory.) For help in planning such an essay, refer to the Guide for Planning an Essay, which appears in Springboards to Writing, Chapter One on page 25.

2. Here are some topics which have not been directly mentioned in the questions asked so far. Perhaps one of them could be a writing springboard for you:

   (a) Why Man Went to the Moon.
   (b) How Will the Moon be Useful?
   (c) Now that we have landed on the Moon, discuss: What Next in Space Exploration?
   (d) Before we explore space, we should (should not) solve the problems of this planet.
   (e) Today's Science Fiction Is Tomorrow's Reality.
   (f) Describe the life on a planet which is advanced enough to send saucers to survey the earth.
   (g) Impressions of life on earth by visitors from outer space.
   (h) The government should (should not) control information given to the public.

Nobody knows my name

five

UPI Photo.

SPRINGBOARDS TO THINKING

For informal, not written, response . . . to stimulate your thinking

1. What mood is the artist trying to create with the picture and its title?
2. Does the expression on the boy's face imply that more is unknown about him than just his name? What groups of people, in addition to teenagers, are often looked at as a group instead of as individual people?
3. What is it about today's world that makes people feel unimportant? Why are so many young people involved in what is known as a "search for identity"?
4. How do you think the Peace Corps volunteer in the photograph feels about his work? Would the feeling "nobody knows my name" apply to him? Why or why not? Might it apply to the other people in the photograph? Why or why not?
5. While many older people are Peace Corps volunteers, most of them are young people. What would you imagine is the reason that such work appeals so very strongly to young men? . . . to young women?

109

The Case for Drafting All Boys—and Girls

DR. MARGARET MEAD

(1) Young Americans in every part of the land are finding their voices. Whatever the issue, more and more of them—girls as well as boys—are declaring themselves. When they speak up it is most often to protest: "It isn't fair!"

(2) This is a generation that does not readily accept things as they are. There are some young people, of course, who are merely restive—the black-helmeted boys who race into a town on their motorcycles and the boys and girls who converge in masses on holiday resorts. And some, like the students at an Eastern college who marched all day out of "general discontent," seem to be protesting mainly for the sake of protest.

(3) But others, an ever-growing number, are concerning themselves seriously and vigorously with public issues. Through sit-ins, stand-ins, teach-ins, marches and demonstrations, on campus and off, they are debating and taking positions—a wide variety of positions—on civil rights, academic freedom and responsibility, the forms of voluntary service young people should be allowed to give, the kind of war they are willing or unwilling to support, whether those who are called upon to bear arms should not also have the right to vote, and above all, the inequities of the draft. Faced with adult responsibilities, they are protesting their status as nonadults. Confronted by problems of policy, they are demanding their right to take part in decisions that affect their lives and the lives of others, as students, as wage earners (or as uneducated and unemployable young people), and as parents and citizens. In short, they want a voice in the affairs of the country. Especially they want to be heard when, on any issue, they protest: "It isn't fair."

(4) Today the focus of protest is the draft. The sense that what is happening in the draft isn't fair has made it the central issue on which a great many dissatisfactions converge. And the inequities of the draft may make it a stumbling block for a whole generation. The most obvious inequities are those that affect the lives of young men—not only the relatively small number who are called to military service but also those who are deferred, perhaps indefinitely, and those who are rejected permanently. But there are other inequities, less obvious but equally serious. For this system, because it concentrates on young men, sets girls and young women apart as if they did not exist. And because it concentrates only on military service, it is a threat to this generation's growing sense that what happens to any of them will affect the future of all of them.

(5) It is significant that the strongest protests among young people against the present system do not come from those who have the least

hope of preferment—the dropouts, the unskilled and those who have the brains but not the means to go to college or professional schools. Rather it is the students in our colleges and universities, those whom the present system most favors, who are most loudly protesting the essential unfairness of making their less-privileged age mates carry the heaviest burdens of hardship and danger. What we are seeing is not a widening rift between those who have some possibility of choice and those who have none. Instead, we are witnessing an upsurge of discontent among those most favored.

(6) It is significant also that girls see the draft as an issue on which they too should take a stand, as they have on other contemporary issues. Together with boys, they have worked for civil rights, they have served in the Peace Corps and other voluntary organizations that allow them to give practical expression to idealism, and they have joined actively in the dialogue on the issues of war and peace. All this has placed them in a different relationship to the young men of their generation even where, as in the draft, their interests and their very existence are disregarded.

(7) The system of the draft thus brings to a head, as young people themselves see it, the question of whether it is fair to ask only a portion of a generation to give involuntary service to their country; whether it is equitable to exclude all the rest of that generation—all the girls, all the boys who lack the qualifications necessary to meet military requirements, and all the boys who are exempted for reasons beyond their control.

(8) And so a new question is raised, a question that many people are asking today: Would a universal national service be more equitable?

(9) There are those who will object to any innovation. But for those who are sensitive to the long history of our American struggle to reconcile responsibility, privilege, and freedom and for those who are tuned to the protesting voices of contemporary young Americans, the idea of universal national service will have a special appeal. By setting aside older ideas and instead shaping a program to our own expectations, we may transform a service asked of and given by all young people into something that is peculiarly American—a worthy sequel to our conception of universal free education for every child in the United States, regardless of race and color, creed and class.

(10) Universal national service is still only an idea. But for a moment I should like to suppose . . .

Suppose *all* young people were required to register at the age of 18. Each one, girl and boy, would be given a series of educational and medical examinations that would place all young people within the whole group of their generation in the country. Each would also be given an opportunity to state the kind of service to the country he or she could in good conscience give. No one would be exempt—or disregarded—in the old sense. No one would be relieved of the obligation to give two years, let us say, to the country, working under direction and living on the same subsistence allowance as everyone else. But equally, no one would be

111

excluded from the privilege of being individually and carefully assessed, helped and brought as close as possible to our best standards for education, skill, health, civic knowledge and responsibility. No one would be excluded from an opportunity to know and work with young people like and different from himself or herself. No one would be excluded from the experience of leaving home and the home neighborhood and discovering a new environment and a different set of demands and possibilities. No one would be excluded from the opportunity to develop a special talent merely because he or she lacked the expected foundation of knowledge or skill or even the awareness of how such a talent could be developed.

(11) Those who did not know how to plan a trip or read a map or make up a budget or talk to a stranger or fill out a form or follow written directions would have a chance to learn. Those who had been overprotected, who had been in "good" schools since nursery-school days, associating only with other children exactly like themselves, studying until they felt that book knowledge was running out of their ears, would have a chance to discover new directions and work in new settings. By the time they are 18, many of our most privileged children have had 15 years of schooling without any chance to put their learning to work, while a very large proportion of our least privileged children have had to survive ten or more years of utterly unrewarding sitting in dreary classrooms, learning less and less, falling further and further behind, suffering defeat of hope and denigration of individuality. Both would profit by living and working within a new group of peers in an unfamiliar place, by the discovery that they had recognized rights and obligations and by the experience of finding out that they were neither exempt nor excluded from responsibility.

(12) Universal national service would not mean that every boy and every girl would be set the same task. On the contrary, it would mean the mobilization on a national scale of a great variety of activities to meet the needs of our country and our young people. It would fulfill our most basic obligations to our young men and women and provide them with appropriate means of giving service. It would open new doors for a great many. But it would not provide individual freedom of choice in any simple sense. At eighteen, young people are moving toward adult life; they themselves are asking for adult status. Combining all this would mean the development of a new sense of what is fair and equitable—for everyone.

(13) Looking to the future, it would be necessary for some—boys and girls—to learn the skills essential to our industrial world and for some to begin the training required to produce the next generation of scientists, engineers, physicians, nurses, teachers, and technicians. What we hoped to accomplish by deferring certain students from the draft—that is, to provide for the necessary quota of trained and qualified men—would still be important. But now we could include young women as well, setting goals for their achievement that few girls have had in the recent past. And those, boys and girls, who are excluded today from the exercise of their talents would be given a chance to find themselves. And we would

still need to meet the requirements, different at different times, of our armed services. The difference would be that those who were selected to carry this responsibility would not be the *only* ones who were called on for service. Nor would we be faced by the all but insoluble dilemma of finding special ways of showing appreciation for those who volunteer and of compensating adequately those who are serving involuntarily.

(14) However it was organized in detail, universal national service would not absolve young men and young women from responsibility. All of them, whatever they are doing, would be committed for a certain time to some form of activity as citizens, full citizens, with a voice in what they were doing and responsibility for what they had in hand. Eighteen-year-olds, both the privileged and underprivileged, are unready for parenthood in a complex world. But they are ready for many forms of adult activity that involve the companionship of girls and boys as equals, as individuals, all of whom have a stake in what they are accomplishing. And all of them would benefit by the experience of a kind of life, for a limited period, in which obligation, privilege, and responsibility were combined, in which no distinction was made between rights and duties as they took part in the very varied and necessary tasks of protecting, conserving, and developing the country in which they expected to live as self-sustaining adults, free to make their own choices and decisions.

(15) The current protest, "It isn't fair," has grown out of the uncertainties and inequities of segregating one ill-defined group in a whole generation. A universal national service may be the one equitable answer.

READING SURVEY

1. Main Idea
What is the central theme of this essay?

2. Major Details
(a) Why is it that not only boys, but also girls, protest the draft?
(b) What is Margaret Mead's plan for a universal national service?
(c) How would this plan benefit young people?

3. Inference
(a) In general does Margaret Mead's essay reflect respect for, or disapproval of, young people today?
(b) To whom is Margaret Mead addressing her plan?

4. Opinion
(a) What is your opinion of the plan for a universal national draft?
(b) If this plan were adopted, what service would you like to give?

VOCABULARY BUILDING

Lesson One: The Vocabulary of Social Change: Part I

This is an age of social change. Because people often do not like what they see going on in the world, they want to improve society. In this essay there are many words which form part of the vocabulary of social change. Some of them are:

protest	(paragraph 1)
restive	(2)
converge	(2)
status	(3)
rift	(5)
universal	(8)
insoluble	(13)
absolve	(14)
complex	(14)
stake	(14)

THE BACKGROUND STORY: This is the age of *complaining* (protest) about social conditions. Many young people are *restless* (restive) about the problems of our *complicated* (complex) society. However, many adults do not think that the problems are serious. This has caused a growing *split* (rift), known as the "generation gap," between the older and younger members of our society.

But the problems of our world are not *without solution* (insoluble). Since both the older and younger generation have a *share* (stake) in the improvement of society, they should *come together in a common purpose* (converge) to take steps to *set free from the consequences of their guilt* (absolve) those who have been inhuman to their fellow men. Certainly a *nation-wide or world-wide* (universal) respect for the opinions of all age groups would benefit all of mankind, but this cannot happen until each group is willing to give up the idea that it has a special *rank* (status) in society.

EXERCISE 5A: On separate paper, give a specific example of each of the following:

1. An example of the rift between the older and younger generations.
2. An example of a status symbol.
3. An example of the words on a picket sign carried by a social protester.
4. An example of why a teenager might be restive.
5. An example of a universal problem for all inhabitants of this planet.

EXERCISE 5B: The social protester uses many of the words discussed here. Fill in the word which he might use in the blanks below.

1. He wants the group to respect his rank.   ——————————

2. He hopes that his ideas and actions can meet for a common purpose.   ——————————

3. He wants society to wash itself of its former errors.   ——————————

4. He hopes that there will be a healing of the recent campus political split.   ——————————

5. He knows that to get attention for his plan it might be necessary to encourage open complaining.   ——————————

6. He wants change to begin and, therefore, is impatient and restless.   ——————————

7. He is sure that most problems are not impossible to solve.   ——————————

8. He hopes that his ideas for change will get full-scale acceptance.   ——————————

9. He thinks it would benefit all if each person felt he had a share in things.   ——————————

10. He knows that this is a complicated and difficult world.   ——————————

Name: _____ Date: _____

Lesson Two: The Vocabulary of Social Change: Part II

Here are some more words from the essay which are part of the vocabulary of social change:

inequities	(paragraph 3)
dialogue	(6)
equitable	(7)
innovation	(9)
reconcile	(9)
transform	(9)
peers	(11)
mobilization	(12)
dilemma	(13)

THE BACKGROUND STORY: It seems that many people think that there is a need to *change* (transform) our society through *creative new ways* (innovations) so that things will be more *just* (equitable). But many of these people have a *predicament* (dilemma) about how to arrange the *putting into motion* (mobilization) of changes. It would be most helpful if the younger and older generations would *share ideas and have conversation* (dialogue) about the *unjust things* (inequities) which need to be repaired. Nevertheless, many older people find it difficult to *compromise and adapt* (reconcile) themselves to the participation of young people in the affairs of our society. As a result, each age group prefers to keep close to the *members of its own age group* (peers) where understanding of one another is easier.

EXERCISE 5C: On separate paper, give a specific example of each of the following:

1. An example of an innovation that you think might work.
2. An example of a group of your peers.
3. An example of an inequity in society today.
4. An example of a topic which could be better understood if there were dialogue about it between the younger and older generations.
5. An example of protest mobilization that you have read or heard about.

EXERCISE 5D: The social protester uses many of the words discussed here. Fill in the word he might use in each of the blanks below.

1. She is interested in creative new ways of doing things. _____

2. She is perplexed about how to solve the world's problems. _____

3. She knows that she should be able to place into motion all good efforts and ideas. _____

4. He often prefers members of his own age group. _____

5. She knows that it is difficult for some people to come to terms with the real problems of the world. _____

6. She wants to have conversation with others about the problems of our society. _____

7. She sees many unfair things happen daily. _____

8. She wants society to be just to all. _____

9. She knows that it will be impossible to change all inequities to justices overnight. _____

SPELLING

Lesson One: Spelling Demons

Here are more words that are frequently misspelled. Using the helpful techniques given in Chapter One, you should make it a point to learn these new Demons, which were taken from "The Case for Drafting All Boys—and Girls."

academic	benefit	dilemma	individually
accomplish	budget	environment	knowledge
adequately	citizen	especially	necessary
among	concentrate	exercise	organization
appreciation	conscience	existence	possible
appropriate	contemporary	fulfill	suppose

Name: _____ Date: _____

Lesson Two: Capitalization

The misuse of capital letters is as serious an error as a misspelled word. Unfortunately, some careless writers do not realize this and merely ignore the rules of capitalization. As you read the material that follows, you will begin to realize that a key word to remembering capitalization is *particular*. If you keep this word in mind, you should have less trouble applying these simple and easy to understand rules when you write.

1. CAPITALIZE:

the name of a particular person	*Martin Luther King, Jr.* *Elizabeth Taylor*
a title that precedes the name	*President Nixon* *Admiral Dewey*
a title that replaces the name	the *Pope* the *Secretary of State*
the name of a race of people	*Negro* *Indian*
the name of an organization or a department of the government	the *Knights of Columbus* *Republicans* *Congress* the *Coca-Cola Company*
the pronoun I	Slowly *I* turned the key in the lock.

2. CAPITALIZE:

the name of a particular place	*New York* *Great Britain*
the name of a particular region	*the South* the *Northeast*
the name of a particular street	*Fifth Avenue* *Elm Street*
the name of a particular building	the *Empire State Building* *Independence Hall*
the names of the planets and stars with the exception of earth, sun, and moon	*Mars* *Venus* the *Milky Way*

3. CAPITALIZE:

the names of languages	*French* *Spanish*
the name of a particular school course	*Physics 14A* *Geometry 26D*
the names of publications	the *New York Times* *Look* magazine
the name of a particular school or college	*Van Buren High School* *Yale University*
brand names	*Heinz Ketchup* *Ford Mustang*

4. CAPITALIZE:

the days of the week and the months of the year	*Monday* *September*
the names of particular holidays	*Christmas* *New Year's Day*
the names of historical events and periods	*World War Two* the *Renaissance*

5. CAPITALIZE:

all words denoting a particular deity	*God* *Buddha, Allah*
all words referring to God	We cannot understand *God's* ways, but *He* surely understands our ways.
all names of religions and religious writings	*Christianity* the *Bible*, the *Koran* *Zen Buddhism*

Now the firsts—which you probably know quite well.

6. CAPITALIZE:

the first word of a sentence and the first word of a direct quotation	The actor exclaimed, "Do not touch me!"
the first word and all important words in the title of a book, play, short story, essay, poem	The Fall of the House of Usher Catcher in the Rye
the first word and all nouns in the salutation of a letter	Dear Mr. Lyons: My dear Sir:
the first word of the close of a letter	Sincerely yours,

EXERCISE 5E: Capitalize whichever words need to be capitalized.

2250 stewart road
san francisco, california
april 4, 1969

general mark coleman
the pentagon
washington, d.c.

dear general coleman:

   in my sociology class at downstate college, we recently discussed your article "the draft and our nation's future," which appeared in the february issue of the *reader's digest*. although the class agreed with most of what you wrote, there was quite a heated debate concerning the conclusion of your article, where you stated, "because war and violence are a basic part of man's nature, we will always need armed forces to police and protect us." we were all dismayed to discover that the secretary of defense held such a negative attitude.

   if our world is to survive, we must learn to think of peace as man's normal state. according to the word of god as set down in the bible, war is an abnormal condition that must not be tolerated. instead of studying war strategy, the congress would do better to study the doctrines of christianity and judaism. we have memorial day to honor those who died in our wars. shouldn't we have a peace day to honor those who are living in peace? we are spending billions of dollars in an attempt to reach mars and venus, while we have made a rather small effort to live peacefully right here on earth. in short, we must learn to promote peace if our nation —and the world—is to have a future.

very truly yours,

the students of sociology 8b
professor david watkins

EXERCISE 5F: Fill in the blanks with any missing letters.

1. Ac___demic studies give us the kno___le___ge to fu___fil___ our goals ade_____tely.

2. It is ne_____sary to con_____trate in order to solve a dil_____ma.

3. A___propr_____ate exer_____se is espe_____ally good for the aged.

4. An individ_____ly controlled env___r_____ment will soon be pos-_____ble.

5. We can ben___fit from an ap___re_____ation of contemp_____ary art.

6. The cons_____ence of each cit_____en must guide his e___ist___nce.

7. Working with a limited bud___et, the World Health Organ_____ation

is sup___osed to ac___omplish minor miracles am___ng the sick peoples of the world.

Name: _____   *Date:* _____

AGREEMENT OF SUBJECT AND VERB

As you already know from the discussion of sentence fragments, every complete sentence must have a subject and a verb, which can be either singular or plural in form. Logically, a singular verb should be used with a singular subject and a plural verb with a plural subject. Thus we write:

A protest march takes time to organize.

Dilemmas take time to solve.

George and Helen take the bus to work.

Note that in the subject the -s ending is a sign of the plural and in the verb it is a sign of the third person singular (he, she, it, one). Although this case of subject-verb agreement is quite simple, there are some instances in which it is not so easy to be sure of agreement.

(a) Words that come between a subject and its verb do not change the number of the subject.

The train with the beach crowds leaves at noon.

The men in the office work long hours.

The number of the subject is not changed by expressions introduced by such words as *together with, in addition to, including, except, as well as.*

Professor Tobin, as well as his students, was surprised.

The President, together with his cabinet members, has left for vacation.

☞ YOU DO THIS:

In the following sentences cross out the incorrect verb form.
1. The players on the first team (was, were) the best.
2. A child, like his parents, (learn, learns) by copying.
3. The budget for the space programs (is, are) quite high.

(b) When subjects are joined by *either . . . or, neither . . . nor, not only . . . but also,* the verb agrees with the subject closest to it.

Neither Joe nor his sisters like to study.

Either the captains or the umpire calls time out.

Subjects joined by *and* are usually plural and take a plural verb. However, when *each* or *every* precedes singular subjects joined by *and,* a singular verb should be used.

Mike and Sally exercise every day.

Every man and woman has the need to accomplish something.

122

☞ **YOU DO THIS:**

In the following sentences cross out the incorrect verb form.
1. Neither the instructor nor his students (enjoy, enjoys) a dull class.

2. Each boy and each girl (is, are) to benefit from the grant.

3. Either the chairs or the table (has, have) to be returned.

(c) In sentences beginning with *here is, there is,* and *where is,* be especially careful to look ahead and determine the subject. Make it and the verb agree.

There are three reasons for the rift.
Here is the latest innovation.

The introductory *it* is always followed by a singular verb.

It is the most appropriate gift possible.
It is the citizens who will make the nation strong.

The title of a written work, even when plural in form, takes a singular verb.

The Grapes of Wrath is one of Steinbeck's best works.
The *New York Times* prints all the news fit to print.

☞ **YOU DO THIS:**

In the following sentences cross out the incorrect verb form.
1. It (is, are) the students who make a college great.

2. *The Masters* (was, were) written by C. P. Snow.

3. Where (is, are) the astronauts going to land?

(d) When used as subjects, *each, every, everyone, everybody, anybody, nobody, someone, somebody, something, everything, either, neither, nothing* regularly take singular verbs.

Everyone is fascinated with space exploration.
Each of us lives a rather complex existence.

None, some, any, and *all* may be either singular or plural. Decide which is correct from the context of the sentence.

None are so appreciative as those who have little.
None is so appreciative as he who has little.

123

Class, number, family, group, and other collective subjects take a singular verb when the subject is regarded as a unit. A plural verb is used when the subject refers to the individuals of a group.

The whole family is going on the trip.

The family have gone their separate ways.

☞ YOU DO THIS:

In the following sentences cross out the incorrect verb form.

1. Neither (is, are) capable of doing the job well.

2. The class (want, wants) to create its own curriculum.

3. None (is, are) so fulfilled as he who has love.

(e) Words stating an amount (time, money, weight, etc.) are usually singular and take a singular verb.

Two weeks is the usual vacation.

Six ounces of cough syrup is what I ordered.

Subjects which are plural in form but singular in meaning usually take singular verbs. These include: economics, civics, mathematics, physics, news, measles, mumps, ethics.

Economics is my favorite subject.

Measles is a common childhood disease.

Words such as *trousers, scissors, eyeglasses, thanks, riches,* and *means* usually take a plural verb.

The scissors are on the table.

The millionaire's riches are to be given to charity.

☞ YOU DO THIS:

In the following sentences cross out the incorrect verb form.

1. Ethics (is, are) the study of what is right and wrong.

2. Five dollars (is, are) all I have left.

3. Your thanks (is, are) all that I want.

EXERCISE 5G: Using the verb given in front of each sentence, fill in the correct form of the verb in the blank space provided. Keep all the verbs in the present tense.

1. *to operate*: Neither the toaster nor the radio _____ properly.

2. *to challenge*: The teacher, as well as his students, _____ my right to protest.

3. *to exercise*: One of my friends _____ to keep physically fit.

4. *to have*: Each man and woman _____ the knowledge to succeed.

5. *to be*: *The Perils of Pauline* _____ an old movie serial.

6. *to be*: There _____ a number of methods for solving a dilemma.

7. *to dissolve*: Both sugar and salt _____ in water.

8. *to protest*: People like Joe _____ every inequity in society.

9. *to be*: Aeronautics _____ a relatively new field.

10. *to want*: Everyone in our unstable society _____ universal peace.

11. *to enjoy*: The family _____ many of the same sports activities.

12. *to try*: Either Helen or her sons _____ to answer the questions.

13. *to be*: Six pounds of flour _____ what I ordered.

14. *to reveal*: A probe into ghetto conditions _____ a lack of basic health standards.

15. *to separate*: The lunar module, in addition to several rockets, _____

_____ from the spacecraft in flight.

Name: _____ *Date:* _____

16. *to come*: Across the river _____ the two bull elephants.

17. *to be*: Either you or I _____ supposed to attend the meeting.

18. *to cause*: Mumps _____ the parotid glands to swell.

19. *to hold*: Brooks Brothers _____ a sale every Easter.

20. *to be*: It _____ the citizens who determine a nation's future.

EXERCISE 5H: Rewrite each of the sentences below, making sure that the verb agrees with the new subject given.

Example: Joe never leaves the office before six.
    The men never leave the office before six.

1. The probe was dangerous.

    The probes _____

2. Just two of the rockets were fired to launch the satellite.

    Just one _____

3. Helen and Rochelle protest the inequities in our society.

    Only Helen _____

4. Ten letters take a long time to write.

    Nine weeks _____ to pass.

5. Among the many gifts were three genuine Ming vases.

    _____ a genuine Ming vase.

6. Either the government or the citizens determine the nation's future.

    Either the citizens or the government _____

7. They are extremely complex designs.

    It _____

8. *Oliver Twist* was written by Charles Dickens.

    Great Expectations _____

   Name: _____ *Date:* _____

9. Both of the dilemmas are enough to cause a headache.

Either of the dilemmas _____

10. The compass is not accurate.

The scissors   sharp. _____

11. Our federal laws, as well as the Constitution, guarantee our rights.

The Constitution, as well as our federal laws, _____

12. The worker in the bubble-gum factory was optimistic.

The workers _____

13. Your riches influence my decision.

Your news _____

14. Every girl likes to receive a Valentine.

Girls _____

15. Does a diamond disintegrate in acid?

_____ diamonds _____

16. Unfortunately, there is a deplorable ghetto in every major city.

_____ ghettos _____

17. Physics, although difficult, is fascinating.

Puzzles _____

18. Neither David nor the girls were gullible.

Neither the girls nor David _____

19. Everyone is fickle.

All _____

20. Tom, together with Mark and Sal, is studying aeronautics.

Mark and Sal, together with Tom, _____

Name: _____ Date: _____

PRONOUN AGREEMENT

A pronoun takes the place of a noun (the name of a person, place, or thing), thus helping to prevent repetition. Some of the frequently used pronouns are: I, me, my, mine, myself, you, he, his, him, she, her, one, it, we, us, they, them, these, this, that, who, which, what, both. There are also pronouns that do not take the place of any specific noun. These include: someone, anyone, some, none, everyone.

☞ YOU DO THIS:

Underline the pronouns in the following sentence.

What do you think of someone who will not allow himself to have a good time with his friends?

A pronoun must agree in number with the word or words for which it stands. Thus we write:

Mike said that he would fulfill his plans.
The astronauts left their command module to walk in space.

These examples are easy enough to understand. But there are some common problems in agreement of pronouns and the words for which they stand. These problems are similar to those discussed in the preceding section on the agreement of subject and verb.

(a) Use a singular pronoun to refer to such words as: someone, somebody, something, everybody, everyone, everything, nothing, anybody, anyone, nobody, no one, one, person, man, woman, either, neither, each.

Everyone should learn to benefit from his mistakes.
A person should practice what he preaches.

Collective nouns such as *group, team, class,* and *family* take a singular pronoun when the nouns refer to the group as a whole and a plural pronoun when the nouns refer to the individual members of the group.

The team is practicing for its biggest game.
The team are going their separate ways after this game.

☞ **YOU DO THIS:**

Fill in the correct pronouns in the spaces provided.

1. Each of us has _____ own insoluble problems.

2. The family have decided to take _____ careers more seriously.

3. Anyone can play the piano if _____ will practice.

(b) Use a plural pronoun when you are referring to two or more words joined by *and*.

Lynn and David are transforming their basement into a playroom.

When two words are joined by *either . . . or* or *neither . . . nor*, the pronoun should agree with the word that is the closest.

Either Dan or Ted will read his article.
Neither the general nor his officers have revealed their secret.

☞ **YOU DO THIS:**

Fill in the correct pronouns in the spaces provided.

1. Neither the girls nor Joe will study _____ homework.

2. Philadelphia and San Francisco are known for _____ hospitality.

3. Either the coach or his players will accept _____ award.

EXERCISE 5I: Select the correct pronoun from each set given.

The walls and ceilings in the apartment had lost (its, their) color. Either Bill or professional painters would have (his, their) job cut out for them. Wanting to do the job himself in order to save money, Bill decided that the best place to start repainting was in (his, their) kitchen. Of course, some people do not like to do (his, their) work alone, and Bill quickly decided to ask three of (their, his) best friends to join him. Everyone was invited to bring (his, their) paintbrush. But once they had arrived, neither his friends nor Bill really wanted to do (their, his) share —especially on such a hot summer day. Instead they wanted to watch TV and see (its, their) hometown baseball team play (their, its) weekly doubleheader. What could Bill do? Should a person argue with all of (his, their) best friends? He had a better solution to (their, his) problem. He simply called two more friends and asked them to come over. As soon as they arrived, the TV suddenly lost (his, its) audience. All of Bill's friends returned to (his, their) painting. After all, who wanted to watch TV when two gorgeous wenches were painting in the kitchen?

Name: _____ Date: _____

EXERCISE 5J: Rewrite the following sentences, making sure to correct any errors in verb and pronoun agreement.

1. Jack Mason, as well as many of his friends, work at a second job to augment their income.

   _____

   _____

2. The mumps are easily recognizable because they cause a good deal of swelling.

   _____

   _____

3. Either of the innovations are sure to make their mark.

   _____

4. The man with the most contemptible ways are ostracized by society for their low morals.

   _____

   _____

5. Everyone have to learn to be articulate and tactful if they want to succeed.

   _____

   _____

6. Your eyeglasses is in its case on the table.

7. Neither the astronauts nor their spacecraft are prepared for their next mission.

   _____

   _____

8. The ten pounds of potatoes are packaged in their own air-tight plastic bag.

   _____

   _____

Name: _____ Date: _____

9. The bucket of moon metals are not disintegrating although they have been in the furnace for an hour.

_____

_____

10. None are so smart as he who knows himself.

_____

11. Every person who are oppressed should fight for their freedom.

_____

_____

12. Down the stairs comes Jack and Helen with their puppy.

_____

13. The class is protesting their status as nonadults.

_____

14. The number of volunteers were surprisingly small for the job they had to do.

_____

_____

15. The Peace Corps, like many similar organizations, are known for their humanitarian work.

_____

_____

16. Either you or I are going to solve our complex dilemmas.

_____

17. *Leaves of Grass*, known for their lyric picture of America, were written by Walt Whitman.

_____

_____

Name: _____ Date: _____

EXERCISE 5K REFRESHER:
1. Find and correct any errors in verb or pronoun agreement.
2. Find any sentences that are not part of the development and delete them.
3. Check the arrangements of examples. If necessary, rearrange them into logical order—either more-to-less important or less-to-more important, whichever you think most appropriate.

The five letter word _draft_ has more than three times their size in varied meanings. Some of their meanings are familiar to us while other definitions are not as well known. All of us is aware of the definition which means that people are selected to do a compulsory job. The draft is not popular with many boys. Just as most students know that the first version of an essay is called a rough draft, architects know that a drawing of building plans are called an architect's draft. Beer lovers all over the world knows that when beer is on draft, glasses can be filled from a large keg rather than from small bottles. Also, when one catches a cold, which happens to all of us at one time or another, the infection is sometimes blamed on the patient's having stood in a draft. Perhaps one of the least known meanings of draft are a catch of fish made with one pull of a net. And of course, all baseball managers follow the spring drafts because bidding for rights to new players have important impact on each team's capability. Although only five letters long, _draft_ is an extraordinary word. Knowing this, can anyone safely continue to say, "Let's abolish the draft."

Name: _____ Date: _____

SPRINGBOARDS TO WRITING

1. As a result of looking at the drawing and the photograph, reading the essay, or answering the questions which followed each, you might have some thoughts about the central theme—universal national service. (Look back at those pages to refresh your memory.) For help in planning such an essay, refer to the Guide for Planning an Essay, which appears in Springboards to Writing, Chapter One on page 25.

2. Here are some topics which have not been directly mentioned in the questions asked so far. Perhaps one of them could be a springboard for you:

   (a) The case for or against the present draft system.

   (b) What do you think of conscientious objectors, draft card burners, and the boys who move to Canada to escape the draft?

   (c) The case for or against a volunteer military army.

   (d) The value of working for the Peace Corps.

   (e) Is brotherly love really possible?

   (f) Discuss a problem that seems to you to be a current issue of concern.

   (g) President John F. Kennedy, who started the Peace Corps, said at his inauguration, "The torch has been passed to a new generation of Americans. . . ." Describe: The New Generation of Americans.

Belling, SCULPTURE. *Collection, the Museum of Modern Art, New York. A. Conger Goodyear Fund.*

CHAPTER **six**

SPRINGBOARDS TO THINKING

For informal, not written, response . . . to stimulate your thinking

1. What does this sculpture look like to you? Why?
2. Why do you think the artist used metal rather than marble or clay to make the sculpture?
3. What do you think is the artist's view of our modern world?
4. Do any people you know ever act like robots? Does anyone you know ever treat you like a robot?
5. Why do some people say that we are moving from the time of "nobody knows my name" to the time of "nobody knows my number"?

135

Man and the Machine

ROBERT CUBBEDGE

(1) Whatever the immediate outcome of the labor-management rift, technological change is inevitable; automation in virtually every field of endeavor is merely a matter of time. Whether he likes it or not, the individual worker must learn to adapt to the new processes.

(2) Ironically, automation clearly improves working conditions in most cases. Automated plants are cleaner, neater, and more pleasant to look at; usually, they are also far safer. There are automated grain mills that have nearly eliminated dust. There are foundry workers who never touch the molding sand, except out of curiosity. And there are oil refinery workers who could wear dinner jackets and white gloves on the job and never get them soiled. Automation is not without its hygienic and esthetic advantages.

(3) But from creation of the first tool—the *coup de poing* (a pear-shaped chipped-stone tool; literally "blow of the fist")—man, the worker, has been the maker and master of his machines. With the advent of automation, he will still be the maker, but his mastery will be more theoretical than actual. The change is fraught with all kinds of emotional and psychological hazards. No longer will the product of man's sweat be visible to his eye, nor lovingly held in the hand.

(4) For five years, Charles Walker, director of research in technology and industrial relations at Yale University, investigated the emotional responses of workers in an automated steel plant. The men, all known as semi-craft workers, had spent their previous adult lives in plants employing the old steelmaking methods. Working directly with their product, they had used various kinds of familiar tools to control production with their own hands. When this steel mill was automated, they were switched to remote-control processes.

(5) Automation, they were told, would free them from using their hands and allow them to take on more responsible tasks, step up steel production, and reduce muscular fatigue on the job.

(6) The men indeed found their work lightened, Walker reported, but there were drawbacks: "They admitted that their muscles were not tired and that physical drudgery had been lifted from their shoulders, but they complained that nervous fatigue, from just standing and watching the machine, had been substituted."

(7) In some forms of automation, Walker observed, "muscular fatigue disappears and there is an immediate release of tension." This is the type in which automatic signals tell the worker when some adjustment must be made, at which time he acts more as a repairman than as an operator. But

From *Who Needs People?* by Robert Cubbedge, 1963, Robert B. Luce, Inc., for David McKay, Inc.

in the automation under study at this specific steel mill, the worker was not warned by signals. He was forced to stand and watch the machine, constantly alert. To avoid costly breakdowns, he was expected to intervene promptly whenever anything went wrong. A foreman complained: "In the old mill you controlled the machine; now it controls you."

(8) Walker reported further that in this steel mill, there was at first the usual resentment against automation because of the displacement of fellow-workers by robots; later, all the displaced workers were given other jobs in the same firm. It was found after a considerable amount of time, then, that the majority of workers had adjusted to automation; psychological fatigue lessened, and they began to get more satisfaction out of their jobs. Only a few asked to be returned to their old jobs in other plants belonging to the company.

(9) None of this eliminated the basic problem of man vs. automation. Even after their nervousness and tensions disappeared, the steelworkers still had a serious morale problem. As Walker noted: "They still indicated that they wanted more direct participation in the solution of steel production problems than they now had." How to give them this added satisfaction is a matter now under study by many groups of scientists and labor and management authorities.

(10) Doctors and psychologists are interested, too, and with good reason, as increasing connections with stress-illnesses appear. Although workers one day will adapt themselves to automation, this stress can only increase at the outset. The highest incidence of gastric ulcers in the hourly-paid class is now found among skilled machinists, who exert less physical effort than do most of their fellow workers. It has also been reliably estimated that twenty per cent of all employees in industry are borderline emotional-disorder cases. And a recent medical survey of heart diseases revealed that unskilled laborers are among the least likely of all occupational groups to have heart attacks; among those most susceptible to heart attacks, however, are people working with computing machines.

(11) Part of the same problem is the reaction of workers to reduced contact with their fellows, as a result of reduction in their numbers and increase in distance between workplaces. A study similar to the Walker investigation, by William A. Faunce of Michigan State University, showed that the commonest causes of complaint among 125 automated workers were increased noise; need for closer attention to work; and, most important, loneliness and isolation from other workers. At least one British union has already asked for "lonesome pay." Solitary confinement, it claimed— and not without some justification—is one of the most dreaded forms of punishment. In truth, many people become highly erratic unless they are kept in contact with others.

(12) From Rolleston, England, came this sad story: Once the envy of his bachelor friends, Horace Moulds worked in the packing department of a sugar factory with 52 girls. He was understandably happy in his job

137

until, one day, automation came and machinery replaced the girls. Apparently, he decided he had nothing left to live for; at any rate, the coroner ruled his subsequent death a suicide. "He worried over the machines," said the coroner. "They replaced ninety-nine percent of the human element and it was possible Mr. Moulds could not adapt himself to automation."

(13) Related to the problem of loneliness is the problem of boredom—which, of course, is not peculiar only to automation. In fact, it is perhaps more typical of old-style conventional mechanization than of automation. But some operative jobs, under automation, may still be highly routine and boring. In Coca-Cola bottling plants, for instance, the old method of inspection was to put four bottles of finished Coca-Cola in front of a strong light and have an inspector watch for any foreign matter in the liquid. Then someone initiated a conveyor system in which the bottles ran continuously. This was a much faster process, but the job was so boring that a bottle of Seven-Up had to be run through every now and then to make sure the inspector was still awake!

(14) Another troublesome factor is the tendency of the individual to become hostile if his personality is ignored. Michigan State's Faunce quotes a typical automated worker: "They [the supervisors] never say hello—they treat you like a machine. They used to be friendly. Now they seem under a strain."

(15) One more point to ponder: While automation may virtually eliminate many types of accidents and individual occupational diseases, the risk of isolated, but disastrous, accidents still exists; in a few rare instances, the dangers are actually increased. We must recognize, therefore, that the decline of physical risk can be offset by the emotional hazards of greater responsibility. One worker, obviously under extreme nervous tension, told Faunce: "I pushed the wrong button and stuff flew all over. I was lucky [in not being hurt] but it cost the company $13,000 to fix the machine."

(16) It was found, further, that automation may stimulate the mental activity of workers—with desirable or undesirable effects, depending on the presence of constructive outlets and opportunities to use them. One worker told Walker: "On my old job my muscles got tired. I went home and rested a bit and my muscles were no longer tired. On this new automatic mill your muscles don't get tired but you keep thinking even when you go home."

(17) Who knows but that it may be necessary to have amusement gadgets built into automated devices?

(18) Certainly, "goofing off" will be a problem—out of boredom if nothing else. In some industries, it already is a problem—particularly where machines operate unaided by man but automatically give off a signal when they get into trouble. Tests have shown that when a man has nothing to do but watch for a sudden light on a control board or a similarly erratic and infrequent signal, his mind tends to wander. Thus, when

the signal does come, he may be daydreaming and miss it entirely. The result can be costly—even, perhaps, disastrous. When whole factories are controlled by one man in front of a control board, this will be a king-sized problem.

(19) The Hancock Telecontrol Corporation of Milwaukee has perfected a device, right out of George Orwell's novel, *1984*, that may have particular application one day in this field. An electronic monitoring system, the Hancock machine was installed recently in the Milwaukee plant of Cutler-Hammer, Incorporated, itself a leading manufacturer of electrical equipment and control apparatus. "Big Brother's" eyes are lights in a balcony control room tied in to each punch press in the plant. When a punch press is running, its light glows a steady green. When the punch press stops, a red light pops on. At his option, the worker may activate a flashing red light to indicate mechanical trouble, a shortage of material, or any other problem that may have interrupted production.

(20) Hancock Telecontrol argues that the system will cut idle time and raise incentive pay, put a foreman at the operator's "beck and call," and give workers "quite a psychological boost." "You look at this panel," rhapsodized a company spokesman, "and you see your whole plant at work."

(21) The local lodge of the International Association of Machinists had another description for the machine, however. "It's like an electronic spy system," asserted a union official. He noted pointedly that the system can record each machine's output on a graph, thus constituting a potentially frightening bludgeon for management to wield against its employees. The union's idea of an adequate safeguard against such an eventuality was a twenty-one point program for restrictions on use of the machine. Among the points were the following:

1. Workers must be given duplicates of the system's records of their performance.

2. In any dispute over the records, the worker's word must be final.

3. The machine must not be used for time studies or disciplinary action.

(22) Even with safeguards, "Big Brother" will clearly have an uphill fight for popularity. It typifies one of the most common objections to automation—that it debases the worker. This objection has long been heard in connection with mass production. It will grow louder with increases in automation.

(23) Will automation in fact increase the tendency to subordinate man to the machine? The problem is most perplexing in the current transitional period. What of the future?

(24) There is every reason to believe that the conditions of worker debasement will be greatly alleviated with the advent of a fully automated society. This supposition is based on the premise that very few workers will be needed to feed the machines or carry on the extremely dull, routine jobs. As a consequence, it will be possible to place more workers in jobs that furnish a greater amount of self-satisfaction.

(25) Man is not by nature an efficient technological unit; therefore, the machine quickly surpasses him in its ability to do routine jobs and do them better. It seems logical to replace these routine jobs by a machine with electronic controls and place man in that work that takes advantage of his greatest potential—his ability to think and reason. If automation accomplishes this end, it will be performing a social as well as an economic service.

(26) In this connection, it is interesting to note the changes in the percentages of skilled, semiskilled, and unskilled workers during the twenty-five years ending in 1955. Skilled workers represented 12.9 per cent of the labor force in 1930 and 13.7 per cent of the labor force in 1955. Semiskilled workers rose even more rapidly, from 16.4 per cent to 23.2 per cent. But, during the same period, the percentage of unskilled workers in the labor force fell from 28.4 to 18.6. The table points out a definite reduction in the percentage of unskilled workers during the past 25 years. This decline is certain to be speeded by the introduction of automated equipment. The hand-trucker of today, replaced by a conveyor, may become tomorrow's push-button assembly man; the assembly worker may become a toolmaker; the toolmaker may become an electronics engineer.

(27) Actually, the development of automation has been slowed by the shortage of engineers and technicians and competent personnel trained in maintaining, producing, and designing the necessary equipment. During the past few years, Detroit has been plagued by unemployment caused by reduction in the numbers of workers needed in the production of automobiles; yet not a day passes without several pages of advertisements in Detroit newspapers in search of skilled and semiskilled people for the new technologically advanced industries.

(28) The report of the Congressional subcommittee on Economic Stabilization stated that the most disturbing thing that came to the Congressmen's attention was the near-unanimous conclusion of the witnesses that the nation is faced with a threatened shortage of scientists, technicians, and skilled labor.

(29) Not all workers can be transformed into design engineers, of course. However, the consensus seems to be that there will be an abundance of skilled jobs fully within the capabilities of the present work force, provided workers are properly trained and motivated.

(30) We have seen that with the advent of automation, the output per man-hour and the skills and responsibilities of individual workers will increase. Wages, therefore, will tend to increase accordingly.

(31) There are numerous examples of installation of automatic equipment resulting in higher wages for workers. Richard E. Sullivan, chairman of the School of Commerce at the University of Wisconsin, has described an illustrative case. A company employing 215 people installed automated pieces of computer-type equipment over a period of thirty-one months. No workers were dismissed, and all jobs were markedly upgraded as a result of the installation. Before automation, the average weekly salary

had been $57; after, the average weekly salary had increased to $71. Even when these increases are adjusted for the concurrent general increase in wages, it is evident that higher skill requirements were rewarded by higher pay.

(32) It is likely, moreover, that present wage structures and job evaluation systems will become valueless and will need upward revision throughout industry for the era of automation. Individual wage incentives will not be practical, because individual effort will not be associated directly with output. As a substitute, it may be desirable to install a group incentive plan which will include the entire plant as a working unit. The UAW-American Motors profit-sharing plan and the Steel Workers-Kaiser agreement would seem to be a long step in this direction.

(33) Each individual firm must, of course, formulate its own job evaluation plan. Only after an accurate analysis of job requirements can the right man be found to fill each job. In such a plan, the factor of responsibility will bear more weight than ever before—which, alone, should require a complete revision of current job classifications. In addition, existing contract clauses and plant customs related to seniority will probably be found unsatisfactory in the light of the new needs presented by automation. In all likelihood, the ability to learn will gradually replace experience, or perhaps even the ability to do the job, as a standard for continued employment.

(34) To sum up, it would seem obvious that worker skills will be upgraded by automation, and that the factory of the future will be a model of working safety and comfort. Machines will do the dirty, the repetitive, and dangerous jobs—leaving the worker to become more effective, perhaps more creative, in his own right. This will require the training of workers in new skills and techniques. Wages will increase as the responsibilities of individuals increase and as jobs are upgraded. Wage standards will be based on job responsibility rather than output, and seniority rules will be limited by the individual's willingness and ability to learn. Automation may not deliver a Utopia, but, at its best, it can certainly point the way.

READING SURVEY

1. Main Idea

What is the central theme of this essay?

2. Major Details

(a) How has automation improved working conditions?

(b) What effects of automation are of concern to doctors and psychologists?

(c) Why is "goofing off" more of a problem with automation?

3. Inference

(a) Read paragraph seven again. What is the foreman's attitude toward automation as implied by his complaint?

(b) Read paragraph twenty-one again. Judging from the rules it has made, what do you think is the attitude of the workers' union toward automation?

4. Opinion

(a) Do you agree with the last sentence of the essay? Explain.

(b) Do you think that the problems brought about by automation can be solved with job retraining and psychology? Explain.

VOCABULARY BUILDING

Lesson One: The Vocabulary of the Machine in Mass Society

I   In many ways the machine dominates modern life. Because machines provide faster methods of production, huge masses of products can be made
in little time. This mass of products, combined with the growing mass of
population on our planet, causes many people to say that this is the age
of "The Mass Society." There is a vocabulary of the machine in the mass
society. Some of the words appear in this essay:

technological	(paragraph 1)
automation	(1)
mechanization	(13)
computer	(31)

As you will see, these words have similar meanings. There is a good
reason for this: each word is related to the use of machines which perform the work of humans.

An invention is considered a *technological* invention when it employs a
specialized, scientific method to increase productivity and eliminate
human operations.

Under *automation* most production is controlled by self-acting devices
which operate quickly and take the place of human efforts.

A *mechanization* process is one which uses machinery, often manually
operated, to avoid small-step human operations.

A *computer* is a machine which performs number calculations faster and
more accurately than humans can.

EXERCISE 6A: Fill in the blank with the appropriate word.

1. The change-over to machines that are not necessarily automatic is

   called _____.

2. Progress possible because of inventions which use technical methods

   to achieve practical purposes is called _____
   advance.

3. A machine which can perform most of its operations by itself would

   be considered an example of _____.

4. A machine which can perform skillful, fast operations with numbers

   is a _____.

143   *Name:* _____ *Date:* _____

II   Without a doubt the machine which has attracted the most interest from
our mass society is the computer. Here are some words which are used
when computers are discussed:

program
computerized
data
input
output
cybernetics

When you construct a complete coded system which represents all points
to be calculated by a computer, you construct a *program*. (When you
do this, you are called a *programmer*.)
When you do something by means of a computer, you have *computerized*
it.
When you are looking for information, you are gathering *data*.
When you put information into a computer, you feed it *input*.
When you get information out of a computer, it feeds you *output*.
When you compare the automatic control system of the human brain with
that of an electronic, computerized communications setup, you are en-
gaged in the study of *cybernetics*.

EXERCISE 6B: Fill in the blanks with the appropriate word.

1. "I need more information!"   _____
2. "There's just too much to keep track of
   around here. It's time we did things by
   computer."   _____
3. "Where is the pile of cards which must be
   fed into the computer?"   _____
4. "Have you finished putting the company's
   payroll records into a coded system?"   _____
5. "I can't believe it! Look at what the com-
   puter has just fed out to us!"   _____
6. "But Professor, we must remember that
   while the computer is able to do complex
   mathematical calculations quickly and accurately, it does not have the all-important
   human ability to 'read between the lines.'"   _____

Name: _____ Date: _____

Lesson Two: The Vocabulary of Man in Mass Society

The increased use of machines, including computers, in our mass society has had its effects on man. He often feels unimportant, in part because a single individual seems not to count in the midst of such a huge population, and in part because machines are being invented which are more skillful and faster than any single individual can be. There is a vocabulary of Man in the Mass Society. Some of the words appear in this essay and they can be logically grouped:

Some feelings man has about himself on the job:	**fatigue**	(5)
	tension	(7)
Some attitudes man has about others on the job:	**resentment**	(8)
	hostile	(14)
Some words about jobs:	**drudgery**	(6)
	routine	(24)
	efficient	(25)
	incentive	(32)
	debases	(22)
	upgraded	(31)

When a man feels tiredness, he feels *fatigue*.

When a man feels tight and nervous, he feels *tension*.

When a man takes offense at, and feels annoyed about, something done to him by others, he feels *resentment*.

When a man acts unfriendly and angry, he is *hostile*.

When a job demands tiresome, menial work, it is *drudgery*.

When a job demands boring repetition of an ordinary performance, it is *routine*.

When a job demands an effective worker who gets a task done quickly and well, the job demands an *efficient* worker.

When a job well done will bring personal satisfaction, extra money, or a promotion, the worker will have an *incentive* to do the job well.

When a job will lower the esteem of a worker either in his own eyes or in the eyes of others, he will dislike the job because it *debases* him.

When a job will raise the esteem or skills of a worker either in his eyes or in the eyes of others, he will like his job because it can *upgrade* him.

EXERCISE 6C: On separate paper, give a specific example of each of the following.

1. Something which might cause you fatigue.
2. Something which might give you tension.
3. Something which might make you feel resentment.
4. A job that you think would be drudgery.
5. A job that would demand an efficient worker.

Name: _____ Date: _____

EXERCISE 6D: Choosing from the list to the left below, substitute the one word which has the same meaning as the italicized word or words in this paragraph.

fatigue
tension
resentment
hostile
drudgery
routine
efficient
incentive
debased
upgrade

When we were leaving the candy factory today, Joe asked me not to have *a feeling of annoyance* (   ) about what had happened. Joe is all right, but those other men in my crew make me *angry and unfriendly* (   ). After all, I always work hard when a *bonus* (   ) is offered to the crew that will do a new job in the most *skillful, quick* (   ) way. Of course, during the competition we were all under *pressure* (   ) to push ourselves beyond the *boring repetition* (   ) of a task into alert production. Although it is always a relief to get away from the *tiresome and menial work* (   ) of every day, the men feel *tiredness* (   ) of another sort. Even so, in the competition today each of us on the crew tried hard to *raise the level of* (   ) the whole group so we could win. Yet, after all my efforts today and on other days, I was *humiliated and brought down* (   ) in front of the foreman because the men said that they had done all the work while I fell asleep behind the marshmallow dippers. Some jokers!

SPELLING

Lesson One: Spelling Demons

Here are more words that are frequently misspelled. Using the helpful techniques given in Chapter One, you should make it a point to learn these new Demons, which were taken from "Man and the Machine."

abundance	description	laborer	numerous
adjust	disastrous	machinery	peculiar
apparatus	disease	manufacturer	performance
complaint	endeavor	medical	salary
continuously	extremely	muscle	substitute
curiosity	interrupt	nervous	technique

Name: _____ Date: _____

Lesson Two: Commonly Confused Words

You may sometimes misspell a word because you confuse it with another word that is similar in appearance. Unlike the Sound-Alikes given in Chapter Two, the sets of words listed below are not pronounced alike, but there is a close resemblance in their spelling; often the difference is just a letter or two. Because they are very commonly used words, you should try to learn them well.

1. *accept* (to receive)
   I would be happy to accept the dinner invitation.
   except (excluding)
   Everyone except Joe passed the English test.

2. *advice* (a recommendation)
   My father gave me good advice concerning my future plans.
   advise (to give a recommendation)
   I advised Jack to see a doctor.

3. *affect* (to change or influence)
   The bad weather will affect my plans for the day.
   effect (to cause; the result)
   The doctor is working to effect a cure.
   Alcohol has a strange effect on many people.

4. *breath* (an exhalation)
   I could smell liquor on his breath.
   breathe (to inhale and exhale)
   It is unhealthy to breathe polluted air.

5. *choose* (to select—present tense)
   Because I am lazy, I always choose the easiest courses.
   chose (to select—past tense)
   Hal chose a Buick as his next car.

6. *clothes* (garments)
   Joe changed his clothes before going out for dinner.
   cloths (pieces of fabric)
   Mary has a drawer full of dusting cloths.

7. *costume* (a suit or dress)
   Helen wore a gypsy costume to the masquerade ball.
   custom (the usual course of action)
   It is a custom to tip a waiter.

8. *desert* (to leave or abandon; a dry, wasted region)
Do not desert those in need.
The Sahara Desert is in North-Central Africa.
dessert (the last course of a meal)
Strawberry shortcake is my favorite dessert.

9. *later* (coming after)
Mike promised to do his homework later.
latter (the second of two things)
The millionaire has both a Rolls Royce and a Jaguar XKE; the latter is a very expensive sports car.

10. *loose* (not tight)
The car has a loose wire.
lose (to misplace)
I had better tighten this button before I lose it.
loss (the fact of being misplaced)
The fire caused great financial loss.

11. *moral* (an ethical issue)
There is a moral to be learned from many children's fables.
morale (mental state)
The soldiers' morale was improved greatly by the visiting entertainers.

12. *quiet* (silent)
You must be quiet in a library.
quite (completely)
He was quite tired after the long trip.

A SPECIAL NOTE: Memory tricks may help you to distinguish between these often confused words:
Remember that *except* means *exclude*.
The expression "cause and effect" will help you link *effect* with "to cause."
Chose rhymes with hose.
A *cost*ume has a *cost* but a custom does not.
A glass of *ale* will lift the soldier's mor*ale*.
Strawberry shortcake is a de*ss*ert.
Three vowels in a row are very q*uie*t.

148

EXERCISE 6E: Underline the correct word from the set of words in parentheses.

When I (accepted, excepted) the invitation to the love-in, I didn't know (quiet, quite) what to expect. I had been (adviced, advised) to wear colorful (cloths, clothes), so I (choose, chose) blue slacks and a (loose, lose, loss) pink shirt. The (later, latter) was a left-over from a Halloween (costume, custom) party. The love-in was being held in a local park, which was so crowded that I could hardly (breath, breathe) as I pushed my way through the mass of long hair, flowers, and psychedelic hand-me-downs. In the midst of all this, I found my friends polishing their guitars with dusting (clothes, cloths). Following the (costume, custom) at love-ins, a strange girl asked me to (choose, chose) a flower from several she carried, while a bearded philosopher offered (advice, advise) on the draft, taxes, and the (moral, morale) issues of the day. The fast beat of the guitar music and the friendliness of the group soon lifted my (moral, morale) and I started to (loose, lose, loss) my shyness. We all sang along with the rock tunes and then (later, latter) in the day we enjoyed a meal of cookies and beer with pumpkin seeds for (desert, dessert). As the dusk approached, the police were suddenly and unaccountably upon us and I found myself running until I was out of (breath, breathe). (Accept, Except) for a few stragglers, we all managed to escape. When I returned to the park that evening, it was (quiet, quite) and (deserted, desserted), giving me a chance to think about the (affect, effect) of the gathering. For the first time I sensed the (loose, lose, loss) of feeling and communication among the people of our society. By staging love-ins, young people hope to (affect, effect) the future mood of the world.

Name: _____ Date: _____

EXERCISE 6F: Unscramble the letters in parentheses to form the missing words in each sentence. If necessary, check your spelling with the list of Demons in this chapter.

1. Most actors are (ROUSNEV) _____ before a (ANMFO-RPERCE) _____.

2. If (DISSEEA) _____ goes unchecked, the result can be (ATORSSUDIS) _____.

3. John Gunther's (SCRIPSEDNTIO) _____ of Russia certainly arouses the reader's (OISRUCIYT) _____ _____.

4. Joe's bowling (TIQUENECH) _____ is quite (CULPERIA) _____.

5. The trapeze artist fell during his act because he had forgotten to (JUADST) _____ his (AAAPPRUTS) _____ _____.

Name: _____ Date: _____

EXERCISE 6G PROOFREADING FOR SPELLING: Use the proofreading techniques given in Chapter Four to find and correct any misspelled words in the following paragraph. If necessary, check your spelling with the list of Demons in this chapter.

Unhappy workers continously go out on strike in order to interupt the work of the manefacterer. The workers' compliant is usually that their salry does not reflect the abundence of the nation. And in this age of technology, numorous picket signs remind us that mashinery is no subsitute for an excellent laboror. Retirement funds and medicle benefits are also becoming extremly important issues. While the labor leaders endevor to resolve the dispute, the workers picket and pray for relief for their aching leg musles.

Name: _____ Date: _____

FROM PARAGRAPH PRINCIPLES TO ESSAY WRITING

Frequently you will be required to write essays for some of your college courses. Such assignments usually require the presentation of information about a selected subject. An essay which is written to convey information is called *exposition*.

In many ways an expository essay has the same structure as a paragraph, except that the essay has more extended discussion and uses additional specific examples. If you have used any of the Springboards to Writing at the end of each chapter, you have written an expository essay. Perhaps a few pointers will guide you in planning your essays:

The Paragraph	*Purpose*	The Essay
the topic sentence	to state, limit, and control the main idea	the introductory paragraph
development with use of facts, examples, incident, definition, or comparison and contrast	to develop the main idea with specific points	the main body paragraphs (there should be at least three of them)
(in certain cases: the concluding sentence)	to conclude by coming back to the general main idea	the concluding paragraph)

Notice from the comparison chart above that an expository essay should have at least five paragraphs altogether. Keep this in mind when selecting a topic. Some topics might be suitable for a book but too broad for a five-paragraph essay; other topics might be suitable for a paragraph but too limiting for a five-paragraph essay. For example, suppose that you wish to write a five-paragraph essay on the general topic of automation:

GOOD TOPIC: Automation is evident in the home.
TOO BROAD: Automation is helpful.
TOO LIMITING: Our automatic dishwasher is a General Electric.

Before you can be sure that a topic is good for an essay, it is best to think ahead to *each of the three main points* which you will discuss in *each of the three paragraphs of the main body of the essay*. Try to think of three sensible, interesting main ideas, each of which can be stated in a good topic sentence and which can be developed with one of the five methods presented in Chapters One and Two. If you cannot, the chances are that the topic you have chosen is not suitable.

As you think ahead to the three main points which you plan to make, write them down. Looking at the three main points you have listed will make it more visibly clear whether or not a topic is suitable for a five paragraph essay. Compare the plan for each of the following topics, and notice the judgment made for each plan:

	A *Automation is Evident in the Home*	B *Automation Is Helpful*	C *Our Dishwasher is a General Electric*
Introduction	introduce the three main ideas that follow	←	←
Main Body (3 main ideas)	I. heat and light II. labor-saving devices III. leisure	I. science II. business III. home	I. how it works II. what it does III. its usefulness
Conclusion	summarize the three main ideas	←	←

Judgments:

A is fine; not too broad or to limiting.
B is too broad; each development would be shallow and general.
C is too limiting; the main points are similar and repetitious.

☞ YOU DO THIS:

Which topic is more suitable?
1. a. The Pressing Machine Uses Steam.
   b. Recent Significant Advances in Industrial Automation.
   c. Industrial Advances through the Ages.

2. a. Medicine.
   b. Penicillin Is White.
   c. Significant Medical Discoveries of 1970.

Many times even when a student can sense that a topic is good, he cannot think of three main points for the three main body paragraphs. Often it is not difficult to think of two main points; it is the third point that can become troublesome. In planning, first allow yourself to come up with your own ideas. If you run out of ideas, here are a few idea patterns—which you should feel free to adapt, rearrange, modify, and change—to help you find three main points of value:

Total Essay Pattern

1. Introduction
2. Main Body I. _____ main point one
3. Main Body II. _____ main point two
4. Main Body III. _____ main point three
5. Conclusion

Main Body Idea Patterns

I. past
II. present
III. future

I. science
II. business
III. the arts

I. personal
II. family
III. social group

I. political
II. economic
III. social (or substitute for any:
religious)

I. the individual
II. the community (or nation)
III. the nation (or world)

I. home
II. business (or school)
III. leisure time

I. childhood
II. adulthood
III. old age

I. physical
II. psychological
III. spiritual

I. personality
II. character
III. ability

I. students
II. workers
III. financiers (or owners or bosses)

EXERCISE 6H: Here are suggested topics for a five-paragraph essay. Improve each topic if necessary.

1. Dating Habits.

_____

2. The Newest United States Space Satellite.

_____

3. Racial Tensions.

_____

154

4. An Intellectual Usually Likes to Read.

_____

5. Why Some Students Are Restive.

_____

EXERCISE 6I: Read the essay topic given. Think ahead to three main ideas which you might use to develop the topic.

1. Cigarettes: Good or Bad.   I. _____

                              II. _____

                              III. _____

2. The Superior Sex.   I. _____

                              II. _____

                              III. _____

3. What is Love?   I. _____

                              II. _____

                              III. _____

4. Possible Future Space   I. _____
   Discoveries.
                              II. _____

                              III. _____

5. Typical Misleading Ad-   I. _____
   vertisements.
                              II. _____

                              III. _____

Name: _____ Date: _____

6. Dating Habits of College Students.

I. _____

II. _____

III. _____

7. The Case for (against) Desegregation.

I. _____

II. _____

III. _____

8. Peers Can Be Pests.

I. _____

II. _____

III. _____

9. Unscrupulous Business Practices.

I. _____

II. _____

III. _____

10. Notorious Bandits of the Old West.

I. _____

II. _____

III. _____

EXERCISE 6J: For each of the general topic areas given, create a suitable topic for a five-paragraph essay. In each case, think ahead to three main ideas which you will discuss; your plan should clearly show that the essay topic you have created is suitable.

1. General topic area: Science.
   Suitable topic for a five-paragraph essay:

_____

Plan: Think ahead: Main Body I: _____

Main Body II: _____

Main Body III: _____

2. General topic area: People.
   Suitable topic for a five-paragraph essay:

   _____

   Plan: Think ahead: Main Body I: _____

   Main Body II: _____

   Main Body III: _____

3. General topic area: Cars.
   Suitable topic for a five-paragraph essay:

   _____

   Plan: Think ahead: Main Body I: _____

   Main Body II: _____

   Main Body III: _____

4. General topic area: Medicine.
   Suitable topic for a five-paragraph essay:

   _____

   Plan: Think ahead: Main Body I: _____

   Main Body II: _____

   Main Body III: _____

5. General topic area: Politics.
   Suitable topic for a five-paragraph essay:

   _____

   Plan: Think ahead: Main Body I: _____

   Main Body II: _____

   Main Body III: _____

Name: _____ Date: _____

1. The essay "Man and the Machine" is more than five paragraphs long, yet it retains the pattern of introduction, main body, and conclusion. How many paragraphs are in the main body? _____

2. The main body is organized to present three major points. For each of the sets of paragraphs listed below, give the major point presented. Select three from the list of choices.

    major point choices:

    paragraphs 3–12 _____   (a) emotional reactions

    paragraphs 13–23 _____   (b) workers' skills and wages

    paragraphs 24–33 _____   (c) need for government action

                                                    (d) boredom and "Big Brother"

3. Paragraph two is an excellent example of an expository paragraph. Find and underline its topic sentence and its concluding sentence. Do they work well together? What are the three examples used to support the topic sentence?

(a) _____

(b) _____

(c) _____

Name: _____ Date: _____

THE INTRODUCTORY PARAGRAPH

It is important to write an introductory paragraph that will convince the reader that the essay will be worth reading. To be completely effective, this opening paragraph must accomplish two things: it must *state the topic of the essay* and it must *capture the reader's interest*. Any one of several devices may be used to fulfill the latter purpose.

(a) Emphasize the importance of the topic.
(b) Ask a provocative question.
(c) Use an appropriate quotation.
(d) State the divisions of the topic.
(e) Use a stimulating incident or anecdote.

Naturally, the method that you choose will depend on the nature of the topic and on your own preferences. Any one of these devices can help make the reader receptive to an essay. After each device is explained below, there is an example of an introduction that could be used for an essay entitled: The Case for Mechanization.

(a) *Emphasize the importance of the topic*: The writer may impress the reader by explaining the current interest in the topic or by indicating that the subject may influence our lives. For example:

From the articles about labor disputes that crowd the daily newspapers, it is clear that mechanization is now as important an issue as wages. Whether they are auto workers or candy makers, employees frequently go out on strike to protest the use of labor-saving machines. But the strikes and the eventual settlements do not really solve the basic problem, for the fear of technological progress will not diminish until the workers come to realize the many advantages of a mechanized society.

(b) *Ask a provocative question*: The reader's interest can be stimulated by asking a question that does not have an easy answer. The essay that follows should then be concerned with finding a possible answer. For example:

We marvel at the news of a computer that can do the work of an office full of bookkeepers or a sugar-packaging machine that operates more quickly and efficiently than fifty women. Yet at the same time, we fearfully question our own usefulness in an automated society. Will the machine replace man as the producer of the world's goods and services? Will man eventually become obsolete?

159

(c) *Use an appropriate quotation*: A quotation is an easy and effective device to use—if it is used sparingly. The daily newspapers are a good source of quotations suitable for current topics. If the subject is of a more general nature, the book *Bartlett's Familiar Quotations*, which you can find in the reference section of the library, may provide appropriate material. For example:

"Armed with his machinery man can dive, can fly, can see atoms like a gnat; he can peer into Uranus with his telescope, or knock down cities with his fists of gunpowder." When Emerson made this comment a century ago, he was only hinting at the usefulness of machines that can improve both man's material and mental well-being.

(d) *State the divisions of the topic*: A brief idea of the plan of the essay, if stated in an effective manner, can hint at the interesting points which you intend to cover. For example:

Contrary to a belief held by many people, the machine is not an electrical monster that will eventually devour mankind. Man's astounding accomplishments increase as machines enrich our lives. Technological advance has made possible discoveries in medical science which help preserve life; in space explorations which will undoubtedly produce a plethora of new resources; and in industrial innovations which can release the worker from routine, menial tasks. Surely the machine is not a monster—it is a marvel!

(e) *Use a stimulating incident or anecdote*: The use of an interesting incident or anecdote can act as a teaser to lure the reader into the remainder of the essay. Be sure that the device is appropriate for the subject and focus of what is to follow. For example:

Stopping at a construction site recently, I watched a giant scoop gouge huge craters out of the earth. Overcome with a sense of man's uselessness, I felt resentful. Turning to a fellow sidewalk superintendent, I said, "That machine is doing the job of one hundred men with shovels!" The man, frowning at my selfish reaction, said tactfully, "Or a thousand men with spoons!" His few words jolted me; suddenly I realized that without progress in mechanization, our lives would be difficult and backward.

THE CONCLUDING PARAGRAPH

Because no reader likes to be jarred by an abrupt ending, a concluding paragraph should be used to give the essay a feeling of completeness. An effective conclusion should *reemphasize the topic of the essay*, leaving the reader with a strong impression of what has been said. Any one of the following methods may be used:

(a) Make a plea for change.
(b) Draw the necessary conclusions from what has been said.
(c) Summarize the major points of the essay.

When choosing a method for ending an essay, remember that the conclusion should flow naturally out of the body of the paper; it should not appear to be tacked on. After each method is explained below, there is an example of a conclusion that could be used for an essay entitled: The Case for Mechanization.

> (a) *Make a plea for change*: A conclusion may make a plea for a change of attitude or for specific action. The following paragraph does both:

The public must be helped to realize that the numerous advantages of mechanization far outweigh the disadvantages. But at the same time, we must have an organized program of job retraining for those workers who are replaced by machines. It is evident that more people need to be trained to operate the new mechanical inventions. When society fully understands mechanization, the technological future of the world will become limitless.

> (b) *Draw the necessary conclusions from what has been said*: Based on the facts given in the essay, you may use the concluding paragraph to form certain judgments about the topic. For example:

Thus it can be seen that the machine has catapulted us into a new potential for progress, the outcomes of which can only be imagined. Often man is as hesitant to readjust his practices to include the products of progress as he is to try the untried. Yet we know that man, because of his ability to reason, is different from other animals; let us hope that in the future, man's reaction to mechanization will reflect the supposed superiority of *Homo sapiens*.

(c) *Summarize the major points of the essay*: A restatement of the major points—using new words—will help the reader to remember what he has read. A summary is usually most effective in a long theme. A summary would seem repetitious at the end of a short theme. For example:

The machine, then, is a metal marvel that not only aids the business-man, but also the average worker. With machines taking over the tedious jobs, men are free to do more responsible and satisfying tasks, often at higher salaries. Because physically strenuous and time-consuming jobs are left for the machines, workers face fewer health hazards and have more leisure time to pursue new interests. If workers could take a less short-sighted view of the machine, they might see its significant advantages for themselves and their children.

A SPECIAL NOTE: Aside from the methods given above, certain devices presented in the section on the introductory paragraph can be useful in concluding paragraphs: for example, the quotation, the question, and the incident or anecdote.

Common Errors to Avoid in Introductions and Conclusions

1. Never use expressions such as: "Now I will tell you about," "I would like to discuss..." or "In my paper I will explain...." These expressions, and others like them, make the structure of your essay too obvious.

2. Avoid absolute statements such as: "This proves that...." or "If we take this action, the problem will be solved." To be as accurate as possible, you need to qualify these statements: "This seems to prove that...." or "If we take this action, we will be helping to solve the problem."

3. Avoid using clichés and overworked quotations. An essay on marriage would not benefit from a reminder that love and marriage go together like a horse and carriage. "To err is human, to forgive divine" has long since lost its freshness and would add nothing to an essay.

4. Never apologize for what you are going to write or for what you have written. If you begin your theme with "I don't know very much about this subject," you will immediately lose the reader's interest. In addition, if you end a theme with "Of course there are many other opinions about this subject, and I certainly do not know everything," you will destroy the impact of your essay. If you really do feel unsure about your opinions, change your topic to something that you can be more positive about.

5. Make sure that the introduction and conclusion are an integral part of the whole essay; they should not seem tacked on. The introduction should state the topic of the *entire* theme, and the conclusion should relate to the general topic rather than one specific point.

6. The size of the introduction and conclusion should be kept in proportion to the size of the whole essay. An introduction or conclusion of 200 words would certainly be too long for a theme of about 500 words. However, a long paper may require a 200-word introduction or conclusion.

EXERCISE 6L: Referring to the list of errors to avoid, evaluate the effectiveness of the following sets of introductions and conclusions. Make any corrections that you think will improve these introductions and conclusions. Some of them may have to be completely rewritten.

I The following introduction and conclusion are from a 500-word expository theme on the topic:

The Case against Computerized Dating

Introduction

The minute that I met Alice I was sure that the computer knew its business. Alice was exactly the kind of girl that I had described in the computer dating questionnaire. She had blond hair, blue eyes and was a Kim Novak look-alike. In fact, Alice told me that she was often mistaken for the actress. On the way to a local movie, we met my friend Jack, who quickly turned green with envy as he eyed my date. When I had called Alice for the date, Jack had insisted that I would end up with an ugly wallflower. Well, he certainly could not have been more wrong. Aside from being beautiful, Alice was witty, outgoing, and intelligent and had an interest in racing cars, a sport that I have followed since I was about ten years old. Some day I hope to be able to buy my own racing car so that I can enter the Indianapolis 500. After three hours, however, Alice and I were all talked out about racing and our conversation came to a complete halt. We both tried to break the awkward silence, but I soon concluded that we were not meant for each other after all. This one date made me realize why the computer can never be a successful matchmaker.

Conclusion

As I have proven in my essay, computer dating is not a good way to meet a compatible date.

163

II The following introduction and conclusion are from a 500-word expository theme on the topic:

A Plan for Racial Equality

Introduction

Segregation is a deplorable situation that must be ended immediately. We must learn to treat others as we would have them treat us. After all, we are all the same under the skin. As Abraham Lincoln proclaimed, "All men are created equal."

Conclusion

The government, then, should strictly enforce federal laws against segregation and should provide free job training and higher education for minority groups. When these things are done, we will have true racial equality.

III The following introduction and conclusion are from a 500-word expository theme on the topic:

The Need for Censorship in Books

Introduction

The use of sex in books is popular today. The neighborhood bookstands are overrun with cheap paperback books that feature unclad girls on the cover and racy writing inside. In addition, a glance at the bestseller list indicates that eight of the ten books listed deal extensively with sex.

Conclusion

Therefore, the federal government should organize a committee to review books before their publication to weed out pornography. In addition, there should be strict enforcement of a law forbidding minors to purchase books intended only for mature adults. If these actions are taken, we will be helping to protect our children against the dangers of obscene literature.

IV The following introduction and conclusion are from a 500-word expository theme on the topic:

Flying Saucers Do Exist!

Introduction

Do flying saucers and little green Martians really exist? Perhaps the celestial beings are not green and do not come from Mars. But as I will show in my essay, we are being visited by life from outer space.

Conclusion

I must admit that my knowledge of this subject is somewhat limited and the mystery of UFO's must be investigated further. But based on the evidence given, it seems to me that flying saucers do exist.

V The following introduction and conclusion are from a 500-word expository theme on the topic:

The Case against the Present Draft System

Introduction

I have many reasons for being against the present draft system.

Conclusion

Under the present draft system, an intelligent young man with money can avoid being drafted. A friend of mine went to college and graduate school merely to obtain a student deferment. When it seemed that the Selective Service had finally caught up with him, he took a job as a teacher to get an occupational deferment. There must be thousands of men who use similar methods to elude the draft.

EXERCISE 6M ESSAY ANALYSIS: Answer these questions about the essay "Man and the Machine."

1. What device does the author use as the basis of his introduction?

   _____

2. Where in the introduction does the author state the topic of the essay?

   _____

3. What method does the author use to develop the conclusion?

   _____

4. Would another method have been more effective for concluding this essay? Why?

   _____

   _____

EXERCISE 6N: Look back at the essay plans and topics which you created for Exercise 6J on pages 156–157. On separate paper, write an appropriate introduction and conclusion for each essay.

Name: _____ Date: _____

1. Find and correct any verb agreement errors or pronoun agreement errors.
2. Rework the sentences so that there are at least three samples of subordination and one of coordination.

Improved education for all people, no matter what his age, could be one important use of the machine. Many such devices of automation already exists. They are excessively expensive. More must be produced. Then the cost will decrease.

Soon a student will be able to learn at their own speed. No longer will he have to rush to keep up with rapid learners. No longer will he get bored while waiting for slow learners. The key to the new methods in automated education are the telephone wires. They will be used for more than just conversation. Near the home phone will be a microfilm reader, a television receiver, an automated typewriter and other aids. The student will be able to telephone the library, request a book, and then read the necessary pages on their microfilm reader. All lecture courses will be available on video tape, starring teachers who have been trained in clear speaking. Also, when requested, technical information will be sent to the automated typewriter in a form scientifically planned for the human brain to understand and absorb.

People often jokingly say that teachers will soon be replaced by machines. However, with the use of machines in education the teacher become more important than ever. It will be the job of the teacher to do what no machine can ever do - supply the human touch. Only the human teacher can be sympathetic, can understand a student's confusion and clear it up, and can encourage the type of creative thinking that lead to the invention of more machines.

Name: _____ Date: _____

SPRINGBOARDS TO WRITING

1. As a result of looking at the metal sculpture, reading the essay, or answering the questions which followed each, you might have some thoughts about the central theme—the machine in the mass society. (Look back at those pages to refresh your memory.) For help in planning such an essay, refer to the Guide for Planning an Essay, which appears in Springboards to Writing, Chapter One on page 25.

2. Here are some topics which have not been directly mentioned in the questions asked so far. Perhaps one of them could be a writing springboard for you:

   (a) Choose one:

      Automation in the Home.
      ... Medicine.
      ... the Office.
      ... the Factory.

   (b) What makes a good boss (foreman)?

   (c) Personal expression and efficient production: Can they go together?

   (d) The psychological effects of the mass society on man.

   (e) Is this the society of "Big Brother"?

   (f) Unions—good or bad?

   (g) Machines yet to be invented.

   (h) The automated society of 2001.

   (i) Mass-produced products—good or bad?

   (j) What life would be like without machines.

   (k) Use this quotation as the central topic of an essay:

   One machine can do the work of fifty ordinary men. No machine can do the work of one extraordinary man.

   Elbert Hubbard, The Philistine

 1. (SILENT)

 2. (MUSIC UP)

 3. SOLO SINGER: (VO) New Ultra Brite Toothpaste...

 4. (MUSIC)

 5. ...a taste you can really feel.

 6. New Ultra Brite..

 7. gives your mouth...

 8. (SFX: SOUND OF KISS)

 9. (MUSICAL ACCENT)

 10. ...sex appeal.

 11. (MUSIC UNDER) ANNCR: (VO) New Ultra Brite Toothpaste the craziest taste, the freshest...

 12. breath, the brightest teeth.

 13. Put them all together...

 14. they...spell...

 15. sex appeal. (MUSIC UP) SOLO SINGER: (VO) New Ultra Brite...

 16. gives your mouth... (SFX: SOUND OF KISS AND MUSICAL ACCENT)

 17. ...sex appeal.

 18. (MUSIC UNDER) ANNCR: (VO) After Ultra Brite everything else is just toothpaste.

Ultrabrite ad: © Courtesy Palmolive Company.

Tab ad: Copyright © 1969 The Coca-Cola Company. Reproduced through the courtesy of The Coca-Cola Company.

D'Agostino ad: Courtesy D'Agostino Supermarkets, Inc.

SPRINGBOARDS TO THINKING

For informal, not written, response . . . to stimulate your thinking

The Ultra Brite Ad
1. Read the entire sequence on the television storyboard for Ultra Brite Toothpaste. What story is told?
2. Why is the emphasis on sex appeal rather than health?

The Tab Ad
1. Why, if this is an ad for Tab, is most of the ad space given to the people rather than the product?
2. What is the connection between the people pictured, the slogan, and the product?

The D'Agostino Ad
1. This is an ad for D'Agostino Supermarkets. Why is most of the ad space given to a picture of a girl?
2. What is the effect of saying that there will be a love-in at the supermarket? What is the effect of saying, ". . . but please don't kiss the butcher."?

Love Is a Fallacy

MAX SHULMAN

Cool was I and logical. Keen, calculating, perspicacious, acute, and astute—I was all of these. My brain was as powerful as a dynamo, as precise as a chemist's scales, as penetrating as a scalpel. And—think of it!—I was only eighteen.

5 It is not often that one so young has such a giant intellect. Take, for example, Petey Burch, my roommate at the University of Minnesota. Same age, same background, but dumb as an ox. A nice enough fellow, you understand, but nothing upstairs. Emotional type. Unstable. Impressionable. Worst of all, a faddist. Fads, I submit, are the very negation of

10 reason. To be swept up in every new craze that comes along, to surrender yourself to idiocy just because everybody else is doing it—this, to me, is the acme of mindlessness. Not, however, to Petey.

One afternoon I found Petey lying on his bed with an expression of such distress on his face that I immediately diagnosed appendicitis. "Don't

15 move," I said. "Don't take a laxative. I'll get a doctor."

"Raccoon," he mumbled thickly.

"Raccoon?" I said, pausing in my flight.

"I want a raccoon coat," he wailed.

I perceived that his trouble was not physical, but mental. "Why do you

20 want a raccoon coat?"

"I should have known it," he cried, pounding his temples. "I should have known they'd come back when the Charleston came back. Like a fool I spent all my money for textbooks, and now I can't get a raccoon coat."

25 "Can you mean," I said incredulously, "that people are actually wearing raccoon coats again?"

"All the Big Men on Campus are wearing them. Where've you been?"

"In the library," I said, naming a place not frequented by Big Men on Campus.

30 He leaped from the bed and paced the room. "I've got to have a raccoon coat," he said passionately. "I've got to!"

"Petey, why? Look at it rationally. Raccoon coats are unsanitary. They shed. They smell bad. They weigh too much. They're unsightly. They—"

"You don't understand," he interrupted impatiently. "It's the thing to

35 do. Don't you want to be in the swim?"

"No," I said truthfully.

"Well, I do," he declared. "I'd give anything for a raccoon coat. Anything!"

My brain, that precision instrument, slipped into high gear. "Any-
40 thing?" I asked, looking at him narrowly.

"Anything," he affirmed in ringing tones.

I stroked my chin thoughtfully. It so happened that I knew where to
get my hands on a raccoon coat. My father had had one in his undergraduate days; it lay now in a trunk in the attic back home. It also hap-
45 pened that Petey had something I wanted. He didn't *have* it exactly, but
at least he had first rights on it. I refer to his girl, Polly Espy.

I had long coveted Polly Espy. Let me emphasize that my desire for
this young woman was not emotional in nature. She was, to be sure, a
girl who excited the emotions, but I was not one to let my heart rule my
50 head. I wanted Polly for a shrewdly calculated, entirely cerebral reason.

I was a freshman in law school. In a few years I would be out in practice. I was well aware of the importance of the right kind of wife in fur-
thering a lawyer's career. The successful lawyers I had observed were,
almost without exception, married to beautiful, gracious, intelligent
55 women. With one omission, Polly fitted these specifications perfectly.

Beautiful she was. She was not yet of pin-up proportions, but I felt
sure that time would supply the lack. She already had the makings.

Gracious she was. By gracious I mean full of graces. She had an erect-
ness of carriage, an ease of bearing, a poise that clearly indicated the best
60 of breeding. At table her manners were exquisite. I had seen her at the
Kozy Kampus Korner eating the specialty of the house—a sandwich that
contained scraps of pot roast, gravy, chopped nuts, and a dipper of sauer-
kraut—without even getting her fingers moist.

Intelligent she was not. In fact, she veered in the opposite direction.
65 But I believed that under my guidance she would smarten up. At any
rate, it was worth a try. It is, after all, easier to make a beautiful dumb
girl smart than to make an ugly smart girl beautiful.

"Petey," I said, "are you in love with Polly Espy?"

"I think she's a keen kid," he replied, "but I don't know if you'd call it
70 love. Why?"

"Do you," I asked, "have any kind of formal arrangement with her?
I mean are you going steady or anything like that?"

"No. We see each other quite a bit, but we both have other dates.
Why?"

75 "Is there," I asked, "any other man for whom she has a particular fond-
ness?"

"Not that I know of. Why?"

I nodded with satisfaction. "In other words, if you were out of the picture, the field would be open. Is that right?"

80 "I guess so. What are you getting at?"

"Nothing, nothing," I said innocently, and took my suitcase out of the
closet.

"Where are you going?" asked Petey.

171

"Home for the weekend." I threw a few things into the bag.

85 "Listen," he said, clutching my arm eagerly, "while you're home, you couldn't get some money from your old man, could you, and lend it to me so I can buy a raccoon coat?"

"I may do better than that," I said with a mysterious wink and closed my bag and left.

90 "Look," I said to Petey when I got back Monday morning. I threw open the suitcase and revealed the huge, hairy, gamy object that my father had worn in his Stutz Bearcat in 1925.

"Holy Toledo!" said Petey reverently. He plunged his hands into the raccoon coat and then his face. "Holy Toledo!" he repeated fifteen or
95 twenty times.

"Would you like it?" I asked.

"Oh yes!" he cried, clutching the greasy pelt to him. Then a canny look came into his eyes. "What do you want for it?"

"Your girl," I said, mincing no words.

100 "Polly?" he said in a horrified whisper. "You want Polly?"

"That's right."

He flung the coat from him. "Never," he said stoutly.

I shrugged. "Okay. If you don't want to be in the swim, I guess it's your business."

105 I sat down in a chair and pretended to read a book, but out of the corner of my eye I kept watching Petey. He was a torn man. First he looked at the coat with the expression of a waif at a bakery window. Then he turned away and set his jaw resolutely. Then he looked back at the coat, with even more longing in his face. Then he turned away, but with
110 not so much resolution this time. Back and forth his head swiveled, desire waxing, resolution waning. Finally he didn't turn away at all; he just stood and stared with mad lust at the coat.

"It isn't as though I was in love with Polly," he said thickly. "Or going steady or anything like that."

115 "That's right," I murmured.

"What's Polly to me, or me to Polly?"

"Not a thing," said I.

"It's just been a casual kick—just a few laughs, that's all."

"Try on the coat," said I.

120 He complied. The coat bunched high over his ears and dropped all the way down to his shoe tops. He looked like a mound of dead raccoons. "Fits fine," he said happily.

I rose from my chair. "Is it a deal?" I asked, extending my hand.

He swallowed. "Its a deal," he said and shook my hand.

125 I had my first date with Polly the following evening. This was in the nature of a survey; I wanted to find out just how much work I had to do to get her mind up to the standard I required. I took her first to dinner. "Gee, that was a delish dinner," she said as we left the restaurant. Then

I took her to a movie. "Gee, that was a marvy movie," she said as we left the theater. And then I took her home. "Gee, I had a sensaysh time," she said as she bade me good night.

I went back to my room with a heavy heart. I had gravely underestimated the size of my task. This girl's lack of information was terrifying. Nor would it be enough merely to supply her with information. First she had to be taught to *think*. This loomed as a project of no small dimensions, and at first I was tempted to give her back to Petey. But then I got to thinking about her abundant physical charms and about the way she entered a room and the way she handled a knife and fork, and I decided to make an effort.

I went about it, as in all things, systematically. I gave her a course in logic. It happened that I, as a law student, was taking a course in logic myself, so I had all the facts at my finger tips. "Polly," I said to her when I picked her up on our next date, "tonight we are going over to the Knoll and talk."

"Oo, terrif," she replied. One thing I will say for this girl: you would go far to find another so agreeable.

We went to the Knoll, the campus trysting place, and we sat down under an old oak, and she looked at me expectantly. "What are we going to talk about?" she asked.

"Logic."

She thought this over for a minute and decided she liked it. "Magnif," she said.

"Logic," I said, clearing my throat, "is the science of thinking. Before we can think correctly, we must first learn to recognize the common fallacies of logic. These we will take up tonight."

"Wow-dow!" she cried, clapping her hands delightedly.

I winced, but went bravely on. "First let us examine the fallacy called Dicto Simpliciter."

"By all means," she urged, batting her lashes eagerly.

"Dicto Simpliciter means an argument based on an unqualified generalization. For example: Exercise is good. Therefore everybody should exercise."

"I agree," said Polly earnestly. "I mean exercise is wonderful. I mean it builds the body and everything."

"Polly," I said gently, "the argument is a fallacy. *Exercise is good* is an unqualified generalization. For instance, if you have heart disease, exercise is bad, not good. Many people are ordered by their doctors *not* to exercise. You must *qualify* the generalization. You must say exercise is *usually* good, or exercise is good *for most people*. Otherwise you have committed a Dicto Simpliciter. Do you see?"

"No," she confessed. "But this is marvy. Do more! Do more!"

"It will be better if you stop tugging at my sleeve," I told her, and when she desisted, I continued. "Next we take up a fallacy called Hasty Gen-

eralization. Listen carefully: You can't speak French. I can't speak French.
Petey Burch can't speak French. I must therefore conclude that nobody
at the University of Minnesota can speak French."

"Really?" said Polly, amazed. "*Nobody*?"

I hid my exasperation. "Polly, it's a fallacy. The generalization is
reached too hastily. There are too few instances to support such a conclusion.

"Know any more fallacies?" she asked breathlessly. "This is more fun
than dancing even."

I fought off a wave of despair. I was getting nowhere with this girl,
absolutely nowhere. Still, I am nothing if not persistent. I continued.
"Next comes Post Hoc. Listen to this: Let's not take Bill on our picnic.
Every time we take him out with us, it rains."

"I know somebody just like that," she exclaimed. "A girl back home—
Eula Becker, her name is. It never fails. Every single time we take her
on a picnic—"

"Polly," I said sharply, "it's a fallacy. Eula Becker doesn't *cause* the rain.
She has no connection with the rain. You are guilty of Post Hoc if you
blame Eula Becker."

"I'll never do it again," she promised contritely. "Are you mad at me?"

I sighed deeply. "No, Polly, I'm not mad."

"Then tell me some more fallacies."

"All right. Let's try Contradictory Premises."

"Yes, let's," she chirped, blinking her eyes happily.

I frowned, but plunged ahead. "Here's an example of Contradictory
Premises: If God can do anything, can He make a stone so heavy that He
won't be able to lift it?"

"Of course," she replied promptly.

"But if He can do anything, He can lift the stone," I pointed out.

"Yeah," she said thoughtfully. "Well, then I guess He can't make the
stone."

"But He can do anything," I reminded her.

She scratched her pretty, empty head. "I'm all confused," she admitted.

"Of course you are. Because when the premises of an argument contra-
dict each other, there can be no argument. If there is an irresistible force,
there can be no immovable object. If there is an immovable object, there
can be no irresistible force. Get it?"

"Tell me some more of this keen stuff," she said eagerly.

I consulted my watch. "I think we'd better call it a night. I'll take you
home now, and you go over all the things you've learned. We'll have another session tomorrow night."

I deposited her at the girls' dormitory, where she assured me that she
had had a perfectly terrif evening, and I went glumly home to my room.
Petey lay snoring in his bed, the raccoon coat huddled like a great hairy
beast at his feet. For a moment I considered waking him and telling him

that he could have his girl back. It seemed clear that my project was
220 doomed to failure. The girl simply had a logic-proof head.

But then I reconsidered. I had wasted one evening; I might as well
waste another. Who knew? Maybe somewhere in the extinct crater of her
mind, a few embers still smoldered. Maybe somehow I could fan them into
flame. Admittedly it was not a prospect fraught with hope, but I decided
225 to give it one more try.

Seated under the Oak the next evening I said, "Our first fallacy tonight
is called Ad Misericordiam."

She quivered with delight.

"Listen closely," I said. "A man applies for a job. When the boss asks
230 him what his qualifications are, he replies that he has a wife and six children at home, the wife is a helpless cripple, the children have nothing to
eat, no clothes to wear, no shoes on their feet, there are no beds in the
house, no coal in the cellar, and winter is coming."

A tear rolled down each of Polly's pink cheeks. "Oh, this is awful,
235 awful," she sobbed.

"Yes, it's awful," I agreed, "but it's no argument. The man never answered the boss's question about his qualifications. Instead he appealed
to the boss's sympathy. He committed the fallacy of Ad Misericordiam.
Do you understand?"

240 "Have you got a handkerchief?" she blubbered.

I handed her a handkerchief and tried to keep from screaming while
she wiped her eyes. "Next," I said in a carefully controlled tone, "we will
discuss False Analogy. Here is an example: Students should be allowed
to look at their textbooks during examinations. After all, surgeons have
245 X-rays to guide them during an operation, lawyers have briefs to guide
them during a trial, carpenters have blueprints to guide them when they
are building a house. Why, then, shouldn't students be allowed to look
at their textbooks during an examination?"

"There now," she said enthusiastically, "is the most marvy idea I've
250 heard in years."

"Polly," I said testily, "the argument is all wrong. Doctors, lawyers, and
carpenters aren't taking a test to see how much they have learned, but
students are. The situations are altogether different, and you can't make
an analogy between them."

255 "I still think it's a good idea," said Polly.

"Nuts," I muttered. Doggedly I pressed on. "Next we'll try Hypothesis
Contrary to Fact."

"Sounds yummy," was Polly's reaction.

"Listen: If Madame Curie had not happened to leave a photographic
260 plate in a drawer with a chunk of pitchblende, the world today would not
know about radium."

"True, true," said Polly, nodding her head. "Did you see the movie? Oh,
it just knocked me out. That Walter Pidgeon is so dreamy. I mean he
fractures me."

175

265 "If you can forget Mr. Pidgeon for a moment," I said coldly, "I would like to point out that the statement is a fallacy. Maybe Madame Curie would have discovered radium at some later date. Maybe somebody else would have discovered it. Maybe any number of things would have happened. You can't start with a hypothesis that is not true and then draw
270 any supportable conclusions from it."

"They ought to put Walter Pidgeon in more pictures," said Polly. "I hardly ever see him any more."

One more chance, I decided. But just one more. There is a limit to what flesh and blood can bear. "The next fallacy is called Poisoning the Well."
275 "How cute!" she gurgled.

"Two men are having a debate. The first one gets up and says, 'My opponent is a notorious liar. You can't believe a word that he is going to say.' . . . Now, Polly, think. Think hard. What's wrong?"

I watched her closely as she knit her creamy brow in concentration.
280 Suddenly a glimmer of intelligence—the first I had seen—came into her eyes. "It's not fair," she said with indignation. "It's not a bit fair. What chance has the second man got if the first man calls him a liar before he even begins talking?"

"Right!" I cried exultantly. "One hundred per cent right. It's not fair.
285 The first man has *poisoned the well* before anybody could drink from it. He has hamstrung his opponent before he could even start. . . . Polly, I'm proud of you."

"Pshaw," she murmured, blushing with pleasure.

"You see, my dear, these things aren't so hard. All you have to do is
290 concentrate. Think—examine—evaluate. Come now, let's review everything we have learned."

"Fire away," she said with an airy wave of her hand.

Heartened by the knowledge that Polly was not altogether a cretin, I began a long, patient review of all I had told her. Over and over and over
295 again I cited instances, pointed out flaws, kept hammering away without letup. It was like digging a tunnel. At first everything was work, sweat, and darkness. I had no idea when I would reach the light, or even *if* I would. But I persisted. I pounded and clawed and scraped, and finally I was rewarded. I saw a chink of light. And then the chink got bigger and
300 the sun came pouring in and all was bright.

Five grueling nights this took, but it was worth it. I had made a logician out of Polly; I had taught her to think. My job was done. She was worthy of me at last. She was a fit wife for me, a proper hostess for my many mansions, a suitable mother for my well-heeled children.
305 It must not be thought that I was without love for this girl. Quite the contrary. Just as Pygmalion loved the perfect woman he had fashioned, so I loved mine. I determined to acquaint her with my feelings at our very next meeting. The time had come to change our relationship from academic to romantic.

310 "Polly," I said when next we sat beneath our oak, "tonight we will not discuss fallacies."

"Aw, gee," she said, disappointed.

"My dear," I said, favoring her with a smile, "we have now spent five evenings together. We have gotten along splendidly. It is clear that we 315 are well matched."

"Hasty Generalization," said Polly brightly.

"I beg your pardon," said I.

"Hasty Generalization," she repeated. "How can you say that we are well matched on the basis of only five dates?"

320 I chuckled with amusement. The dear child had learned her lessons well. "My dear," I said, patting her hand in a tolerant manner, "five dates is plenty. After all, you don't have to eat a whole cake to know that it's good."

"False Analogy," said Polly promptly. "I'm not a cake. I'm a girl."

325 I chuckled with somewhat less amusement. The dear child had learned her lessons perhaps too well. I decided to change tactics. Obviously the best approach was a simple, strong, direct declaration of love. I paused for a moment while my massive brain chose the proper words. Then I began:

330 "Polly, I love you. You are the whole world to me, and the moon and the stars and the constellations of outer space. Please, my darling, say that you will go steady with me, for if you will not, life will be meaningless. I will languish. I will refuse my meals. I will wander the face of the earth, a shambling, hollow-eyed hulk."

335 There, I thought, folding my arms, that ought to do it.

"Ad Misericordiam," said Polly.

I ground my teeth. I was not Pygmalion; I was Frankenstein, and my monster had me by the throat. Frantically I fought back the tide of panic surging through me. At all costs I had to keep cool.

340 "Well, Polly," I said, forcing a smile, "you certainly have learned your fallacies."

"You're darn right," she said with a vigorous nod.

"And who taught them to you, Polly?"

"You did."

345 "That's right. So you do owe me something, don't you, dear? If I hadn't come along you never would have learned about fallacies."

"Hypothesis Contrary to Fact," she said instantly.

I dashed perspiration from my brow. "Polly," I croaked, "you mustn't take all these things so literally. I mean this is just classroom stuff. You 350 know that the things you learn in school don't have anything to do with life."

"Dicto Simpliciter," she said, wagging her finger at me playfully.

That did it. I leaped to my feat, bellowing like a bull. "Will you or will you not go steady with me?"

355 "I will not," she replied.

177

"Why not?" I demanded.

"Because this afternoon I promised Petey Burch that I would go steady with him."

I reeled back, overcome with the infamy of it. After he promised, after
360 he made a deal, after he shook my hand! "The rat!" I shrieked, kicking up great chunks of turf. "You can't go with him, Polly. He's a liar. He's a cheat. He's a rat."

"Poisoning the Well," said Polly, "and stop shouting. I think shouting must be a fallacy too."

365 With an immense effort of will, I modulated my voice. "All right," I said. "You're a logician. Let's look at this thing logically. How could you choose Petey Burch over me? Look at me—a brilliant student, a tremendous intellectual, a man with an assured future. Look at Petey—a knothead, a jitterbug, a guy who'll never know where his next meal is coming
370 from. Can you give me one logical reason why you should go steady with Petey Burch?"

"I certainly can," declared Polly. "He's got a raccoon coat."

READING SURVEY

A SPECIAL NOTE: This is the middle chapter of your textbook. Most of the material in this chapter is designed to help you avoid making errors in logic. The story you have just read is not expository like the other essays in your text. It has been included because it provides an entertaining midway break as it introduces you to the fun and usefulness of logic.

1. Main Idea
What is the central theme of this essay?

2. Major Details
(a) Why does Petey want a raccoon coat?
(b) Why does the student who is telling the story want to teach Polly logic?
(c) What is the punch line of the story?

3. Inference
(a) What impression of Polly does Max Shulman give you?
(b) What impression of the student telling the story does Max Shulman give you?

4. Opinion
(a) Do you think that Polly made the better choice? Why or why not?
(b) Do you think that a knowledge of logic could be helpful to you? Why or why not?

VOCABULARY BUILDING

Lesson One: The Vocabulary of Logic

When people are told that their logic is incorrect—or illogical—it means that their reasoning is wrong. It is not always easy to use clear and correct reasoning. Words about logic will help you understand the principles of good reasoning. Some of them appear in the essay and others are added for your convenience:

I. A Few Errors in Logic:

fallacy (title)
generalization (line 160)
contradictory (line 196)
ambiguous
arbitrary
rationalization

II. When Talking About Ideas:

analogy (line 243)
hypothesis (line 256)
premise (line 196)
abstraction
relevant

I A Few Errors in Logic

That argument is inaccurate and therefore it is false; it is a *fallacy*.

That argument assumes that all things are alike or uses one example to prove the whole; it is a *generalization*.

That argument is the opposite of your former argument. You state one point and then deny it with your next point; it is *contradictory*.

That argument was selected without reason, just because you felt like using it; it is *arbitrary*.

That argument can be taken in more than one way; it is *ambiguous*.

Examples

Since it rains every time we take John anywhere, we never take him on a picnic.

Everybody likes chocolate ice cream.
Since Mike likes to ski, all boys must like to ski.

All policemen I know are brutal. However, Patrolman Foster is a kind, gentle man.

All students will fail no matter how hard they study.

She's a nice girl.

That argument is full of untrue reasons for what you are doing; you are trying to mask your real motives with reasons that sound good; it is a *rationalization*.

I know I'm dieting, but if I don't eat a piece of Joan's pie, she will be angry.

EXERCISE 7A: Select the best answer. Circle your choice.

1. You are rationalizing by
    (a) eating that food.
    (b) giving reasonable ideas and opinions.
    (c) trying to fool yourself with untrue excuses.
2. An arbitrary ruling is one that is
    (a) made on someone's whim.
    (b) fair to all concerned.
    (c) evil.
3. That is a contradiction because
    (a) I do not agree with you.
    (b) it is the opposite of what you said five minutes ago.
    (c) it is what happens when muscles tighten.
4. A fallacy is an argument that is
    (a) going downhill.
    (b) completely untrue.
    (c) unfair.
5. Your statement is ambiguous because it
    (a) can be taken two ways.
    (b) is ambitious.
    (c) is brilliant.
6. A generalization is a statement which is
    (a) important to all army officers.
    (b) an oversimplification from one example.
    (c) one example which proves the rule.

II **When Talking About Ideas**

Examples

When you compare the parts of items or situations, you are drawing an *analogy*.

Saying that all men steal is like saying that all dogs bite.

When your explanation is tentative and open to further scientific testing, it is a *hypothesis*.

Chris Columbus made the hypothesis that the world is round; then he decided to test it.

The basic or introductory part of your idea is its *premise*.

In planning disarmament, we proceed from the premise that no one wants to blow up the world.

Name: _____ Date: _____

When you think about something that is not an object but rather an idea or ideal, it is an *abstraction*.

... Love
... Happiness
... Brotherhood

When something has a bearing on current matters, it is *relevant*.

While a discussion about the octopus is not relevant to today's youth, a discussion of drugs is.

EXERCISE 7B: Select the best answer. Circle your choice.

1. An abstraction is not as easy to discuss as a real object because
   (a) an abstraction is artistic.
   (b) an abstraction is not an absolutely fixed thing.
   (c) an abstraction is distracting.
2. Relevant topics are popular because they
   (a) are up-to-date.
   (b) reveal secrets.
   (c) bring happiness.
3. When you draw an analogy, you
   (a) make a picture.
   (b) make a summary.
   (c) make a comparison.
4. The premise of your argument is its
   (a) beginning.
   (b) middle.
   (c) ending.
5. A hypothesis is
   (a) an injection.
   (b) a logical conclusion.
   (c) a temporary assumption.

Lesson Two: Words to Describe the Mind

There are many words which describe characteristics of the mind. Some of them appear in this essay:

keen	(line 1)
perspicacious	(line 1)
calculating	(line 1)
acute	(line 1)
astute	(line 2)
cerebral	(line 50)
canny	(line 97)
persistent	(line 184)
cretin	(line 293)

Name: _____ Date: _____

A mind that is logical is often said to have the qualities of sharpness and exactness. Six of the words listed above convey such qualities. Often they are substituted for one another; they are synonyms.

keen . . . . sharp and penetrating
perspicacious . . . sharp and shrewd
calculating . . . . shrewd and scheming
acute . . . . sharp and penetrating
astute . . . . shrewd and clever
canny . . . . shrewd and knowing

The remaining three words in the list can best be explained as follows:

Cerebral activities are activities of the mind which appeal to intellectuals. Such activities range from concentrated thinking to problem solving to puzzle play.

A person has a *persistent* mind when he refuses to give up even in the face of opposition or discouragement.

A *cretin* is an idiot.

EXERCISE 7C: From the list of six synonyms above, fill in the words at the points of each arrow below. A number of the six words will be used more than once.

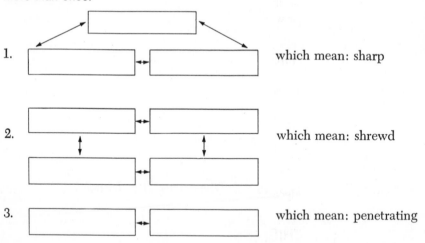

1. which mean: sharp

2. which mean: shrewd

3. which mean: penetrating

EXERCISE 7D: Fill in the blanks with the correct word.

1. cretin _____

2. persistent _____

3. cerebral _____

Choose from:
sharp
stupid
intellectual
continuing

Name: _____ Date: _____

SPELLING

Lesson One: Spelling Demons

Here are more words that are frequently misspelled. Using the helpful techniques given in Chapter One, you should make it a point to learn these new Demons, which were taken from "Love is a Fallacy."

bigger	exactly	huge	library
confuse	examine	immense	manner
connection	exclaim	importance	opponent
desire	exquisite	instance	opposite
dimension	fashion	intelligence	persistent
emphasize	guess	irresistible	restaurant

Lesson Two: Spelling Rule—*IE* and *EI*

Many of the words in Max Shulman's essay can be learned easily with the help of this one simple spelling rule.

Use *i* before *e*
Except after *c*,
Or when sounded like *a*
As in neighbor or weigh

☞ **YOU DO THIS:**

Fill in *ie* or *ei* in each of the following words.

bel____ve   perc____ve   rev____w

____ghteen   pat____nt   rec____ve

Here are some examples:

field   dece*i*ve   fre*i*ght   conce*i*ve   ve*i*l   y*i*eld

☞ **YOU DO THIS:**

Fill in *ie* or *ei* in each of the following words.

shr____k   c____ling   interv____w
v____n   n____ce   w____ght

A SPECIAL NOTE: Here are some words which you see frequently which—if you look at them closely—are exceptions to the above rule.

either   *foreign*   *weird*   *seize*   *leisure*   *neither*

183

EXERCISE 7E: Fill in *ie* or *ei* in each of the following words.

1. misch____f

2. r____gn

3. rec____pt

4. hyg____ne

5. for____gn

6. ____ghth

7. ach____vement

8. conc____ted

9. cash____r

10. rel____ve

11. n____ther

12. sl____gh

13. fr____nd

14. conc____vable

15. l____utenant

16. pr____st

17. dec____tful

18. ingred____nt

19. w____rd

20. b____ge

EXERCISE 7F: For each section below, use the Demons given in this chapter. Each Demon should be used only once.

A. Nine of the Demons have double letters in them. Write them here and either circle or enlarge any letter(s) that seem to be difficult.

_____ _____ _____

_____ _____ _____

_____ _____ _____

B. Four of the Demons begin with the letters *ex*. Write them here and either circle or enlarge any letter(s) that seem to be difficult.

_____ _____

_____ _____

C. Of the Demons not yet listed in this exercise, seven have smaller words of *four* letters in them. Write them here, underline the four-letter word, and either circle or enlarge any letter(s) that seem difficult.

_____ _____ _____

_____ _____ _____

_____

Name: _____ Date: _____

CLEAR THINKING: LOGIC

Although proper grammatical usage is important for good writing, an essay will not be successful if it is built on faulty reasoning. You must think and write clearly, giving effective evidence to support well-thought-out ideas.

As you read the following paragraph about the draft, pay close attention to the reasoning used to build the argument:

> I wholeheartedly disagree with Senator Claghorn's proposal to establish a universal national draft. The stupidity of the plan is apparent when one considers that the Senator has been divorced three times and is now being sued for back alimony payments by his last wife. In addition, our enemies the Russians use this draft system, which makes me wonder if perhaps the Senator is a Communist. Instead of drafting fine young men, the government should send all of the convicted murderers to fight our wars. After all, these criminals like to kill people. This would be the democratic thing to do in the home of the free and the land of the brave.

ANALYSIS: The writer of this paragraph seems to have some very strong feelings about his subject but, unfortunately, he gives no proof to support his argument that a universal national draft is a bad idea. The Senator's marital troubles may indicate that he is not a good marriage risk, but these problems certainly have no bearing on the worth of the man's idea. Instead of discussing the plan, the writer prefers to **attack the man** who proposed it.

The writer then reasons that the plan cannot be any good because our enemies already use it. We may have ideological differences with the Russians, but that does not mean that everything they do is necessarily bad. **Guilt by association** is being used to destroy the proposal.

The counterproposal will not hold up under examination because, while it may be true that some murderers enjoy committing their crimes, it is ridiculous to assume that this is true of all killers. Thus, it is a **generalization** to say that all convicted murderers like to kill people.

185

Even if it were true that all murderers liked to kill, too many questions have not been considered in formulating this new proposal: can murderers be trusted? Is there a moral argument against such a plan? When dealing with a complex problem, you need to analyze and examine your subject from many points of view before coming to any conclusions. The writer, who has created a plan based only on his own personal feelings, is guilty of **oversimplifying** his solution.

The writer ends his argument by carefully linkink his own proposal with democracy, freedom, and bravery—words which have good connotations for Americans. With the same purpose in mind, the writer identifies Senator Claghorn's plan as Communistic, a term which has negative connotations. Thus, the writer has tried to **feed our prejudices**.

☞ YOU DO THIS:

The following paragraph is built on some of the same confused thinking that has just been discussed. Find the errors and label each with its appropriate name. On separate paper, explain why it is wrong.

Because they are often misleading, advertisements should be read with a critical attitude. One can rarely know the truth about a product. The methods used in advertising are similar to the brainwashing techniques of the Red Chinese. In addition, the president of a large advertising firm is Mr. R. I. Win, the worst pro-football quarterback ever. One advertisement designed by his firm claimed that a product called "Hair Seed" could grow hair on bald spots. Because that ad made false claims, I know that all ads lie. If all advertisements were banned, the public would never have to worry about being cheated. Until then, however, we must remember that tricksters are always out to cheat and rob; we must always be on guard against those who want to take advantage of poor, helpless people who are honest, upstanding citizens.

II As you read the following paragraph about college life, pay close attention to the reasoning used to build the argument:

College students should concentrate on having a good time and should never pay attention to intellectual growth. Studying too much can lead to serious consequences. Just last week R. T. Zank, the school bookworm, suffered a nervous breakdown right after his chemistry final. But Sammy Swinger, the handsome football quarterback who never opens a book, is sure to succeed because he is so well liked.

ANALYSIS: The writer of this argument makes his first error in logic when he indicates that there are only two alternatives. A student spends all of his time either studying or having a good time. But there are other courses of action which have not been mentioned. For example, a student may spend part of his time studying and part of his time socializing. The situation is not as black and white as the writer's **either-or argument** would have us believe.

The Story of R. T. Zank proves only that the writer is not a very clear thinker. It is highly doubtful that studying was the sole cause of Zank's nervous breakdown. If the writer had explored the case, he most probably would have discovered that Zank had some serious personal problems. Thus, a **false cause** is being used to prove the argument.

The case of Sammy Swinger falls apart under examination because the writer does not supply the proper evidence to prove that the football player will succeed. The fact that Sammy is well liked certainly does not mean that he will be successful. **Relevant evidence** must be used to back up an argument.

☞ YOU DO THIS:

The following paragraph is built on some of the same confused thinking that has just been discussed. Find the errors and label each with its appropriate name. On separate paper, explain why it is wrong.

> The congestion in our cities is becoming unbearable. To see this we have only to look at our city's complex budget, which the mayor is unable to control. Of course, one of the worst results of overcrowding is corruption in government. In addition, decent places to live are difficult to find because the supply cannot keep up with the demand. Without a doubt, unless half of our city-dwellers move to farms, mankind will perish.

III As you read the following paragraph about cigarette smoking, pay close attention to the reasoning used to build the argument:

> Cigarette smoking is certainly not harmful to health. My grandfather began smoking cigarettes when he was eleven, and he lived to be ninety-five. My Uncle Jim, who smokes four packs of cigarettes a day, is a healthy seventy-two. In addition, Mike Marvel, the ace baseball player, says that Puffo Cigarettes make him feel relaxed and refreshed before a big game. besides, everybody smokes cigarettes so it can't be wrong.

187

ANALYSIS: The writer of this paragraph uses two examples to try to prove that cigarette smoking is not harmful to health. These illustrations may help to clarify the argument, but they certainly do not prove the writer's case. Two men are not representative of the millions of people who smoke. A reputable research study using a much larger sampling would be **adequate evidence** to convince the reader. (Max Shulman calls this fallacy a hasty generalization in his essay.)

The writer then makes the mistake of citing a baseball player's comment as added proof. Whenever an authority is to be used, one must decide if the person is an authority on the subject of the essay. Mike Marvel may know a good deal about baseball, but he does not know any more about cigarette smoking than anyone else. One might also wonder if the authority had any hidden motives for making his statement. In this case, the baseball player endorsed Puffo Cigarettes because he was being paid. Therefore, he certainly was not an **appropriate authority**.

The writer ends his argument with yet another poor attempt at proving his opinion. Although a good many people do smoke cigarettes, it is a ridiculous generalization to claim that everybody does. It is more accurate to limit the statement by saying that many people smoke cigarettes. In the same way, strong words such as "never" and "always" usually have to be limited to "sometimes" and "often." It is important to **qualify** positive statements to make them more accurate.

Even if it were true that everybody smokes cigarettes, this still does not prove that smoking is not harmful to health. One hundred fifty years ago many people believed that slavery was a good thing, but that did not mean it was. The **everyone-is-doing-it argument** does not prove anything, for even the majority can be wrong.

☞ YOU DO THIS:

The following paragraph is built on some of the same confused thinking that has just been discussed. Find the errors and label each with its appropriate name. On separate paper, explain why it is wrong.

> Recently I have read that the insecticide DDT may be responsible for upsetting the balance of nature. However, this is absolutely not true. My Uncle Hank, a farmer who for many years has depended on DDT to save his crops, says that there is nothing wrong with it. Also, Mr. J. P. Spray, the president of Bug-Puncher International, Inc., says that DDT is not at all harmful. Finally, I think that DDT must be safe because so many farmers use it.

IV As you read the following paragraph about flying saucers, pay close attention to the reasoning used to build the argument:

> If flying saucers do exist, they might be dangerous to our society. Thus, we should be afraid of flying saucers, if there are such things, because they could do a good deal of harm to the people of earth. Peter, my next door neighbor, claims that he doesn't consider flying saucers dangerous. In fact, he says that he would enjoy riding in a flying saucer from another planet because he loves to ride in airplanes. Personally, I do not think that flying saucers are a danger because I do not think they even exist; after all, I have never seen one.

ANALYSIS: The writer begins by presenting the logical statement that flying saucers might be dangerous if they really exist. But instead of immediately trying to prove his statement, he merely uses new words to repeat the very same argument in the next sentence. Because the reader is just being led in a monotonous circle, this error is called **circular reasoning**.

Peter is also an illogical thinker. When Peter compares riding in a flying saucer with riding in an airplane, he forgets that, although the vehicles might be somewhat similar, there are probably some very big differences between the two. Things that are being compared must be similar in all major aspects or the result is a **false comparison**. (Max Shulman calls this fallacy a false analogy in his essay.)

The argument falls apart completely with the concluding statement that flying saucers do not exist because the writer has never seen one. It is invalid to argue that something does not exist because one has no **personal knowledge** of it.

☞ YOU DO THIS:

The following paragraph is built on some of the same confused thinking that has just been discussed. Find the errors and label each with its appropriate name. On separate paper, explain why it is wrong.

> Following the news about politicians can be both exciting and dull. Sometimes interesting political people catch our attention while at other times the news about politicians seems ordinary and boring. Politicians, fascinating one moment, can become uninteresting the next. Of course, some people think that politicians are dishonest, but I disagree. After all, they, like doctors, serve the public; and if a doctor does not do a good job, the news will spread quickly. Moreover, I can be sure that politicians are honest because in all my years of going to political meetings, I have never met a dishonest politician.

EXERCISE 7G: Analyze each of the following statements for its soundness of reasoning. A space is provided for your brief analysis.

1. A trial marriage is a good idea. After all, major appliances such as refrigerators and television sets can be purchased with money-back guarantees. If a person can take an appliance on approval, he should be able to do the same with his mate.

2. Dr. Spock, the famous baby doctor, says that the draft system is inequitable.

3. People with red hair are very hot tempered.

4. Senator Shwin's plan for tax reform is no good because the Senator is a drunkard who has been arrested on drunk-driving charges.

5. There is no God because I have never seen evidence that He exists.

6. People who mind their own business never get into trouble.

7. Joe has long hair and a beard so he must be a hippie.

8. If we drop an atomic bomb, we will put a quick end to all of our problems with other nations.

9. Helen had another one of her gallbladder attacks right after eating pizza, so she had better not eat pizza any more.

Name: _____ Date: _____

10. Everybody else cheats on examinations, so why shouldn't I?

_____

11. The Cheetah Automobile is the worst car on the market. Not only have I had trouble with mine, but I know at least six people who complain continually about their Cheetahs.

_____

12. Love and marriage go together like a horse and carriage.

_____

13. I always thought that Pablo was a fine man until I saw him with Bugsy Fletcher, a known criminal.

_____

14. Vote for Tom Johnson for mayor! He is just as American as apple pie. But Vito Marcos, his opponent, has the sly appearance of a Mafia leader.

_____

15. I am sure that Tony will be a good company president because he has raised two fine sons, both of whom became successful lawyers.

_____

16. The federal government should stop spending so many billions of dollars on the space program and should use that money to feed the nation's hungry people. There is no reason for poverty in America while we are using up so much money on a project to send men into outer space.

_____

17. Drinking should be banned in this country. Otherwise, people will get into all kinds of drunken brawls.

_____

　　　　Name: _____ Date: _____

18. One should always tell the truth.

_____

19. Lana Lamour, the Hollywood sexpot, says that she developed her voluptuous measurements by eating Yippie Yogurt.

_____

20. If the government's civil-rights laws were strictly enforced, there would be no more racial problems.

_____

EXERCISE 7H: Answer each of the following questions about logic.

1. Give an appropriate authority for: Football Is a Dangerous Sport.

_____

2. Give adequate evidence for: Women Are (Are Not) Bad Drivers.

_____

_____

3. Correct this generalization: Eighteen-year-olds are mature enough to vote.

_____

4. Avoid circular reasoning in developing: Men Are Strong.

_____

_____

_____

Name: _____ Date: _____

5. Rework this oversimplification: If I had a good deal of money, all my problems would be solved.

_____

_____

6. Qualify this statement: All teenagers are irresponsible.

_____

_____

7. Without using personal knowledge defend: Turnips taste awful.

_____

_____

_____

8. Change this false comparison: Learning to drive is as easy as apple pie.

_____

9. Without attacking the man, develop a statement about Adolph Hitler's philosophy.

_____

_____

_____

10. Avoid using guilt by association in making a statement about a friend who is active in the SDS (Students for a Democratic Society).

_____

_____

_____

Name: _____ *Date:* _____

11. Avoid feeding our prejudices when making up an advertisement about cosmetics.

_____

_____

_____

12. Avoiding the argument "everybody is doing it," argue: Kissing must be good.

_____

_____

_____

13. Correct this false cause: Television is responsible for the violence in America today.

_____

_____

14. Avoiding the either-or argument, develop this statement: We must wipe out the Communists or they will destroy us.

_____

_____

_____

15. Give relevant evidence for: Local traffic problems are not being met effectively.

_____

_____

_____

Name: _____ Date: _____

EXERCISE 71 ESSAY ANALYSIS: On separate paper, answer these questions about the essay "Love Is a Fallacy."

1. Read lines 330–336. Explain how this is an example of Ad Misericordiam. _____

    _____

2. Read lines 340–347. Explain how this is an example of Hypothesis Contrary to Fact. _____

    _____

3. Read lines 348–352. Explain how this is an example of Dicto Simpliciter. _____

    _____

4. Read lines 359–364. Explain how this is an example of Poisoning the Well. _____

    _____

5. Read lines 58–63 again. From what single example is a generalization made about Polly's table manners? _____

    _____

Name: _____ *Date:* _____

EXERCISE 7J REFRESHER:

1. Make any corrections that will improve the effectiveness of the following introduction and conclusion.
2. Plan ahead by listing three main ideas that would comprise the main body paragraphs of the essay.
3. Correct any errors in verb and pronoun agreement.

Advertisements are Illogical

Introduction

A well-known cigarette advertises that they have "less tar and nicotine than the best-selling filter tip cigarette." But the truth behind the ad is that the best-selling filter tip cigarette has more tar and nicotine than any other cigarette on the market. So the advertisement, which sounds impressive, do not really mean anything. In my essay I will give similar evidence to show that advertisements do not make much sense.

Main Body I. _____

Main Body II. _____

Main Body III. _____

Conclusion

The many examples that I have given proves that the public is being deceived when they read or hear these advertisements. If the government will censor the advertising media, the consumer will no longer be cheated when they make purchases.

Name: _____ Date: _____

SPRINGBOARDS TO WRITING

1. As a result of looking at the advertisements, reading the essay, or answering the questions which followed each, you might have some thoughts about the central theme—logical thinking. (Look back at those pages to refresh your memory.) For help in planning such an essay, refer to the Guide for Planning an Essay, which appears in Springboards to Writing, Chapter One on page 25.

2. Here are some topics which have not been directly mentioned in the questions asked so far. Perhaps one of these arguments could be a writing springboard for you. Use clear logic in presenting your case.
   (a) Newspaper editorials are (are not) illogical.
   (b) Advertisements are (are not) illogical.
   (c) Women are (are not) dumb.
   (d) Money is (is not) happiness.
   (e) All parents are (are not) alike.
   (f) Ignorance is (is not) bliss.
   (g) The heart is wiser than the head.
   (h) The head is wiser than the heart.
   (i) Children under sixteen should (should not) be allowed to see all movies.

UPI *Photo.*

eight

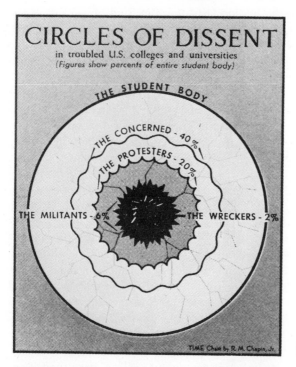

CIRCLES OF DISSENT
in troubled U.S. colleges and universities
(Figures show percents of entire student body)

THE STUDENT BODY

THE CONCERNED - 40%

THE PROTESTERS - 20%

THE MILITANTS - 6%   THE WRECKERS - 2%

TIME Chart by R. M. Chapin, Jr.

Reprinted by permission. Copyright Time, Inc. 1969.

SPRINGBOARDS TO THINKING

For informal, not written, response . . . to stimulate your thinking

1. What does the circle graph show you?
2. How would you define each of the five groups of students so that it is possible to tell the difference between the groups?
3. If this were a graph of your college, would you enlarge or diminish any of the bands?
4. Where would you put yourself in this graph?
5. What is going on in the news photograph?
6. Where would the people in the photograph fit on the graph?
7. Look at the emotions in the picture. What is the emotion of the boy holding up the stick? . . . of the boy holding his head? . . . of the men in the background?
8. This picture appeared in many newspapers. Do you consider it an accurate picture of the student protest movement?
9. On what basis do you think some people claim that the news media distort news events for dramatic effect? Do you agree that there is distortion in the reporting of news? Why or why not? If there is distortion, what sort of problems and dangers could develop?

Four Choices for Young People

JOHN FISCHER

(1) Shortly before his graduation last June, Jim Binns, president of the senior class at Stanford University wrote me about some of his misgivings.

(2) "More than any other generation," he said, "our generation views the adult world with great skepticism . . . there also is an increased tend-
⁵ ency to reject completely that world."

(3) Apparently he speaks for a lot of his contemporaries. During the last few years I have listened to scores of young people, in college and out, who were just as nervous about the grown-up world. Some feel even worse—much worse. The hippies, for example, seem to view the society
¹⁰ around them with a mixture of loathing, incomprehension, and despair. Their appraisal was expressed with admirable succinctness recently by Emmett Grogan, a leader of a West Coast sodality of social dropouts who call themselves The Diggers. "Politics is dead," he announced. "Culture is dead. The whole world stinks."

¹⁵ (4) Such total discouragement probably is shared by only a tiny minor- ity of Americans under twenty-five. But many of the others—perhaps a majority—evidently look at the society they are entering with some degree of bewilderment and mistrust. Roughly, their attitude might be summed up about like this: "The world is in pretty much of a mess, full of injus-
²⁰ tice, poverty, and war. The people responsible are, presumably, the adults who have been running things. If they can't do better than that, what have they got to teach our generation? That kind of lesson we can do without."

(5) These conclusions strike me as reasonable, at least from their point of view. It is true that the world is an unfair and often a terrifying place.
²⁵ It also is true that the conventional wisdom, which the elders try to ladle into the young with such overwhelming generosity, often will have little relevance to the increasingly complex problems of the next two decades. The grown-ups might argue, a little defensively, that the reasons for the mess are somewhat different from what most young people think they are,
³⁰ and that the current crop of adults is neither so stupid nor so corrupt as their youthful critics often assume. Nevertheless, I am delighted to see Jim Binns' generation approaching the future with a certain skepticism. As a one-time semi-pro boxer, I can testify that anyone who keeps his guard up, his eyes wary, and his knees loose has a better chance of sur-
³⁵ vival. And skepticism, after all, is simply a habit of not believing anything until you have some solid evidence that it might be true. Among scientists, I understand, this is known as the scientific method.

(6) The relevant question for the arriving generation is not whether our society is imperfect (we can take that for granted), but how to deal

⁴⁰ with it. For all its harshness and irrationality, it is the only world we've
got. Choosing a strategy to cope with it, then, is the first decision a young
adult has to make, and usually the most important decision of his lifetime.

(7) So far as I have been able to discover, there are only four basic
alternatives:

1. Drop Out.

⁴⁵ (8) Anyone who takes *Ramparts* seriously might think that this solution was invented only yesterday by the Reverend Timothy Leary, and
that it can be practiced successfully only in Haight-Ashbury or Greenwich
Village, with the aid of LSD or some other reality-blunting drug. In fact,
it is one of the oldest expedients, and it can be practiced anywhere, at any
⁵⁰ age, and with or without the use of hallucinogens. It always has been the
strategy of choice for people who find the world too brutal and too complex to be endured. Its notable practitioners include many Hindu mystics,
certain monastic orders dating from the early years of Christianity, several
Buddhist sects, and the skid-row bums slumped on the curb with a pint of
⁵⁵ cheap wine. The hermit of Mount Athos and the millionaire recluse in his
Caribbean hideaway are both dropouts. So were Diogenes and Lao-tse.
So too is the suburban matron whose life centers on her daily bridge game
and a jug of martinis.

(9) This way of life is, by definition, parasitic. In one way or another,
⁶⁰ its practitioners batten on the society which they scorn, and in which they
refuse to take any responsibility. Some of us (The Squares) find this dis-
tasteful—an undignified kind of life, like that of a leech or a kept woman.
But for the poor in spirit, with low levels of both energy and pride, it may
be the least intolerable choice available.

2. Flee.

⁶⁵ (10) This strategy also has ancient antecedents. Ever since civilization
began, certain individuals have tried to run away from it, in hopes of
finding a simpler, more pastoral, and more peaceful life. Unlike the dropouts, they are not parasites. They are willing to support themselves, and
to contribute something to the general community—but they simply don't
⁷⁰ like the environment of civilization: that is, the city, with all its ugliness
and tension.

(11) The joy of simple life among the noble savages has been celebrated
by eloquent propagandists, from Vergil to Rousseau. Their precepts have
been followed by people as diverse as Daniel Boone and Gauguin. When
⁷⁵ I was twenty-one, at a time when American society seemed hopelessly
bogged down in the miseries of the Depression, I attempted it myself. I
applied for a job on an Australian ranch, and if I had been accepted I
might be herding sheep today—no doubt a happier and healthier man.

(12) The trouble with this solution is that it no longer is practical on
⁸⁰ a large scale. Our planet, unfortunately, is running out of noble savages
and unsullied landscapes; except for the Polar regions, the frontiers are

gone. A few gentlemen farmers with plenty of money can still escape to the bucolic life—but in general the stream of migration is flowing the other way. Each year American farming has room for fewer and fewer
85 people. Recently about a million have been moving every year—many of them reluctantly—from the country to the cities. There is some hope that this trend eventually might be reversed; but it would require a massive national effort, extended over several decades.

3. Plot a Revolution.

(13) This strategy always is popular among those who have no patience
90 with the tedious workings of the democratic process, or who believe that basic institutions can only be changed by force. It attracts some of the more active and idealistic young people of every generation. To them it offers a romantic appeal, usually symbolized by some dashing and charismatic figure—a Byron, a Garibaldi, a Trotsky, or a Che Guevara. It has
95 the even greater appeal of simplicity: "Since this society is hopelessly bad, let's smash it and build something better on the ruins." And to anybody with strong Oedipal feelings it provides the special delight of defying the Establishment—that stuffy collection of father-figures whom we all find it so easy to hate.
100 (14) Some of my best friends have been revolutionists, and a few of them have led reasonably satisfying lives. These are the ones whose revolutions did not come off; they have been able to keep on cheerfully plotting their holocausts right into their senescence. Others died young, in prison or on the barricades. But the most unfortunate are those whose
105 revolutions succeeded—men like Djilas and Trotsky. They lived, in bitter disillusionment, to see the Establishment they had overthrown replaced by a new one, just as hard-faced and stuffy.

(15) I am not, of course, suggesting that revolutions accomplish nothing. Some clearly do change things for the better, as in Mexico and (in
110 spite of Djilas' unhappiness) in Yugoslavia. Elsewhere, as in Algeria and in Ghana during Nkrumah's reign, the change clearly was for the worse. My point is merely that the idealists who make the revolution are bound to be disappointed in either case. For at best their victory never dawns on the shining new world they had dreamed of, cleansed of all human
115 meanness. Instead it dawns on a familiar, workaday place, still in need of groceries and sewage disposal. The revolutionary state, under whatever political label, has to be run—not by violent romantics—but by experts in marketing, sanitary engineering, and the management of bureaucracies. For the Byrons among us, this discovery is a fate worse than death.
120 (16) Fortunately the young revolutionists in today's America are safe from such a fate. This government simply is not going to be overthrown by violence, within the foreseeable future. Many recruits of the New Left are unwilling to believe this—and since they can't be bothered to study the history of revolutionary movements, they probably are beyond argu-
125 ment. Bayard Rustin, the leading intellectual of the civil-rights movement,

recently remarked that he has to spend a lot of his time persuading student enthusiasts that the conditions for a successful guerrilla war do not exist in the United States. He seemed unsure whether he had made much headway.

130   (17) At most, these would-be guerrillas might provoke a tragic reaction. So long as they limit themselves to demonstrating and wearing buttons, they will be tolerated. But if they should ever become a real nuisance—if they should attempt enough violence to seriously disrupt the life of the country—then the community will suppress them, quickly and harshly.
135 If that happens, a lot of other people will get suppressed at the same time, and many of the most hopeful impulses in American society will be drowned under a new wave of McCarthyism.

  (18) For the rebels who understand this—the idealists who are determined to remake society, but who seek a more practical method than
140 armed revolution—there remains one more alternative:

4. Try to Change the World Gradually, One Clod at a Time.

  (19) At first glance, this course is far from inviting. It lacks glamour. It promises no quick results. It depends on the exasperating and uncertain instruments of persuasion and democratic decision-making. It demands patience, always in short supply among the young. About all that can be
145 said for it is that it sometimes works—that in this particular time and place it offers a better chance for remedying some of the world's outrages than any other available strategy.

  (20) So at least the historical evidence seems to suggest. Thirty-five years ago, for example, the generation graduating from college also found
150 the world in a mess. The economic machinery had broken down almost everywhere; in this country nearly a quarter of the population was out of work. Hideous political movements were burgeoning in Europe and Asia. A major war seemed all too likely. As a college newspaper editor at that time, I protested against this just as vehemently as student activists are
155 protesting today. I pointed out to my parents' generation, with what I hoped was burning eloquence, that war was insane and inhuman—and that it was stupid to close down factories when people were starving. The doddering old folks who ran the country obviously were bunglers. If they would just step aside, we youngsters would soon straighten things out.
160   (21) Oddly enough, something like that actually happened. The generation which came of age in the 'thirties did get the national economy working again—not by revolution, which was widely recommended by the advanced thinkers of the time, but by slow, pragmatic tinkering. As a consequence, though poverty has not yet disappeared, it has been shrink-
165 ing dramatically for the last three decades. The same generation demonstrated, at considerable cost, that fascism was not the wave of the future. It even created diplomatic machinery for working out peaceful settlements of international disputes. It is true that this machinery has operated

only moderately well; but it has forestalled any major war for nearly thirty years—no trivial achievement in the light of earlier history.

(22) At the same time, my generation was discovering that reforming the world is a little like fighting a military campaign in the Apennines: as soon as you capture one mountain range, another one looms just ahead. As the big problems of the 'thirties were brought under some kind of rough control, new problems took their place—the unprecedented problems of an affluent society, of racial justice, of keeping our cities from becoming uninhabitable, of coping with war in unfamiliar guises. Most disturbing of all was our discovery of the population explosion. It dawned on us rather suddenly that the number of passengers on the small spaceship we inhabit is doubling about every forty years—and that already there aren't enough seats to go around. So long as the earth's population keeps growing at this cancerous rate, all of the other problems appear virtually insoluble. Our cities will continue to become more crowded and noisome. The landscape will get more cluttered, the air and water even dirtier. The quality of life is likely to become steadily worse for everybody. And warfare on a rising scale seems inevitable, if too many bodies have to struggle for ever-dwindling shares of food and living space.

(23) So Jim Binns' generation has a formidable job on its hands. But not, I think, an insuperable one. On the evidence of the past, it can be handled in the same way that hard problems have been coped with before —piecemeal, pragmatically, by the dogged efforts of many people. The victories will be unspectacular: perhaps tomorrow the discovery of a cheaper and more reliable method of birth control, next year the development of a high-yield strain of rice. The real heroes will not be revolutionary demagogues, but the obscure teachers who work out better ways to train underprivileged children . . . the businessmen who manage to upgrade unskilled Negro workers . . . the politicians who devise new institutions to govern our metropolitan areas . . . the journalists who persuade a reluctant citizenry that change not only is necessary, but inescapable.

(24) These individual efforts may add up to a surprising sum of accomplishment. For the arriving generation, from what I have seen of it, shows more potential than its predecessors. It is healthier and better educated. It is more idealistic—that is, more willing to work for the common good, rather than for purely selfish ends. If it is (fortunately) pretty skeptical, it certainly is not complacent.

(25) Provided that a reasonable number of this generation choose the fourth strategy, they probably will accomplish more than they now expect. They can't be sure, of course. As they get on with the job, in their step-by-step fashion, they can be sure of only two things. First, that they will get no help from the dropouts, and precious little from the escapees and the professional revolutionists. Second, that about twenty-five years from now they will be upbraided by their children because they have not done enough, and because they will have failed to foresee the arising problems of the next century.

READING SURVEY

1. Main Idea

What is the central theme of the essay?

2. Major Details

(a) According to John Fischer, what is the relevant question for the arriving generation?

(b) Briefly summarize and define—so that the differences are clear—what is meant by ... drop out

           ... flee

           ... plot a revolution

           ... try to change gradually, one clod at a time.

(c) Who does Fischer think will be the real heroes of our time?

3. Inference

(a) As implied in this essay, what is Fischer's attitude toward young people?

(b) Read paragraphs twenty-one and twenty-two again. When Fischer refers to his youth in the 1930's, what is he implying about today's unrest among young people?

4. Opinion

(a) Given the four choices presented in this essay, which would you choose for yourself? Why?

(b) Read paragraph seventeen again. Do you agree with this prediction? Point to events today which support your opinion.

VOCABULARY BUILDING

Lesson One: Attitudes and Ways of Life

The more people one meets the more one finds that there are many different ideas, attitudes, and preferences which people have about their way of life. In "Four Choices for Young People" there are many words which are useful in a discussion of attitudes and ways of life. Perhaps you will be able to identify something of yourself in these words:

skepticism	(paragraph 2)	idealistic	(13)
mystics	(8)	revolutionary	(15)
monastic	(8)	McCarthyism	(17)
parasitic	(9)	pragmatic	(21)
pastoral	(10)	fascism	(21)
bucolic	(12)	diplomatic	(21)
democratic	(13)		

A person who doubts and criticizes most things is a *skeptic*. Such a person is a *skeptical* listener and reader because his *skepticism* makes him doubt most things that he hears or reads.

A person who prefers his own private, spiritual world is a *mystic*. Such a person likes the *mystical* way of life because as a follower of *mysticism* he believes that the mysteries of man and the universe can be understood only through direct communion with the gods or personal inspiration and insight.

A person who likes to live secluded from the world with no personal comforts—like a monk in a monastery—prefers the *monastic* way of life.

A person who, although capable of supporting himself, chooses to be a *parasite* by attaching himself to someone he can live on without having to give anything in return, lives a *parasitic* way of life.

A person who likes the life of country people and shepherds prefers the *pastoral* way of life. Such a rural and rustic life is also known as a *bucolic* way of life.

A person who favors the political philosophy of government run by and for the masses is a *democrat*. Such a person prefers the *democratic* way of life, which is based on social equality for all and which is usually practiced in a *democracy*. (You can be a democrat without being a Democrat. Only the political party is capitalized.)

A person who is guided by imaginary models of perfection which he tries to imitate is an *idealist*. Such an *idealistic* person expects life to be close to perfect because his *idealism* leads him to set very high standards.

A person who wants to see a sudden and complete change take place is a *revolutionist*. Often such a person's *revolutionary* ideas center on the desire to change a system of government through *revolution* rather than through slower and more orderly evolution.

A person who favors the methods used in the 1950's by the now deceased Senator Joseph McCarthy is a *McCarthyite*. Such a person ruins reputations by widely publicizing half-truths about anyone who seems a handy target. *McCarthyism* supports the use of loaded words and broad hints to imply that someone is antidemocratic, usually as a communist.

A person who has a practical approach to life is a *pragmatist*. Such a person usually prefers *pragmatic* results to idealistic theories.

A person who favors the political philosophy of a central government headed by a dictator, who can impose severe controls and who can suppress all opposition, is a *fascist*. Such a person believes that *fascism* is the best system of government.

A person who is tactful is considered a *diplomat*. The art of *diplomacy* is used by governments in their dealings with other countries. People with *diplomatic* skills are often employed by the government.

EXERCISE 8A: Match the vocabulary words with these classified advertisements:

CLASSIFIED ADS:

HELP WANTED

MEN WHO CAN commune with the gods to help us find our personal meanings in life. Send résumé to Box L.O.V.E.

_____

EXPERIENCED SHEPHERD, with flute if possible, who loves rustic country life. Apply in person to Fields and Meadows, Inc.

_____

NEED MAN TRULY dedicated to the idea of social equality to help a nation that is having trouble. Apply immediately to Box 50.

_____

SITUATIONS WANTED

PRACTICAL solutions my specialty. Write Box 1, 2, 3.

_____

EXPERT doubter and questioner available for any interesting job which requires evaluation. Write Box 0–NO.

_____

EXPERIENCED dictator good at cruel control of people. Write full gory details to Box A.H.

_____

Name: _____   Date: _____

FOR SALE

COLLECTION OF HALF-TRUTHS and scare words useful when publicly accusing someone of being a communist. For one price you can ruin many reputations. Especially useful when you have no facts. Send $2 to Box L.I.E. Will be sent in plain wrapper.

ONE SECLUDED spot far from civilization with no comfort or convenience. Write Box 1 for fuller description.

PERFECT MODELS for all aspects of life. Look easy to follow, but a real challenge to the determined. On view daily at the Rose Garden.

FARM IN THE COUNTRY perfect for people who like the quiet rural life. Details from Box C.O.W.

EXCELLENT OPPORTUNITIES

FOR SOMEONE with tact the opportunity to travel and meet many people. Many hidden benefits. Write Box B.

IN A NATION that seems ready for radical change. Good potential. Only the energetic need apply. Box RRR.

LOST AND FOUND

LOST: IN THE MIDDLE OF TOWN, my private list of names and addresses of rich people I can hang onto. Needed for survival. Contact me immediately through Box P.I.G.

Name: _____ Date: _____

Lesson Two: Tracking Down a Reference

When a writer wishes to emphasize or illustrate a point, he will sometimes use as an example the name of a famous person, an event in history, or a character in literature or mythology. Such references can be valuable and interesting. But the writer rarely includes enough details for the reader to fully understand the reference. Thus, it becomes the task of the reader to track down the reference.

The following will discuss the references used in "Four Choices for Young People." It will also indicate how you can track down many of the references which you encounter in your reading—and which you might want to begin using in your writing.

Name References

Revolutionary Leaders

Garibaldi	(paragraph 13)		
Trotsky	(13)		
Che Guevara	(13)		
Djilas	(14)		

National Figures

Daniel Boone	(11)
Nkrumah	(15)

Artists, Poets, and Philosophers

Timothy Leary	(8)
Lao-Tse	(8)
Diogenes	(8)
Vergil	(11)
Rousseau	(11)
Gauguin	(11)
Byron	(13)

1. *Revolutionary Leaders*
   Garibaldi, Guiseppi (1807–82): An Italian patriot, soldier, and hero who wanted Italy to become a Republic.

   Trotsky, Leon (1887–1940): A Russian intellectual who favored world-wide revolution. He was a major figure in the Russian Revolution of 1917, which marked the beginning of the U.S.S.R. Later, however, he was exiled for opposing Stalin's policies.

   Guevara, Ernesto ("Che") (1928–1967): A Cuban who was important in Castro's revolution. He later went to other Latin American countries to try to start other revolutions.

   Djilas, Milovan (1911–   ): A Yugoslav who helped Tito's revolution. Later he was jailed for speaking against cruel government policies.

2. *National Figures*
   Boone, Daniel (1734–1820): An American frontiersman who, with courage and determination, led pioneers to Kentucky and founded Boonesville.

209

Nkrumah, Kwame (1909–   ): Former Prime Minister of Ghana who led his country to independence from England. Later he began to jail and silence all opposition to his government.

3. *Artists, Poets, and Philosophers*

Leary, Timothy (1921–   ): Once a professor, now a mystic who introduced the world to LSD.

Lao-Tse (about 640 B.C.): A Chinese mystic who taught that the ideal state is one of mystical contemplation and freedom from desires.

Diogenes (about 412–323 B.C.): A convinced skeptic who believed that the simple life was virtuous and, therefore, he discarded all his belongings and lived in a tub.

Vergil (70–19 B.C.): The author of the epic *Aeneid* who felt that the bucolic life was ideal.

Rousseau, Jean-Jacques (1712–78): A philosopher who believed that man is corrupted by civilization and should return to nature.

Gauguin, Paul (1848–1903): An Impressionist painter who, at first a successful banker, turned to painting at the age of thirty-five. When he was forty-five, he left civilization and moved to Tahiti to paint pictures of the natives.

Byron, George (1788–1824): An English poet who was lame and unhappy. He traveled a great deal and wrote poems filled with loneliness and bitterness.

EXERCISE 8B: Refer back to the essay "Four Choices for Young People" and explain why the author, John Fischer, used each reference discussed above. You can quickly locate each reference in the essay by using the paragraph numbers provided with the vocabulary list. (Notice that John Fischer groups many of the names together.) Use your own paper to write out your explanations.

A SPECIAL NOTE: Just as you can find the meaning of words which are new to you by looking them up in the dictionary, so also can you find the meaning of references which you do not understand. The reference section of your school library most likely has dictionaries, encyclopedias, almanacs, yearbooks, indexes, and atlases. Any trained librarian can help you consult the book most suited to your needs. When tracking down a reference, try this:

Reference Needed	Possible Sources (ask librarian for others)
person living or dead	*The Columbia Encyclopedia* (one volume, 1963) *Current Biography* or *Who's Who*
character from literature or mythology	*The New Century Handbook of English Literature* (1956) *Mythology of All Races* (1935)
historical event	*World Almanac* (new volume each year) *Information Please Almanac* (new each year) any index or dictionary of history
place	*The Columbia Encyclopedia* (1963) any atlas or geographical dictionary

If you wish to begin using references in your writing, remember three important guidelines:

1. Be sure that the reference is not too obscure. It should be well known and easily available from basic reference books.

2. Be certain that the reference completely fits the situation you wish to illustrate.

3. Be careful not to overuse references.

SPELLING

Lesson One: Spelling Demons

Here are more words that are frequently misspelled. Using the helpful techniques given in Chapter One, you should make it a point to learn these new Demons, taken from "Four Choices for Young People."

campaign	escape	management	recommend
community	fortunately	noble	region
consequence	fourth	persuade	responsible
contribute	guard	political	rough
definition	inevitable	population	succeed
despair	majority	quarter	tomorrow

Lesson Two: The Apostrophe

Disregarding or misusing the apostrophe is as serious an error as misspelling the word. Careless writers do not realize that the apostrophe is as much a part of the word as each letter. Because it has only three major uses, the apostrophe is easy to learn and use properly.

I *Contractions*: The apostrophe is used in contractions to indicate that a letter or letters have been left out.

it is = it's	do not = don't
let us = let's	we have = we've
have not = haven't	they had = they'd

☞ YOU DO THIS:

Form contractions out of the following sets of words. Be sure to use the apostrophe where needed.

could have = _____   were not = _____

I have =   _____   you are = _____

we will =   _____   she had = _____

II *Plurals*: To form the plural of a letter of the alphabet, a number, or a symbol, use *'s*.

6's   three c's   &'s

If the number is written out, use only the *s*.

fours   sevens   nines

☞ YOU DO THIS:

Insert any necessary apostrophes in the following sentences.

1. Joe won the poker game with three 9s and two 4s.

2. Helen always got Bs and Cs on her compositions because she used too many &s.

III *Possession*: To form possessives, first write the name of the possessor—whether it be singular or plural. Then add *'s* to the end of the name. If it already ends in *s*, add just the '. As follows:

Helen's hat   Dickens' *Tale of Two Cities*
the teacher's integrity   the ladies' club
man's fate   two boys' uniforms

To form the possessives of noun combinations, use the apostrophe only after the last noun in the combination.

my sister-in-law's car   the chief of police's remarks

A SPECIAL NOTE: Do not use an apostrophe with the possessive pronouns: his, hers, yours, ours, theirs, its, whose.

☞ YOU DO THIS:

Rewrite each of the following phrases to form possessives using an apostrophe.

the books of the children _____

the guns of the soldiers _____

the case of the attorney general _____

EXERCISE 8C: Follow the directions for each section.

A. Form contractions out of the following sets of words.

1. I will = _____   6. they are = _____

2. will not = _____   7. Mike is = _____

3. there is = _____   8. would not = _____

4. are not = _____   9. that is = _____

5. does not = _____   10. who would = _____

Name: _____ Date: _____

B. Rewrite each of the following phrases to form possessives using an apostrophe.

1. the purring of the cat _____

2. the purring of the cats _____

3. the honesty of Mr. Ross _____

4. the strength of the country _____

5. the cooking of my mother-in-law _____

6. the work of the men _____

7. the problems of the cities _____

8. the problem of the city _____

9. the orders of the commander-in-chief _____

10. the population of the regions _____

C. Insert apostrophes where necessary in the following sentences.
1. Its necessary to mind your Ps and Qs if youre to succeed.
2. The singers voices could be heard for blocks as they sounded their As.
3. The worlds troubles are todays headlines and tomorrows history.
4. I couldnt understand the essay because the writers ?s look like Ss and his 8s look like 0s.
5. As part of Charles political campaign, he addressed a local teachers association.

EXERCISE 8D: Using the definitions given as clues, fill in this puzzle. If necessary, check your spelling with the list of Demons in this chapter.

Down

1. to get away
2. neighborhood
3. administration
4. not smooth
5. a large area
6. virtuous
7. the meaning of a word
8. to influence
9. twenty-five cents
10. to give along with others, as to a charity
11. A well-planned _____ can help a politician to win the election.
12. the number of people in a society

Across

7. loss of hope
13. unavoidable
14. to suggest
15. to be in charge of
16. to protect
17. to attain a goal
18. the result
19. luckily
20. first, second, third, _____
21. The Republicans and the Democrats are _____ parties.
22. the day after today
23. opposite of minority

THE COMMA

Although the comma seems to be a troublesome mark of punctuation, it can be mastered by learning just six principles that cover the great majority of uses. It is also helpful to remember that the comma represents a short pause in speech. But since not all people pause in exactly the same places, rules must be relied upon for correct usage. Be sure that you have a reason for every comma that you use. If you are not sure that a comma is needed, it is usually wise to leave it out.

Use the comma:

(a) to separate items in a series.
(b) to separate two complete sentences joined by *and, but, for, nor, or.*
(c) to separate coordinate adjectives.
(d) to set off introductory material.
(e) to set off interrupters.
(f) to set off certain conventional material.

(a) *The comma is used to separate items in a series.* Each item may be just one word or a whole string of words, but the series must have at least three items.

Patterns: Item 1, Item 2, Item 3
                    OR
          Item 1, Item 2, and Item 3

Examples: The restaurant is small, elegant, expensive.
          A diplomat must be tactful, articulate, and friendly.
          The convict ran across the yard, climbed over the wall, and escaped to freedom.
          The students complained that the course was too hard, that the grades were too low, and that the teacher was too boring.

☞ YOU DO THIS:

Insert any necessary commas in the following sentences.
1. A good dictionary should state the definition of the word indicate its pronunciation and give possible synonyms and antonyms.
2. Sleep exercise and proper diet contribute to good health.

(b) *The comma is used to separate two complete sentences joined by and, but, for, nor, or.* The two sentences to be joined should be related in thought and of equal importance. (See Chapter Four, page 95 for a more complete discussion of coordination.) It is important to remember that the comma is used only when one of these five words is being employed to join *two complete sentences.*

Pattern: Complete Sentence, $\begin{Bmatrix} \text{and} \\ \text{but} \\ \text{for} \\ \text{nor} \\ \text{or} \end{Bmatrix}$, Complete Sentence.

Examples: She had prayed he would live, but she knew he would die.
She would never forget his face, nor would she forget his warm eyes.

NOTE: If the two sentences are very short, the comma may be omitted.
The elephant bellowed wildly and its mate answered.

☞ YOU DO THIS:

Insert any necessary commas in the following sentences.
1. The pastoral way of life may seem delightful at first but it can become very boring after a while.
2. Hal bought a new baseball glove and then immediately tried to sell it for ten dollars or five dollars and a catcher's mask.

(c) *The Comma is used to separate coordinate adjectives.*

An adjective describes a noun or pronoun. It makes the meaning of a noun or pronoun more specific. The adjective is usually placed as close as possible to the word it describes. As with verbs, the slot method can be used to identify adjectives.

That is (a) ———————————————— thing.

Now let's use some words from "Four Choices for Young People" to test the method.

That is a *noble* thing.

That is a *rough* thing.

That is an *inevitable* thing.

217

When two or more adjectives are used to modify the same word, the
the adjectives are coordinate and must be separated by commas.

Pattern: Adjective, Adjective Noun
Example: bright, colorful shirts

Two tests may be used to determine if the adjectives are coordinate:
(a) try to put *and* between them or (b) try to reverse their order in the
sentence.

Coordinate: bright, colorful shirts
                  Test One: bright and colorful shirts
                  Test Two: colorful, bright shirts

Not Coordinate: several colorful shirts
                  Test One: several and colorful shirts (illogical)
                  Test Two: colorful several shirts (illogical)

☞ YOU DO THIS:

Insert any necessary commas in the following sentences.
1. Joe is an articulate public speaker.
2. Dr. Schweitzer was known as an altruistic righteous man.

(d) *The comma is used to set off introductory material.*

The introductory material may be just a single word such as *however,
therefore, moreover, nevertheless,* or *furthermore* ... or a short expression
such as *on the contrary, in fact, for example, on the other hand, in the first
place, in general, to tell the truth, of course, in addition.*

Pattern: Introductory Word or Expression, Complete Sentence.
Examples: Nevertheless, the world's population will continue to grow.
           In fact, the world's population will double by the year 2000.

The introductory material may also be a lengthy phrase or a subordinate
section. (See Chapter Four, page 98) for a more complete discussion
of subordination.)

Pattern: Introductory Material, Complete Sentence.
Examples: After several hours of conversation with some revolutionists,
              Tom decided that the democratic ideals were worth saving.
           Although Rose is an astute thinker, she sometimes makes con-
              tradictory statements.
           Floating out in space, the astronaut felt at peace with the
              world.
           To augment his small income, Joe took a job as a pretzel
              bender.

☞ YOU DO THIS:

Insert any necessary commas in the following sentences.
1. Because the Sahara is such a dry region only very small animals can survive the desert heat.
2. With an inviting smile and a tight skirt a wench will attract many admirers.
3. Protesting his innocence in a loud voice Hal refused to pay the fine for littering.

(e) *Commas are used to set off interrupters.*

An interrupter may be any one of the single words or short expressions that can be used to introduce a sentence. (See rule 4.) Be sure that a comma is placed both before *and after* the interrupter.

Pattern: Complete, Interrupter, Sentence.
Examples: The nation is, of course, under the rule of the majority.
I believe, however, that the majority is capable of making a mistake.

An interrupter may also be a subordinate section that usually begins with *who* or *which*.

                    who
Pattern: Complete, or 〰〰〰〰 , Sentence.
                   which

Examples: Gary, who is fascinated by aeronautics, is going to design a new type of spacecraft.
The Queen Elizabeth, which was docked at Pier 19, sailed on Friday.

In the pattern above, commas are used to surround the subordinate section because the subordination merely *adds information about a specific subject.* In the examples above, Gary is a specific man and the Queen Elizabeth is a specific ship. Therefore, the information given in the subordinate section is ADDED INFORMATION not basic for identification of the subject and you need to ADD COMMAS. But, if the information in the subordinate section is needed to identify the subject, then commas are *not* used.

Examples: The scientist who is fascinated by aeronautics is going to design a new type of spacecraft.
The boat which was docked at Pier 19 sailed on Friday.

If the *who* and *which* sections were removed from the examples above, we would have no idea of which scientist and which boat are being discussed. Because the subordinate information is needed to clearly identify the subjects, commas are *not* used. (See Chapter Four, page 98   for additional discussion of this case of subordination.)

219

NOTE: The *who* or *which* and its verb may sometimes be omitted from the subordinate section, but the same rule still applies: if the subordinate section is merely *added information*, then *add commas*. If the subordinate section is needed to identify the subject, then commas are *not* used.

Examples: Jack, an accountant, is a frugal man.
(Jack, who is an accountant, is a frugal man.)
The lamp sitting on the desk belongs to me.
(The lamp which is sitting on the desk belongs to me.)

☞ YOU DO THIS:

Insert any necessary commas in the following sentences.
1. A bucolic way of life is on the other hand more restful and less exciting.
2. The Statue of Liberty which is situated on Liberty Island was a gift from the French people.
3. The students who can pass this test must be very intelligent.
4. George Washington our first president wore wooden teeth.

(f) *The comma is used to set off certain conventional material.*

Conventional material may consist of dates, addresses, or titles.

On June 6, 1944, the allies invaded Normandy.
My aunt has lived at 24 Oak Street, Austin, Texas, for the last thirty years.
J. T. Racken, M.D., is the President's new physician.

Conventional material may also consist of statistics.

957,357,268   page twelve, line ten
five feet, six inches   Act II, Scene iv

Conventional material may also consist of the complimentary close and the opening in an informal letter.

Sincerely yours,   Dear Joe,
Very truly yours,   Dear Uncle George,

NOTE: In a formal letter the opening is followed by a colon.
Dear Sir: Dear Mr. Riggs:

☞ YOU DO THIS:

Insert any necessary commas in the following material.
1. On February 4 1970 Hal Carter Ph.D. moved to Cleveland Ohio to begin a new job.
2. In volume three page five it states incorrectly that the Eiffel Tower is 180 feet 6 inches high.
3. Gentlemen   Dear Harry   Yours truly

EXERCISE 8E: Insert commas wherever they are necessary in the following sentences. On the two lines provided, briefly justify the use of each comma or set of commas. Some of the following need more than two commas.

1. Although Ted led a rather monastic existence he was never lonely or bored. On the contrary he was occupied constantly with his small playful dogs.

_____

_____

2. A vitamin deficiency can cause serious illness but a plethora of vitamins cannot do any harm. Martin Talbot M.D. explained this fact during a lively interesting dinner party.

_____

_____

3. After a tiring six-month political campaign Senator Marshall wanted to escape to a deserted island. Mrs. Marshall insisted however that they vacation in Las Vegas Nevada.

_____

_____

4. The building at 1602 Palm Avenue Atlanta Georgia is the oldest firehouse in America. The firehouse which is a national landmark is still in use.

_____

_____

5. Peter Leech a wealthy lawyer is an annoying parasite. When I see Peter coming down the street I run into a store hide behind a newspaper or jump behind a bush.

_____

_____

6. The revolutionist who thinks that he can immediately transform the world is a fool. The inequities of society cannot be eliminated quickly nor are they completely insoluble.

_____

_____

Name: _____ Date: _____

7. On November 22 1963 John F. Kennedy was assassinated in Dallas Texas. The President who was an ethical man will always be remembered for his strong position on civil rights.

_____

_____

8. The shiny round satellite left its orbit and then disintegrated before reaching the earth. Nevertheless the scientists were pleased with the mission.

_____

_____

9. A person who is persistent who has an astute mind and who is an articulate speaker will succeed in business. It also helps of course to be married to the boss' daughter.

_____

_____

10. Standing on his head for hours the mystic meditated about the meaning of life. His face a bright shade of red remained expressionless the entire time.

_____

_____

11. A man who is at least six feet ten inches tall has an advantage in a basketball game. While the other players have to jump up to the basket he just has to drop the ball down through the hoop.

_____

_____

12. Were you just trying to avoid an argument or are you really gullible enough to believe Bill's excuse? Even my father who tells some of the biggest lies imaginable would never use such a ridiculous story.

_____

_____

13. Unhappy about the lack of incentive Hal quit his old job. But his new job which required him to do routine tasks was not any better.

_____

_____

14. This dinner you must admit is one of the most unusual meals you have ever had. How often do you eat fried worms rose petals and seaweed?

_____

_____

15. Uncle Harry standing by the window likes to invent unusual things. His latest innovation for example is a motorcycle that can go 1500 miles an hour. Unfortunately he cannot find anyone who can survive the ride.

_____

_____

16. Skeptical about his future as an actor David trained to become a computer programmer. His ability to work with numbers together with his fascination with technology made it easy for him to learn his new profession.

_____

_____

17. The dialogue in Act IV Scene ii is not very good for the author has relied on too many jokes. The play therefore needs rewriting.

_____

_____

18. To avoid making an illogical statement one should think before he speaks. This advice as good as it may be will not help a cretin.

_____

_____

Name: _____ Date: _____

19. In spite of the Emancipation Proclamation and more recent civil-rights laws segregation still exists in many areas of the country. Dr. Martin Luther King who won the Nobel Peace Prize realized this when he asked for complete integration an end to racial violence and better job opportunities for his people.

_____

_____

20. The red glowing sun descended slowly and then disappeared below the horizon. Delighted by this beautiful sight Janet heaved a sigh of quiet contentment.

_____

_____

EXERCISE 8F: Follow the directions for each item. Be sure to use commas wherever necessary.

1. Write a statement about cars using two complete sentences joined by *but*.

_____

_____

2. Describe yourself using at least three items in a series.

_____

_____

3. Describe your home using coordinate adjectives.

_____

_____

4. Use an introductory expression to begin a sentence about cigarette smoking.

_____

_____

5. Write a sentence about your school. Put an interrupter in a subordinate section that requires commas.

_____

6. State your complete home address as part of a sentence.

_____

7. Write a sentence about a type of person you dislike. Use an interrupter that is a subordinate section which requires commas.

_____

8. Write a statement about television using _although_ to begin the sentence.

_____

9. Write a statement about space travel using a short expression to interrupt the sentence.

_____

10. Write an opening and a complimentary close for a letter to the President.

_____

11. Write a statement about a dilemma you have been in. Use two complete sentences joined by _or_.

_____

_____

Name: _____ Date: _____

12. Write a statement about your future plans, using *when* to begin the sentence.

_____

_____

13. Complete the following sentence, giving three actions that you believe should be taken.
The President should _____

_____

_____

14. Describe yourself using coordinate adjectives.

_____

_____

15. Use an introductory word to begin a sentence about censorship.

_____

_____

16. Write a sentence about your favorite singer. Use an interrupter that is a subordinate section which does not require commas.

_____

_____

17. Write a sentence about a person, starting with his name and using an interrupter which states his profession. Do not use the word *who*.

_____

_____

18. Write a sentence about your birthday with the date at the beginning of the sentence.

_____

_____

Name: _____ Date: _____

OTHER MARKS OF PUNCTUATION

Punctuation is not only necessary but is also extremely useful in adding color and style to your writing.

The Period

Use after a complete statement.

The campaign was successful.

Use after most abbreviations.

U.S.   Mrs.   etc.   Ga.

The Question Mark

Use only after a *direct* question.

Did the dog bite you? (direct)
[not: I asked if the dog bit you. (indirect)]

The Exclamation Point

Use after a word, an expression, or a complete sentence that conveys strong emotion.

Oh! What a surprise!
It's an engagement ring!

A SPECIAL NOTE: THE INTERABANG Here is visible proof that the English language changes to meet new needs. The interabang is a recently invented mark of punctuation designed to follow a question which, because it is also an exclamation, needs no answer. Notice that it is formed by combining an exclamation point with a question mark. Because it is just beginning to appear in print, you should use it sparingly.

How about that‽
Isn't that car super‽

The Semicolon

Use between two full sentences that are closely related in thought and are of equal importance. (Notice that the sentence following the semicolon does *not* begin with a capital letter.)

Joe is a very poor reader; it takes him three days to read a comic book.

Use between items in a series when the items themselves contain commas.

At the party I met Frank Parks, a bank president; Ralph Warren, a history teacher; and Helen Carson, a professional singer.

The Colon

Use after an opening statement to direct attention to the material that follows, which is usually an explanation of the opening statement.

Use after the opening of a formal letter, between a title and a subtitle, between numbers indicating chapter and verse of the Bible, and between numbers indicating hours and minutes.

I need the following groceries: ketchup, napkins, and cereal.

You made one big mistake: you used a generalization to prove your argument.

Dear Sir: Dear Mr. Ross:

College Writing: The Rhetorical Imperative

We read Matthew 6:11.

Helen left at 12:30.

The Dash

Use to signal a dramatic pause: use a single dash to emphasize what follows and use a set of dashes as you would a set of commas. (Note that the dash should be used sparingly in formal writing.)

The man walked for hours—as he often did—until it was dark.

It was the one thing she really needed—a mink toothbrush.

Parentheses

Use sparingly to set off an interruption which is not as important as the main material.

Thomas Wolfe (1900–1938) wrote *Look Homeward Angel.*

Sailing (not to be confused with cruising) is difficult.

Quotation Marks

In all of the examples below, notice where the quotation marks are placed in relation to the other marks of punctuation. For example. *The commas and the period are* always *placed inside the quotation marks.*

Use to set off the exact words that someone has said when he is quoted directly. (Notice that when the wording of a person's statement is changed to form an indirect quotation, you do *not* use quotation marks.)

Susan said, "I will leave tomorrow." (direct)

Susan said that she would leave tomorrow. (indirect)

"I believe," said Peter, "that we are sinking."

"What makes you say that?" gurgled his wife.

Use to set off the titles of stories, magazine articles, short poems, and chapters in books. (The titles of longer works, including books and plays, should be underlined.)

"Celestial Crockery" is one of the essays in this book.

The first poem in *Leaves of Grass* is entitled "Song of Myself."

Use to set off words that are being used in a special sense.

Joan is a "nice" girl.

"Charisma" is a difficult word to define.

EXERCISE 8G: Follow the directions for each item. Be sure to use whatever punctuation is required.

1. Write a direct quotation about love. Then change it to an indirect quotation.

   Direct: _____

   _____

   Indirect: _____

   _____

2. Write an exclamation about something you hate.

   _____

3. Using the hydrogen bomb as your subject, write two complete sentences that can be joined by a semicolon.

   _____

   _____

4. Write a direct question about music. Then change it into an indirect question.

   Direct: _____

   _____

   Indirect: _____

   _____

5. Using a dash for emphasis, write a sentence about an animal that disgusts you.

   _____

6. Using air pollution as your subject, write two complete sentences that can be joined by a colon.

   _____

   _____

Name: _____ Date: _____

7. Write a sentence about a current fad, using parentheses to set off an interrupter.

_____

_____

8. Use a complete sentence to state the title of your favorite essay, short story, or poem.

_____

_____

9. Write a sentence about three world capitals that you would like to visit, giving both the city and nation. Be sure to use semicolons for clarity.

_____

_____

10. In a complete sentence, list three things that you would like to own. Use a colon to direct attention to your items.

_____

_____

11. Write a brief note to a doctor about your neighbor's illness. Use three common abbreviations and marks of punctuation that are appropriate in a letter.

_____

_____

_____

_____

_____

_____

Name: _____ Date: _____

12. Using direction quotations, present a three-line dialogue between a policeman and a student protester. For each line identify the speaker in a different place in the sentence.

_____

_____

_____

13. Write a direct question about civil rights. Then change it to an indirect question.

Direct: _____

_____

Indirect: _____

_____

14. Using dieting as your subject, write two complete sentences that can be joined by a semicolon.

_____

_____

15. Using the danger of motorcycles as your subject, write two complete sentences that can be joined by a colon.

_____

_____

_____

16. Using a dash to set off an interrupter, write a sentence about an elephant.

_____

_____

Name: _____ Date: _____

17. Write a direct quotation about democracy. Then change it to an indirect quotation.

Direct: _____

_____

Indirect: _____

_____

18. Write a sentence about someone you dislike, using parentheses to set off an interrupter.

_____

_____

19. In a complete sentence, list at least three qualities that you would look for in the person you would want to marry. Use a colon to direct attention to your items.

_____

_____

_____

20. Using the computer as your subject, write two complete sentences that can be joined by a semicolon. Then rewrite your sentences, joining them with one of the five connectors: and, but, for, nor, or.

Using Semicolon: _____

_____

Using Connector: _____

_____

EXERCISE 8H: Adding all necessary punctuation and capital letters, create sensible sentences in the paragraphs below. Be sure to include all marks of punctuation presented in this chapter (except the interabang).

although it is considered a complex science astrology can be great fun for most people astrologers believe that an individuals personality is influenced by the position of the planets at the time of his birth how well do the following astrological descriptions fit you your family and your friends

a person born under the sign of Aries March 21st—April 20th is a doer rather than a thinker if an Arian is given his way he will often become a demagogue he enjoys being the boss and will do anything to maintain his position on the positive side he is a builder who acts quickly and decisively

Taurus which runs from April 21st to May 20th is the sign of the bull as one would imagine a Taurean is stubborn bullheaded and persistent he is slow to think and to act but once he has made up his mind the dogmatic Taurean will not change it he is an aesthetic person and holds one quality above all others honesty

were you born between May 21st and June 20th if so you are a fickle undependable Gemini but you are also a highly creative person with an astute mind that allows you to understand and act quickly some famous Geminis are John Wayne the film actor George Bernard Shaw the English playwright and Walt Whitman the American poet.

the sign of Cancer rules the period from June 21st to July 22nd a Cancer also called a Moon Child tends to be domineering possessive and demanding but these are often outweighed by his good qualities sensitivity generosity and optimism the Cancer is usually heard to say dont worry everything will be better tomorrow

born between July 23rd and August 22nd the Leo is governed by one personality trait he is an egoist to the point of being a show-off and a ham actor because he is self-assured and impulsive the Leo is never still or quiet he is optimistic and generous in helping others

a person born between August 23rd and September 22nd is a self-centered Virgo the Virgos chief aims are to avoid responsibility and at the same time to achieve selfish goals he has a good mind but is often an illogical thinker nevertheless he is thorough about whatever he does perhaps because of their furtive ways Virgos make excellent politicians statesmen and diplomats

Name: _____ Date: _____

balance is the key to Libra which governs the period from September 23rd to October 22nd the Libran is an emotional romanticist who can sometimes lose his self-control he can become impulsive like a child when balance is restored he becomes calm and level-headed at all times the Libran is a sympathetic vital person.

the lustful Scorpio is born between October 23rd and November 22nd he can be both domineering and tyrannical in order to attain his major goal in life physical satisfaction with a keen mind for support the Scorpio is an idealist who fights for a cause there can be universal peace he insists mutual trust is the answer to everything do you know a driving forceful Scorpio

the Saggitarius November 23rd–December 21st is driven by conflicting personality characteristics he can be frugal and extremely selfish one minute and then without any explanation he can suddenly become magnanimous and openhearted when he is after something he strikes quickly gets what he wants and moves on the Saggitarius most positive trait is that he often uses his canny mind for constructive purposes

Capricorn which runs from December 22nd to January 19th is the sign for a climber the Capricorn may climb through work or he may climb through illicit means although his methods may vary the Capricorn has the drive to climb to the top he can settle for nothing less after reaching the top however he usually asks now what do I do with all of it

from the moment of his birth sometime between January 20th and February 19th the Aquarius is drawn toward public rather than private activity but the nature of the public activity will vary greatly as he plots the overthrow of the government the Aquarius shouts liberty equality freedom in contrast an Aquarius might also be a statesman or humanitarian some famous Aquarians are Adlai Stevenson the American politician Franklin D Roosevelt the 32nd President of the US and Douglas MacArthur the American army general

the weakling of the Zodiac is Pisces February 19th–March 21st he is compatible with others but suffers from being too much of a conformist he is quite content to follow other peoples opinions and actions moreover he will never succeed because he lacks one essential quality initiative but one can admire the fine aspects of his personality loyalty dependability and adaptability.

in his article Practical Astrology John Hutton Ph.D. brings up a point that is important to remember the celestial bodies guide us in a general direction he explains beyond that it is still up to us to determine the specific paths that our lives will take

Name: _____ Date: _____

EXERCISE 8I REFRESHER:

1. Find and correct any sentence fragments.
2. Rework the sentences so that there are at least one example of co-ordination and two examples of subordination.
3. Find and correct any errors in logic.

The young adults of this nation are one of our best natural resources. They are newcomers to the adult world. They are able to see and question things with fresh eyes. Young people have the potential of transforming the world into a more equitable, ethical place. While it is true that many adults would prefer teenagers to observe and obey rather than observe and object. Other adults encourage useful protests in the hope that society will recognize and correct its faults. But the spokesmen for young adult groups demand nothing short of total revolution. Thus we know that all young people want a revolution. However, for a revolution to be successful. The great majority of the citizens would have to cooperate. Because many adults, while recognizing the complex problems in our society, are satisfied with most things. Hence, the likelihood of a successful revolution is small indeed.

Name: _____ Date: _____

SPRINGBOARDS TO WRITING

1. As a result of looking at the graph and the photograph, reading the essay, or answering the questions that followed each, you might have some thoughts about the central theme—four choices for young people. (Look back at those pages to refresh your memory.) For help in planning such an essay, refer to the Guide for Planning an Essay, which appears in Springboards to Writing, Chapter One on page 25.

2. Here are some topics which have not been directly mentioned in the questions asked so far. Perhaps one of them could be a writing springboard for you:

   (a) Develop a convincing argument in favor of one of Fischer's first three choices.

   (b) Additional Choices for Young People (not mentioned by Fischer).

   (c) Develop a convincing argument either for or against Jim Binns' statement in paragraph two of the essay: "More than any other generation, our generation views the adult world with great skepticism ..."

   (d) Fischer predicts that the real heroes of our age will be the hard-working, unnoticed teachers, businessmen, politicians, and journalists who labor to improve our world bit by bit. Think of someone you know or have heard of and write an essay entitled: One of the Real Heroes of Our Time.

   (e) As a young person thirty years from now—your own child perhaps —write an essay in which you describe the state of the world as you see it.

   (f) My Personal Philosophy of Life.

   (g) Choose one: Why I Am an Idealist. . . a Mystic. . . a Skeptic. . . a Fascist. . . a Democrat. . . a Revolutionary. . . a Pragmatist. . . a Parasite.

   (h) Riot, Revolution, and Repression—the New Three R's?

   (i) My Experience in a Riot.

   (j) Revolution Is (Is Not) Possible in the United States.

   (k) What I Would Like to See Changed in our Society—and How I Would Implement My Plan.

George Tooker, THE SUBWAY. Collection, Whitney Museum of American Art, New York.

nine

SPRINGBOARDS TO THINKING

For informal, not written, response . . . to stimulate your thinking

1. Describe what you see in this picture.
2. Why aren't any of the people walking together or at least looking at each other?
3. What does the artist want to convey by giving most of the men the same face?
4. Why do you think the woman is reacting as she is?
5. How would you feel if you were in this subway station?
6. Have you seen any evidence in your own experience that the world is *not* becoming a cold, impersonal place? Explain.
7. Is there anything you could do to make yourself closer to others—and others closer to each other?

Who Cares?

LEONARD GROSS

(1) This country is toying with a dangerous new idea. Twice a world savior, it has begun to wonder if its people will save one another.

(2) The growth of this suspicion can be clearly traced. It was born in New York City at 3:25 a.m., March 13, 1964, when a man attacked 28-year-old Catherine Genovese as she was returning to her home from work. He stabbed her. She screamed for help, and he fled. Twice in the next half hour, he returned to stab her. Repeatedly, she called to her neighbors for help. At least 38 of them heard her, but none of them helped her, and she died.

(3) The story stunned the nation. In succeeding weeks, newspapers the country over produced local versions of what had all the appearances of an epidemic of apathy. Examples:

(4) In Chicago, 60 persons ignored a uniformed policeman's cries for assistance as he battled two youths. In Santa Clara, Calif., several motorists saw a taxicab driver being robbed, but none even summoned police. In San Pedro, Calif., other motorists drove by two policemen struggling to prevent a man from jumping off a 185-foot-high bridge. "We were hanging on for dear life and trying to get someone to stop. But they all drove on like they didn't want to be bothered or get involved," one of the patrolmen reported later. Back in New York City, a Broadway crowd stood by while eight men stomped two; a Bronx crowd would not rescue a naked girl from a rapist's attack, and bystanders fled from a 19-year-old college student who had just been stabbed by one member of a gang of toughs. His statement to the New York *Times* is unforgettable:

(5) "I put my hand down and saw blood. I went over to a car that had stopped to watch. 'Please help me to a hospital,' I said. They rolled up their windows and drove away. I went to another car and asked for help, but they did the same thing, drove away. Then I went to a truck and asked the driver for help. He pulled around me and drove away and left me there. Nobody on the street helped me."

(6) Why does this happen? Why don't people—at least some people—*care*?

(7) Many explanations are being offered. All of them make some sense. None is very pleasant. One is that Americans are becoming too dollar-minded to risk the costs of involvement. Getting involved means being a witness. You lose time, pay, even popularity. A man in a building close to the one in which the young girl from the Bronx was raped railed at reporters for calling attention to the story. It was bad for business, he said.

Now women wouldn't come to his office anymore. In New Orleans, Mabel Simmons, book-page editor of the *Times-Picayune*, saw a woman lying, apparently unconscious, on a sidewalk in the city's business district. No one seemed too concerned. Mrs. Simmons went into a nearby store, where she received permission to call the police. When they asked for the address, she, in turn, asked the store owner. He refused to give it to her. He didn't want the store connected with a police incident. In disgust, she set down the phone and checked the address herself.

(8) Fear of involvement is widespread and pronounced. Sometimes, it it is the fear of hurting someone. More often, it is the fear of getting hurt. One veteran social worker reports, "If a boy is stabbed in the hallway of a project, he can die, and no one will help him. They're all afraid of retaliation." Many Americans are loath to testify at trials, and serve on juries with reluctance. Judge Nathan M. Cohen of Chicago's Criminal Court excused more than 200 persons before he could complete a jury to hear a recent case involving organized crime. Male prospects asking to be released spoke in low voices, fidgeted with their clothing and refused to look the judge in the eye. The case was finally heard by an all-women jury.

(9) In a New Orleans suburb two years ago, a young girl was leaning over her hi-fi set when a bullet shot past her head. Outside, residents found two drunken constables shooting off their guns. But no one—not even the girl's parents—reported the incident to authorities. "We didn't know when we might need them," someone said lamely.

(10) Enforcement authorities blame cumbersome legal processes and a tendency to "understand" rather than punish criminals as causes of citizen reluctance. Despairing of getting satisfaction, people do not press charges. But at least one veteran police chief, Edward J. Allen of Santa Ana, Calif., cites the police themselves as one source of the problem. "They don't integrate. They develop a feeling that they have been set aside by society," he contends. Whatever the causes, there is a decisive feeling of estrangement between the public and law-enforcement agencies that accounts, in part, for the phenomenon of noninvolvement.

(11) Another suggestion offered by authorities is that because we are now provided for in so many ways, the principle of individual responsibility is vanishing from American life.

(12) Aaron M. Kohn, managing director of the New Orleans Metropolitan Crime Commission, Inc., speaks with dismay about the "metropolitan complex," which enables the citizen to rationalize away his obligations to society. Dr. Joe Elkes, psychiatrist-in-chief of The Johns Hopkins Hospital in Baltimore, decries the synthetic quality of contemporary experience, "when staring at the TV replaces good talk with a neighbor; or the phonograph, community singing in the church hall; or the latest what-to-do-next book on child-rearing, a real involvement with one's children." So much do we simulate, says Dr. Elkes, that when a real, live situation impels

action, we are out of the acting habit. In Las Vegas, Nev., some time ago, a Federal narcotics undercover agent was shot while sitting in his car in a residential neighborhood. Many people ran to their doors and peered into the darkness, but none of them ventured outside to investigate. When police asked later why they hadn't, several explained they had been watching *The Untouchables* on television and wanted to see the end of the program.

(13) A frequently mentioned source of noninvolvement is what the technicians call "a breakdown in primary groups"—groups united by culture, language, religion, or common purpose. One American in four moves every year, the small-town resident to the city in search of opportunity, the city dweller to the suburbs in search of peace. In his new environment, he feels no identity, sinks no roots, has no stake. Strangeness frightens him; feeling threatened, he seeks to eliminate risks. He stays in line; he conforms. His world is now so complex that "the only way to survive is to cut a lot of it out," says Dr. Alfred J. Kahn, professor of social-welfare planning at Columbia University. Adds Alvin L. Schorr, a research chief of the Social Security Administration, "The man doesn't want to do too much. He adjusts by shutting things out. It may not work for society. But it works for him."

(14) The problem appears to be greatest in cities where a sense of community is lowest. California's Bay Area offers a striking example. San Francisco is noted for the community pride of its residents. Police Chief Thomas J. Cahill speaks glowingly about the cooperation he receives from the public. If an assault of the Catherine Genovese type occurred in San Francisco? "We'd get fifty calls in five minutes." Oakland, across the Bay, is an unobtrusive city with many migrants and little civic verve. Its police chief, E. M. Toothman, lists ten recent cases of public refusal to become involved—including one in which at least six persons failed to help a 63-year-old man who was being fatally stomped—and offers some dejected views about the moral breakdown of society.

(15) When an individual leaves the neighborhood that knows him, he loses his first line of defense. The New York college student who was stabbed is probably alive today because he managed to make his way to his own block, where neighbors summoned aid.

(16) The relationship of an aroused, unified neighborhood to individual safety shows clearly in the recent history of Hyde Park on Chicago's South Side. Once a secure, middle-class area dominated by the beautiful University of Chicago campus, Hyde Park by 1953 had become a lair of muggers. So unsafe were the streets that the existence of the university itself was threatened. Then one crime—the abduction and disrobing of a woman—aroused the neighborhood. Hyde Park's residents, including some of the best minds in the country, mapped a cleanup. The community was organized. Slums were razed, and new row houses built. A gospel of cooperation was preached. Today, Hyde Park is the envy of neighborhoods

around it. Such is the sense of community that a cry for help brings instant action. Responding to a scream one evening this spring, sociologist Philip Hauser rushed from his house to find a number of his neighbors, all brandishing baseball bats, fire pokers, and other makeshift weapons, chasing a would-be purse snatcher down the street. "I doubt that he tried Hyde Park again," says Hauser. Such community response has helped cut the crime rate nearly fifty per cent since 1953.

(17) "Success can be found only where there exists citizen zeal," states *Mental Health in the Metropolis,* the work of several prominent scholars. "What is needed is community feeling—when inhabitants have a *central* feeling of belonging."

(18) But the problem is that tendencies in our society are leading us away from the kind of life in which community feelings can flourish. As we move further from old ways, we must rely more and more on the individual's will to act.

(19) I have a vision of the way I would like to be. Most people do. "The self-image is what propels one—if one has it," says psychiatrist Elkes of Johns Hopkins. One gets it from the expected sources—father and mother, primarily, teacher and preacher as well. If that self-image is strong enough, it makes you confront events you would rather avoid. You call the police. You stop and give aid. At times, you even take risks.

(20) To a man, the authorities counseling *Look* agree that the question of willingness to take risks, of individual responsibility, goes back to some pretty old-fashioned fundamentals in human relationships.

(21) If you don't pick up a telephone, it's pretty certain that your son won't either. "He doesn't receive the cues, if you don't give them to him," says Dr. Elkes. If you counsel him to conform, get by, keep his nose clean, you'll find he sticks pretty closely to such advice. In Chicago last summer, 5'4" Royace Prather smashed a chair over the head of an armed six-foot robber who was holding up a restaurant cashier. Analyzing his motives recently, he recalled his father, a farmer "who tried to treat people nicely. He got mad at me one time, I remember, when I forgot to say thanks on the telephone to someone when I was in high school. He always returned borrowed things in better shape than he got them. He always believed in helping people."

(22) In the end, the man who responds is the man who feels something for others. If a child is loved, he can take the risk of loving—or helping—others in turn. "You've got to be able to believe that you can get involved in the lives of others without getting hurt," says a Washington, D.C., psychologist.

(23) The man on the sidelines may well be one who was never given a sense of his own worth. Such a man cannot appreciate the worth of others. When others are in trouble, he will not respond.

(24) Clearly, the emerging problem of noninvolvement in the United States is not simply a matter of human indifference. "Apathy is not the

right word," says Dan Carpenter, executive director of the Hudson Guild Settlement House in New York City. "Apparent indifference can be a form of protection, a defense mechanism." Because a man on shore does not rush into the water to save another man from drowning does not necessarily mean that he is apathetic. It may simply mean that he can't swim.

(25) But if he *can* swim, and does not, then he sentences himself to the self-punishment endured by the haunted narrator in Albert Camus' *The Fall*. An established, impeccable French lawyer, he has his world totally under control until he hears a drowning woman's cry one night, and turns away. Years later, ruined, he winds up talking to himself in an Amsterdam bar: "...please tell me what happened to you one night on the quays of the Seine and how you managed never to risk your life. You yourself utter the words that for years have never ceased echoing through my nights and that I shall at last say through your mouth: 'O young woman, throw yourself into the water again so that I may a second time have the chance of saving both of us!'"

(26) The events of recent months are not an indictment. But they *are* a warning. They have exposed a dangerous incapacity in our society of which we have largely been unaware. We are living in a new world, and we are being tested everywhere—in Vietnam, New York, Mississippi—in ways we have never been before. The rediscovery that we need one another, that we are involved in all mankind, that we have got to care, could atone in part for the murder of Catherine Genovese.

READING SURVEY

1. Main Idea

What is the central theme of the essay?

2. Major Details

(a) What are three of the many possible explanations for public apathy that are given in this essay?

(b) What effect does the sense of belonging have on the crime rate of a community?

(c) Read the first and last paragraphs again. What seem to be the two alternatives for the future of the apathetic society?

3. Inference

(a) Read paragraphs four and five again. What makes the college student's statement "unforgettable"?

(b) Read paragraphs twenty-three to twenty-five again. Do you think that Leonard Gross condemns those who do not respond to a call for help?

4. Opinion

(a) Do you agree with the author that a good many people are becoming apathetic? Use your own experiences to tell why or why not.

(b) Leonard Gross states many possible reasons for public indifference. Which reason do you think is most valid? Why?

VOCABULARY BUILDING

Lesson One: The Vocabulary of Apathy

Apathy occurs when people feel that nothing makes a difference anymore or when people do not care about what happens to others. Some observers find that there is an increase in public apathy today. Some of the words which are useful when discussing apathy can be found in this essay:

stunned	(paragraph 3)	estrangement	(10)
apathy	(3)	noninvolvement	(10)
retaliation	(8)	civic	(14)
loath to	(8)	indifference	(24)
reluctance	(8)	apathetic	(24)

Many of these words are close in meaning. Try to understand the meaning of each word by reading the following paragraph and by doing the exercise that follows. Once you have done both, the meanings of the words will be clear to you.

245

Indifference is the key! For many people it makes no difference if their fellow human beings live or die. Often such *apathy* results from people's hesitance and *reluctance* to get involved with others. But *noninvolvement* was not the way of primitive man as he gathered in groups to help protect all members. Yet today men treat each other like strangers. Where once there was friendliness, now there is *estrangement*.

Among the explanations given to explain people's *apathetic* attitudes is the fact that many violent acts can be seen every day on television. Thus, when violence is done to a real person in real life, observers are not astonished or *stunned*. Yet people should have a sense of *civic* responsibility towards the city and its citizens. Nevertheless, it seems that some people do not feel a difference between what happens outside the window and what happens on the television screen. A second explanation is that people are disinclined and *loath to* help someone who is being attacked because they are afraid that the attacker might want to take revenge. The possibility of such *retaliation* makes people afraid to go to anyone's rescue.

EXERCISE 9A: Fill in the empty blanks.

1. When a man fears _____, he is afraid that a criminal will seek revenge.

2. When a man is _____ _____ get involved, he is not inclined to help others.

3. When a man is _____, he feels no concern for others.

4. When a man is hesitant to help someone, he is exhibiting a _____ _____ to get involved.

5. When a man chooses _____, _____, and _____ he chooses not to be a part of the community of mankind.

6. When a man feels an _____ from others, he feels like a stranger to people in general.

7. When a man is a citizen, he has certain _____ responsibilities to his city and his neighbors.

8. When a man is surprised and dazed by something, he is _____

Name: _____ Date: _____

Lesson Two: Forceful Verbs

Many verbs show action. Some actions are quiet and mild while others are louder and more forceful. Often a verb is considered to be forceful when it can be used in the place of a string of words. The use of forceful verbs can help make your writing more exciting and colorful. Some of them appear in this essay:

Form Used in Essay	Name of Verb	
railed	to rail	(paragraph 7)
fidgeted	to fidget	(8)
decries	to decry	(12)
impels	to impel	(12)
abduct	to abduct	(16)
brandishing	to brandish	(16)
razed	to raze	(16)
flourish	to flourish	(18)
propels	to propel	(19)
atone	to atone	(26)

He *harshly scolded* (railed at) her for reporting the crime to the police.

When asked difficult questions, the men *moved restlessly and nervously* (fidgeted) in their seats.

Serious inequities in society *arouse the conscience and thereby force* (impel) many people to demand immediate action.

Many people *express strong disapproval of* (decry) the apathy exhibited in today's society.

The criminal *carried off by force* (abducted) the young girl.

He ran after the criminal *shaking and waving* (brandishing) the baseball bat.

It is often best to *destroy to the ground* (raze) slums and in their place build clean, new apartment houses.

Once the improvements had been made, the town began to *thrive and prosper* (flourish) as it had never done before.

His guilt haunted him and he wanted *desperately to make up for* (atone for) what he had done.

A sudden emergency can *motivate and thrust* (propel) someone into unexpected behavior.

A SPECIAL NOTE: *Impel* implies that our conscience forces us, while *propel* implies that events force us.

Here are some words that you see frequently which—if you look at them closely—are exceptions to the above rule. Notice that many of the exceptions are musical terms borrowed from Italian.

sopranos	altos	autos	echoes
pianos	solos	tobaccos	dynamos

V *F Plurals*: Some words ending in *f* or *fe* merely add *s*, while some change the *f* or *fe* to *ves*. Because there is no rule for this change, you must learn each word individually and use a dictionary when necessary.

calf – calves
knife – knives
life – lives
roof – roofs
belief – beliefs
safe – safes
self – selves

VI *Singulars That Are Plural*: Some words have the same form for both the singular and plural. Notice that most of these words refer to animals, fish, or grains.

deer	wheat
sheep	rye
bass	series
trout	dozen

VII *Irregular Endings*: A few common words have irregular plural endings.

tooth – teeth
goose – geese
mouse – mice
ox – oxen

VIII *Foreign Words*: Many foreign words form their plurals according to the rules of the foreign sources. Some of the plurals you may already know; others you will have to look up in a dictionary.

alumnus – alumni
fungus – fungi
focus – foci
radius – radii
medium – media
bacterium – bacteria
curriculum – curricula
analysis – analyses
axis – axes
basis – bases
crisis – crises
parenthesis – parentheses
criterion – criteria
chateau – chateaux

EXERCISE 9D: Form the plurals of the following words.

1. religion _____
2. tendency _____
3. armful _____
4. box _____
5. brother-in-law _____
   _____
6. defense _____
7. tomato _____
8. auto _____
9. leaf _____
10. radio _____

11. chief _____
12. wolf _____
13. sheep _____
14. foot _____
15. thesis _____
16. ox _____
17. criterion _____
18. series _____
19. maid of honor _____
    _____
20. motto _____

Name: _____ Date: _____

EXERCISE 9E: Fill in the blanks with any missing letters.

The civics prof _____sor stated dramatically that man has the power to destroy our b_____tiful earth in a mat_____r of min__t__s. The s_____rce of the destruction would be that cruel phen__m_____on–the hydrogen bomb. Showing his dis_____t, the teacher reasoned that man will prob_____ly always have a fund__men_____l tend_____y toward violence and destruction. As sev_____al prom_____nt members of the Atomic Energy Com_____sion have stated, "We have the op_____t__-_____ty to create modern wonders with atomic energy. But instead we con_____n ourselves only with the a_____a of def_____e." The lecture continued with an expl__n_____on of how reL__g_____n can serve to bring about peace among the various national gr_____ps. The pro__es-_____r ended with a s_____g_____tion that we should not be af_____d of atomic energy. Rather we should ap_____c_____te all of its more pl_____s_____t uses.

Name: _____   Date: _____

THE UNIFIED ESSAY

A unified essay is one in which all ideas are related and all points link. Many of the skills previously discussed in this book will help you achieve a unified essay. A quick review will illustrate:

Skill Topic	*How It Helps You Achieve a Unified Essay*
Topic Sentence and Paragraph Development	The main idea of each paragraph is clearly stated at its beginning. The rest of the paragraph develops that topic sentence.
Arrangement of Details	Details do not jump around but instead are put in an order that makes sense and flows smoothly.
Paragraph Principles in Essay Writing and Introductions and Conclusions	The total design of the basic expository essay is five paragraphs. The introduction launches the topic, and the conclusion summarizes it. Each of the three main body paragraphs present and develop one main idea.
Logical Thinking	All points are logical and related so that a sensible train of thought is presented.

While these aids help you in the external plan and design of your essay, equally important are devices of *internal* unity. Internal unity is achieved with the use of certain words and types of wording which link sentences and even paragraphs more successfully. They are:

I. Words of Transition
II. Key Words: Deliberate Repetition

I. Words of Transition:

When moving from one idea or example to the next, you might feel that the change is too abrupt.

Too abrupt: Very few people accepted the invitation. They decided to go on with their plans.

Smoother: Very few people accepted the invitation. Nevertheless, they decided to go on with their plans.

To avoid abrupt changes, you can use words of transition. A full list of such words is given in the chart which follows.

When selecting a word of transition, do it with care. Be certain of the type of signal you need—addition, contrast, and so on. Then look through all the words listed in the signal group until you locate the one most suitable and appropriate for the sentences you wish to connect.

Using the list of words of transition, select the correct signal and then give one appropriate word from that signal group.

1. John said furiously, "I never want to see her again. _____ she might be beautiful, but she is mean.

    select: signal: ____summary, ____granting a point, ____suggestion

    word from signal group: _____.

2. "I might not be the smartest person in the world. _____ I know a lie when I hear one," Mike exclaimed.

    select: signal: ____relationship-similarity

    ____relationship-contrast

    ____relationship-cause and effect

    word from signal group: _____

Words of transition should be used sparingly. If you overuse them, your writing will become bulky. Remember that the mind automatically links statements that follow each other. Therefore, you should use words of transition only when needed for clarity. As a general, informal rule, a maximum of three or four words of transition should be used in a paragraph of 150 words.

☞ **YOU DO THIS:**

Look back at paragraph sixteen of "Who Cares?" Find the three words of transition which signal the development of the example:

_____   _____   _____

Now read the paragraph again leaving out these three words. What happens to the story?

_____

Directions: Two steps should be used when you consult this list. First, determine the type of signal you need. Next, select from that signal group the word which is most appropriate to the meaning of your sentences.

Type of Signal	*Words to Use; Signal Group*
To signal an addition:	in addition, furthermore, moreover, also, equally important . . .
To signal an example:	for example, for instance, thus, in other words, as an illustration, in particular . . .
To signal a suggestion:	for this purpose, to this end, with this object . . .
To signal emphasis:	indeed, truly, again, to repeat, in fact . . .
To signal granting a point:	granted that, although, though, even though, while it may be true, in spite of . . .
To signal a summary:	in summary, in conclusion, therefore, finally, consequently, thus, accordingly, in short, in brief, as a result, on the whole . . .
To signal the development of a sequence:	*Value Sequence:* first, second, secondly, third, thirdly, next, last, finally . . . *Time Sequence:* then, once, after, afterward, next, subsequently, previously, first, second, at last, meanwhile, in the meantime, immediately, soon, at length, when, yesterday, today, tomorrow . . . *Space Sequence:* above, across, under, beyond, below, nearby, nearer, opposite to, adjacent to, to the left/right, in the foreground, in the background . . .
To signal a relationship:	*Similarity:* similarly, likewise, in like manner . . . *Contrast:* in contrast to, however, but, still, nevertheless, yet, conversely, notwithstanding, on the other hand, on the contrary, at the same time, while this may be true . . . *Cause and Effect:* consequently, because, since, therefore, accordingly, thus, hence, due to, as a result . . .

EXERCISE 9F: Many of the paragraphs which were written for this book to illustrate methods of paragraph development and arrangement of details are also examples of the correct use of words of transition. Refer to the following three paragraphs and underline all words of transition.

1. Chapter Two, page 42, "The Governor's recently televised. . . ."
2. Chapter Two, page 43, "To study for an examination. . . ."
3. Chapter Two, page 40, "At first glance, Birmingham. . . ."

EXERCISE 9G: Fill in an appropriate word of transition in each blank. In some cases you may decide that no word is needed. Although signal groups are repeated, try to vary the words you select.

1. The police are highly trained. _____ they sometimes make unintentional mistakes which cause grief to themselves and others.

2. Automation is replacing the human worker in certain jobs. _____

   _____ men must retrain themselves for the more skilled jobs which our technology requires.

3. The head of any nation must expect to handle extremely complex

   problems whose solutions are not always simple and popular. _____

   _____ there is the ever present dilemma of the

   economy. _____ there is the problem of maintaining good relations with foreign countries. These and other problems are not only a burden; they are also a challenge.

4. She was apathetic about everything. _____ she really did not care about other people at all.

5. The foregoing collections of facts about air and water pollution are

   overwhelming. _____, we are headed for disaster.

6. On a darkened street the public telephone may be a person's only

   hope in calling for help when needed. _____, in many cities unless a person happens to have a dime handy, the telephone is

   worthless. _____ it seems that a person's life is not even worth ten cents.

Name: _____ *Date:* _____

7. Our entire welfare system is outdated; we need a better one. _____

   _____, it has been suggested that we develop a

   new system which will truly help those unable to work and, _____

   _____, encourage all who can work to earn their
   living and self-respect.

8. Cigarette smoking can cause lung cancer. _____ there
   is the fact that cigarette smoking can contribute to emphysema and
   heart disease.

9. Nothing he ever does turns out right. _____ if he

   tries to carve a turkey, he cuts his finger. _____ if
   he wants to impress a girl he has just met, he trips over the smallest
   pebble or blade of grass.

10. It is impossible to understand. _____ we need
    progress, but is this the price we must pay?

11. She looked out the window. _____ from her she saw

    the windows of Paul's house. _____ her she could
    see the children playing in the street.

12. There has been considerable damage in recent days to the agriculture

    class' experimental garden. _____ it is declared that
    all protesters must gather only on the side lawn of the college.

13. They were much too far out at sea. _____ he could
    see that the storm was closing in rapidly.

14. He picked up the infant. _____ it stopped crying.

15. That is the poorest, dumbest excuse I have ever heard! _____

    _____ it's a big lie.

Name: _____ Date: _____

EXERCISE 9H: Choose three of these five paragraphs to do. Use separate paper. In writing these paragraphs, do not overuse words of transition. Use them only where needed for clarity.

1. Write a paragraph about people's manners. Use appropriate words of transition which signal examples.
2. Write a paragraph describing the block you live on. Use appropriate words of transition which signal space sequence.
3. Write a paragraph in which you give directions on how to do something such as baking a cake, washing a car, or whatever interests you. Use appropriate words of transition which signal time sequence.
4. Write a paragraph which presents both sides of the problem of the military draft. Use appropriate words of transition which signal the relationship of contrast.
5. Write a paragraph which explains why some students cheat. Use appropriate words of transition which signal cause and effect.

II. Key Words: Deliberate Repetition:

Ideas can be connected by the deliberate repetition of certain key words. It is best that the word you choose for deliberate repetition be closely related to the main idea of the paragraph or essay. Of course, while such repetition should occur often enough to achieve unity, it should not be overdone.

(a) *Key words in a paragraph:* Here is a paragraph which was presented in Chapter One as an illustration of a topic sentence developed by example. Notice how key words are used to create internal unity.

Different people like to spend their leisure time in different ways. Some like to watch a sporting event while others prefer to play ball or go skating. Some people like to dance to the gyrating rhythms of popular music while others enjoy nothing as much as an excellent orchestra performance. Some people like to go to big parties while others choose to spend their free time with a few close friends. When it comes to leisure time. there seem to be almost as many preferences as there are people.

☞ YOU DO THIS:

Referring to the paragraph above, answer these questions.

1. In the first sentence, what word is deliberately repeated? _____

_____ Why is it, more than any other in the sentence,

a key word? _____

_____

2. Look at the middle three sentences. What words are deliberately re-

peated throughout? _____

_____

Why are these words, more than any others, key words? _____

_____

3. In the final sentence, what words are deliberately used in order to

form a connection with the first sentence? _____

Are they key words? _____ Why or why not? _____

_____

(b) *Key words to link paragraphs*: Paragraphs, as well as sentences can be linked with the use of key words. Of course, in an expository essay paragraphs are related to each other as long as they follow the essay pattern presented in Chapter Six and reviewed in this chapter. However, if you wish to achieve internal unity as well, it is possible to link paragraphs by finding a key word in the final sentence of one paragraph and deliberately repeating it in the opening sentence of the next paragraph. Notice these sentences, which are taken from a five-paragraph expository essay:

TITLE:	Forests That Burn
THE LAST SENTENCE OF ONE PARAGRAPH:	In brief, millions of dollars worth of lumber is hungrily consumed by flames of fires which need never have begun.
THE OPENING SENTENCE OF THE NEXT PARAGRAPH:	While forest fires needlessly destroy valuable lumber, they clear the way for a menace far more massive in its scope—floods.

☞ YOU DO THIS:

Referring to the above, answer these questions.   ●

1. How many times is the word "fire" used? _____

2. What other word is deliberately repeated? _____

How many times? _____ Why is it a key word? _____

_____

A HELPFUL HINT: If you wish to link paragraphs, it is useful to employ subordination for one or both of the linking sentences. Use the subordinate section to refer to the idea just finished and the independent section to refer to the new idea you are going to discuss. The following is an example of subordination in a linking sentence which opens a new paragraph:

> While forest fires needlessly destroy valuable lumber, they clear the way for a menace far more massive in its scope—floods.

You can see that the main idea just finished concerns one danger of fire, and the main idea being introduced concerns a by-product of that danger.

The use of subordination in sentences which link paragraphs will serve as an extra check for unity: Remember that for correct subordination the two ideas must be *logically related, with one idea more important than the other or one idea closely following the other*. Another example: ●

> Although frying chicken is a fairly easy way to prepare it, roasting it provides many more opportunities for interesting recipes.

●

☞ **YOU DO THIS:**

Assume that the above is a final sentence of one paragraph which is to link with the next paragraph.

1. What would you guess is the topic of the paragraph being closed?

_____

2. What would you guess is the topic of the coming paragraph? _____

_____

3. Would this sentence be an appropriate link if used as the first sentence

of a paragraph? _____

Why or why not? _____

EXERCISE 9I: Many of the paragraphs in this book are good examples of the correct use of key words. Refer to the following three paragraphs and underline all key words.

1. Chapter One, page 20, "The questions asked on a. . . ."
2. Chapter Two, page 39, "When we speak of the born teacher. . . ."
3. Chapter Six, page 162, "The machine, then, is a metal marvel. . . ."

EXERCISE 9J: For each of the following topic sentences, write a unified paragraph using the deliberate repetition of key words. While such repetition should occur often enough to achieve unity, it should not be overdone. Use your own paper for this assignment.

1. Getting an education is expensive.
2. Maturity means more than just growing older.
3. Distractions from studying are tempting.

4. My parents are _____ people.
5. Summer storms can strike suddenly.

EXERCISE 9K: For each of the following you are given the title of an essay and the three main ideas which the essay will cover in its three main body paragraphs. Write a linking sentence to connect paragraphs as directed.

1. Clothing Is a Big Business
    Introductory paragraph
        I. Designer originals
        II. Ready-to-wear clothes
        III. Make-it-yourself clothes
    Concluding paragraph

    (Directions: Write a sentence for the end of paragraph I to link it with paragraph II.)

    _____

    _____

    _____

2. Treasures of the Sea
    Introductory paragraph
        I. Food resources
        II. Oil Resources
        III. Unknown natural re-
            sources
    Concluding paragraph

    (Directions: Write a sentence to begin paragraph III which links it with paragraph II.)

    _____

    _____

    _____

3. Some Causes of Divorce
    Introductory paragraph
        I. Immaturity
        II. Sexual incompatibility
        III. Money difficulties
    Concluding paragraph

    (Directions: Write a sentence to begin paragraph III which links it with paragraph II.)

    _____

    _____

    _____

Name: _____ Date: _____

4. Industrial Wastes Cause Pollution
    Introductory paragraph
            I. Liquid waste
            II. Solid wastes
            III. Gas (smoke) wastes
        Concluding paragraph

(Directions: Write a sentence to begin paragraph II which links it with paragraph I.)

_____

_____

_____

5. The Superior Sex
    Introductory paragraph
            I. Physically
            II. Intellectually
            III. Emotionally
        Concluding paragraph

(Directions: Write a sentence for the end of paragraph I to link it with paragraph II.)

_____

_____

_____

6. Different English with Different People
    Introductory paragraph
            I. When with friends
            II. When with strangers
            III. When with diplomats
        Concluding paragraph

(Directions: Write a sentence to begin paragraph II which links it with paragraph I.)

_____

_____

_____

Name: _____ Date: _____

7. The Various Roles of Women in Business
   Introductory paragraph
       I. Secretary   (Directions: Write a sentence
       II. Supervisor   for the end of paragraph II to
       III. Executive   link it with paragraph III.)
   Concluding paragraph

   _____

   _____

   _____

8. The Horror of Rats
   Introductory paragraph
       I. Description of rats   (Directions: Write a sentence
       II. How rats thrive   to begin paragraph III which
       III. Diseases rats carry   links it with paragraph II.)
   Concluding paragraph

   _____

   _____

   _____

9. The Problems of the Alcoholic
   Introductory paragraph
       I. Home   (Directions: Write a sentence
       II. Work   to begin paragraph II which
       III. Social   links it with paragraph I.)
   Concluding paragraph

   _____

   _____

   _____

    Name: _____ Date: _____

10. Population Control Is Needed
    Introductory paragraph
        I. Our food supply is
          limited
       II. Our supply of natural
         resources is limited
      III. Our space is limited
    Concluding paragraph

(Directions: Write a sentence for the end of paragraph I to link it with paragraph II.)

_____

_____

_____

EXERCISE 9L ESSAY ANALYSIS: Answer these questions about the essay "Who Cares?"

1. In the first three sentences of paragraph eight, what two words of transition are used? _____ _____

   What key word is deliberately repeated? _____

   _____

2. In paragraph nine, what words of transition are used? _____
3. In paragraph twenty-two, what words of transition are used?

   _____

4. In paragraphs twenty-four and twenty-five, what key words are deliberately repeated to link the paragraphs? _____

   _____

Name: _____ Date: _____

1. Find and correct any comma splices and run-on sentences.
2. Make any necessary corrections in punctuation and capitalization.

After reading *Who Cares?* by Leonard Gross one is likely to ask himself the searching question am I apathetic. The reader may very likely exclaim No. I would certainly go to the aid of someone who is being attacked. But has this reader considered the many other types of apathy. A student might ask himself if he really cares about his school subjects? A workers job might mean nothing more than a way to earn money. A citizen may be more interested in sports than he is in important current issues foreign affairs, national economy, and space exploration. Failing to help a motorist with car trouble a driver can find a convenient excuse for his behavior, after all, he would have been late for an appointment if he had stopped. This indifference is quickly becoming an accepted part of mans personality. We must of course combat this frightening trend if man is to remain human he must care.

Name: _____   Date: _____

SPRINGBOARDS TO WRITING

1. As a result of looking at the picture, reading the essay, or answering the questions that follow each, you might have some thoughts about the central theme—the apathetic society. (Look back at those pages to refresh your memory.) For help in planning such an essay, refer to the Guide for Planning an Essay, which appears in Springboards to Writing, Chapter One on page 25.

2. Here are some topics which have not been directly mentioned in the questions asked so far. Perhaps one of them could be a writing springboard for you:
   (a) Why I Am (Am Not) an Apathetic Person.
   (b) Are We Living in an Estranged Society?
   (c) Why We Need One Another.
   (d) If I Were a Witness to a Crime.
   (e) The Law—Protection for the Criminals or the Victims?
   (f) Is there a Growing Rift between the Police and the Public?
   (g) The Case for (against) Neighborhood Vigilante Groups.
   (h) Recommended Measures to Curb Violence in the Streets.
   (i) The Case for (against) Capital Punishment.
   (j) Is Violence on Television Harmful?
   (k) According to a prominent psychiatrist, children copy their parents' attitudes. Agree or disagree: Parents Serve as Models for Their Children.

CHAPTER ten

Courtesy The Register and Tribune Syndicate, Inc.

DESPAIR

FRUSTRATION

LACK OF EDUCATION

SLUM HOUSING

UNEMPLOYMENT

1967, The Register and Tribune Syndicate

CONRAD

©THE LOS ANGELES TIMES, 1967

Domino Theory

SPRINGBOARDS TO THINKING

For informal, not written, response . . . to stimulate your thinking

1. What does the political cartoon show step by step?
2. Why do you think that the political cartoon is labeled "Domino Theory"?
3. On what one domino do the people in the photograph stand? What specific parts of the photograph guided you to your choice?
4. Do you see any evidence in the photograph of the other domino labels? Why or why not?
5. From your own experience or observation, what labels might you assign to some of the blank dominoes in the political cartoon?
6. How could it affect your life if society ignores the falling of the dominoes? What can society do to stop the falling of the dominoes?

"Why, There's Not Enough
Money Here for Prostitution . . ."

BEN BAGDIKIAN

(1) *"I'm going to be a lawyer,"* said Harry, aged six. *"Lawyers make good money. I'm going to keep my money."*

(2) *"I'm going to be a doctor,"* said his seven-year-old brother firmly. *"And I'm going to take care of my family."*

(3) Their eight-year-old sister announced serenely: *"I'm going to be a nurse in a big hospital and wear a real uniform and help people."*

(4) The sweet optimism of youth could have been heard in millions of homes, but this home was rather special.

(5) It was midafternoon but the tenement was dark. Grey plastic sheeting was tacked to the insides of the living room windows except for one window where a stick was propped against the collapsed Venetian blind to keep it against the cracked glass. Plaster was off an expanse of ceiling and walls, and strands of hair on the laths trembled with the passing wind from outside. A double doorway gave onto the kitchen which was almost invisible. Its windows, too, were sealed with grey plastic, presumably to preserve heat. But the darkness was thickened by a crisscross of clotheslines that filled the room with the hangings of what looked like shapeless cloth. In one corner of the kitchen was a small refrigerator, in another a table with three legs and one chair. There was a stained stove bearing a basin full of children's clothes soaked in cold soapy water. Next to the clothes basin was a pan of cold red beans and beside that an iron frying pan containing a single short rib congealed with fat. Through one kitchen door was a bathroom dominated by a toilet covered by boards; it had frozen and burst during the winter. Through another door was "the kids' room," a murky chamber with one window insulated by a roller shade tacked at the top and held down at the bottom sill with a stone. In this room slept seven children, in two beds. Neither bed had a mattress. The children slept on the springs.

(6) *"Look at this book I got from school,"* Harry said, calling from the living room. *"Want to hear me read?"*

(7) Harry read about Dick and Jane and their dog, Spot. Dick and Jane were cleancut, well-dressed, blonde and red-headed Anglo-Saxon children who lived behind a white picket fence in a red-roofed cottage with geraniums in the window. Their mother was a smiling blonde with clear, square teeth. The father wore a snap brim hat, a conservative suit, and carried a briefcase. And they all lived happily in a schoolbook called *Friends and Neighbors.*

(8) Little Harry might as well have read science fiction about Mars. He had never seen a cottage like that, never knew such parents of his own or anyone else, and so far as one could tell had never seen a geranium or a father in a business suit. His own family, for example, had never in his memory eaten a meal together. There weren't enough chairs, dishes, or forks. But Harry was still eager to please. He had not yet learned that other people expected him to be like Dick and his sister to be like Jane, and expected them to have parents like Dick's and Jane's, to live in a house like Dick's and Jane's, and that as a Negro slum kid all of this was as remote to him as the canals of Mars. And unless he was uncommonly lucky, this book and the school it came from would soon seem as remote.

(9) Harry's mother, Mrs. Martin—to use a fictitious name that will not further burden young Harry—is a weary, round-faced, bewildered woman of indeterminate age in appearance but only twenty-seven. Conversation swirled without touching her most of the time, her brow perpetually creased, a half-smile in constant apology. She looked toward the tangle of clothes hanging from the kitchen ropes.

(10) *"The school, they said the kids' clothes had gotta be cleaner and better. Ah kep' theys clothes jess as clean as ah could but now ah washes 'em every night. Kids they get undressed about five-thirty an' then ah washes. Ah gets up at six in the mornin' and sometimes ah irons what ah washed an' hung the night before."*

(11) The Martins are on welfare, aid to dependent children of the unemployed. Their father is seen spasmodically. He is usually drunk. Mrs. Martin is overwhelmed by the household and trying to deal with the outside world, so she is one of the rare cases in which the welfare workers pay most of the bills directly, the $75 a month for rent, the gas and electric bills as they come due, and the $9.45 a month for "household incidentals." She gets $151.90 a month for food for eight.

(12) The father has been drunk most of the time since the winter of 1962. That was when the meat packing company where he had worked for seven years moved to another city with an automated plant. And it was the winter the youngest child, a boy of five months who slept in a supermarket basket for a crib, died of pneumonia.

(13) *"We come from McCrory, Arkansas,"* Mrs. Martin said. *"We'd been born there an' we was 'croppin'. It was pretty bad. We had two kids and they wasn't nothing to eat and the place we lived in, well it rained right in all the time an' we jess had things worse an' worse gettin' seed and fertilizer. 'Bout a year before, mah husban's brother, he came up here to Chicago to work in this meat packin' plant and he wrote back to McCrory and said we should come up. So we did an' at first we stayed with his brother. They had a four-room place here on the West Side and he and his wife and their seven kids they used three of the rooms and my husband and me and the two kids we used the other room. It was that way for about a month, yes I guess it was a month until we got the first pay*

and we found ourselves a house. The pay, it was $84 a week. We was do-ing right well."

(14) She talked without change of expression, or lifting of voice, as though it were a recitation of events that happened to someone else one hundred years ago. She looked weary and apathetic, huddling in the perpetual twilight of her tenement. She seemed always to be counting the children silently and looking over her shoulder. When a footstep is heard outside the children run to a living room window looking over the entry-way to the building, the outside stairway faded and fuzzy through the plastic sheeting and the crusted window. *"Don' go out, don' go out,"* the mother repeats, though no child makes a move to go out. She keeps them in the flat, away from the bleak and melancholy streets. But on the way to school the older children keep their eyes open for an unbroken soda bottle in the carpeting litter over sidewalk and street, for such a bottle may bring a two-cent deposit and enough of these will buy a packaged cupcake or a soda at the basement variety store, an event announced with a thunderclap to the awed children at home. But Mrs. Martin says, *"Don' go out, don' go out,"* because in the alleys there are dangers worse than broken glass.

(15) So when footsteps are heard on the front stoop the children run to the window, their eyes excited. It could be a stranger with something different and exotic; it might be Sister Mary William, the tall tough-talking young Irish nun with a candy cane and words with their mother; it may be their father and he could be all right or he could be drunk and there would be fighting and his demanding money and the children screaming. So the children's eyes are always bright at the window and Mrs. Martin says, *"Don' go out, don' go out."* The footsteps go down the hallway, up the flight of stairs, and out of the Martin's worries.

(16) It was time for them to get undressed. They eat their evening meal at 4 p.m. and are in bed by 8. In a tiny sector of the kitchen, an angle made by walls of clothes hanging on rope, the nun drew Mrs. Martin away from the children. The Irish girl's great peaked white hat ducked under the clothes and she straightened out afterward like a giant, her blue habit looming over the clothesline. *"I think,"* she said to Mrs. Martin slowly and discreetly, *"I'm going to arrange for you to get into a public housing project."*

(17) Mrs. Martin paused for a moment and then her face lifted. *"Public housing? Public housing? Oh, that would be wonderful, jess wonderful. Public Housing. You really think so?"*

(18) *"Yes,"* the nun said, *"there's a place I think I can get you in over on the South Side."*

(19) Mrs. Martin's face froze. *"The South Side? The South Side! Why, ah can't go to the South Side! Ah'd like to stay on the West Side!"*

(20) *"Well,"* Sister Mary William said breezily, *"why don't we wait and see how it turns out."*

(21) The nun ducked under the clothesline and returned to the chil-

dren in the living room, leaving Mrs. Martin alone with her thoughts in the gloom of her triangle of clothes in the kitchen. She ducked under the clothesline into another triangle near the kitchen stove. The suds had disappeared in the cold basin of wash.

(22) Did the children ever see television?

(23) She looked at the visitor while she collected her thoughts and said, "*Well, they see it sometimes at the school and here and there. We ain't had one since I guess maybe it was a year, no maybe two years, I don't rightly remember, but he had jess got through paying for it, $300, an' it was all paid for an' it broke down. We called the repair man an' he said he had to take it out to his shop. An' the repair man, he came back with it the next Tuesday and he had it out in his car an' give us the bill for $60. We din't have no $60 then, right then that day, so he said to let him know when we did. Well, we called him after that but he done moved his shop an' never let us know his new address so we never did see the TV after that.*"

(24) She would not talk of the baby that died except to say that it was a terrible cold winter. "*The toilet it froze and busted from the cold. The radiator it din't hardly work. But the landlord he let us use another bathroom in the back an' don't charge us extra rent.*"

(25) Clothes for the children who go to school are a worry. When they need new shoes or clothing she has to wait until the welfare worker visits.

(26) What about clothes for herself? When was the last time she bought a new dress? Until I asked that question it had been hard to remember that this was a twenty-seven-year-old woman, that a short time ago she came to the great city in eagerness. But now her eyes lost their emptiness and she smiled. Her voice carried as it had not before, so much so the children stopped talking in the living room and listened in amazement.

(27) "*It was six years ago. We was making good money at the meat plant an' he took me out to a dress shop. When he saw how much I really liked that dress he said, 'Honey, you get it.' It cost $30. Oh, that was a dress. I mean it really was a dress. It was pink and it was cut a lot lower than this one and it had sequins all over and they shined and shined and the pink was so pretty.*"

(28) The girl from McCrory, Arkansas was for the first time identifiable with other young women, with a range of emotions, with liveliness in her voice. Then the face began to sag again and the crease returned to her forehead. She wiped her hands automatically on the side of her stained donated dress and one could see that her slip was held up with pieces of knotted twine.

(29) "*'Bout three years ago we was staying in a place where they was leaks, worse than here. An' the dress, it was in a closet where there was a awful leak an' it soaked the dress through an' through. Ah din't know it an' the dress it got mildewed an' I had to throw it out in the garbage.*"

(30) Outside, Sister Mary William looked down the endless line of row

houses, at the trash barrels lolling on their sides, the broken glass laid like a glistening carpet as far as the eye could see. She crunched the broken glass under her awkward black shoes and said:

(31) *"You figure out what's going to happen to Harry Martin when he finds out he's never going to be a lawyer. And his brother's never going to be a doctor. And his sister's never going to be a nurse. The worst most of us have to resign ourselves to is that there's no Santa Claus. Wait until this hits those kids."*

READING SURVEY

1. Main Idea
What is the central theme of the essay?

2. Major Details
(a) Describe Harry Martin's home.
(b) Why is Harry's schoolbook like science fiction to him?
(c) Why did the Martins decide to come north?

3. Inference
Note: Without adding any comment of his own, Ben Bagdikian repeats in this essay a number of stories exactly as they were spoken.
(a) What is the relation between the title and the content of this essay?
(b) Read paragraphs twenty-three and twenty-seven through twenty-nine again. What is the author trying to imply by including these two stories?

4. Opinion
(a) Do you think that this essay portrays a true picture of poverty? Why or why not?
(b) What effect does this essay have on you? Why?

VOCABULARY BUILDING

Lesson One: The Vocabulary of Poverty, Part I

When a person is poor, he lives in a state of poverty. There can be poverty of the spirit, which implies a lack of high moral values, and poverty of the mind, which implies a lack of intellectual development. But the word poverty by itself implies that there is a lack of food, shelter, and clothing. Today there is a new awareness that poverty should be eliminated from our world. Some of the words which are useful when discussing the mood and living conditions of poverty appear in this essay:

tenement	(paragraph 5)	**overwhelmed**	(11)
murky	(5)	**bleak**	(14)
slum	(8)	**melancholy**	(14)
weary	(9)	**gloom**	(21)

A *slum* is a very crowded city area which has run-down buildings, unsanitary conditions, and poor residents. The apartment houses in a slum are referred to as *tenements*, although this word can also refer to cleaner, ordinary apartment buildings.

The atmosphere of poverty is dark and depressing. *Gloom*, a darkness caused by lack of light or cheer, is everywhere. Windows in slums are often *murky* because they are caked with dirt that blocks out light. Both these gloomy dwellings and the attitude of their occupants are *bleak*— empty of warmth or happiness. The hopelessness of this atmosphere makes people sad and dejected to the point of being *melancholy*; worn-out and fed up to the point of being *weary*; and overcome with the weight of matters to the point of being *overwhelmed* by the struggle to survive and continue.

EXERCISE 10A: For each word given below, select the definition closest in meaning.

1. bleak:
   (a) noisy
   (b) cold and colorless
   (c) dark and dirty
2. melancholy:
   (a) fruit or vegetable
   (b) run-down
   (c) sadly depressed
3. slum:
   (a) an industrial city
   (b) dirt and slime
   (c) run-down, poor area
4. murky:
   (a) muddy
   (b) dangerous
   (c) heavy

Name: _____   Date: _____

5. overwhelmed:
   (a) defeated
   (b) overcooked
   (c) interested
6. tenement:
   (a) slum area
   (b) kind of ghetto
   (c) house for dwelling

7. gloom:
   (a) dark and cheerless
   (b) tired and angry
   (c) paste
8. weary:
   (a) rainy
   (b) clouded
   (c) tired

Lesson Two: The Vocabulary of Poverty, Part II

Here are words which do not appear in this essay, but which are helpful when discussing poverty:

pauper	**shanty**
destitute	**migrant worker**
impoverished	**itinerant worker**
deprived (deprivation)	**subsistence**
undernourished	**illiterate**
malnutrition	

A man who is poor is known as a *pauper*. A pauper can be described as being . . .

destitute: extremely poor to possible point of death.

impoverished: poverty stricken.

deprived: having little or nothing.

A pauper suffers *deprivation* in the form of . . .

POOR FOOD: being *undernourished*: underfed to the point of causing poor health.

having *malnutrition*: bad nourishment or no food at all to the point of death by disease.

POOR SHELTER: living in a *shanty*: poorly built hut of wood or metal scraps held together with mud. (A shanty-town is full of shanties.)

POOR WORK: being a *migrant worker* or an *itinerant worker*: travels from place to place in order to harvest crops as they become ripe; works hard, gets low pay, and has to live in shanty-towns.

getting *subsistence pay*: barely enough to stay alive.

POOR EDUCATION: being *illiterate*: unable to read or write at all.

Name: _____ Date: _____

EXERCISE 10B: Fill in the blanks with words from the vocabulary list above.

1. He moves from farm to farm and picks ripe crops. He is an

   _____ or _____ worker.

2. He has no education at all. He is _____.

3. He is penniless. He is a _____.

4. He barely makes enough to live on. His pay is at the _____

   _____ level.

5. He lives in a run-down, countryside shack. He lives in a _____.

EXERCISE 10C: Degrees of hunger and poverty: Fill in the blanks with the remaining words from the vocabulary list above.

1. He is so poor that he has no shelter or food. He will die of exposure

   and starvation. He is _____.

2. He is not eating enough to insure the proper growth of his bones. He

   is _____.

3. He lacks many things. He is _____.

4. He might die from lack of food. He is suffering from _____.

5. He is very poor. He wants for most things. He is _____.

Name: _____ Date: _____

SPELLING

Lesson One: Spelling Demons

Here are more words that are frequently misspelled. Using the helpful techniques given in Chapter One, you should make it a point to learn these new Demons, which were taken from "Why, There's Not Enough Money Here for Prostitution . . ."

address	before	due	remember
alley	began	enough	thought
apology	business	further	variety
appearance	children	hundred	welfare
awful	dependent	melancholy	woman
awkward	different	really	wonderful

Lesson Two: To Split or Not to Split

Some word combinations cause a great deal of confusion because the writer is not sure if the words should be joined or separated. In some cases, the written form will depend on how the words are used in the sentence. In other cases, it is necessary to memorize the proper spelling.

I *Words that may or may not split*: Because the spelling of each of these words will vary according to its meaning, pay special attention to the definitions given.

already (previously)
   The movie had already started when I arrived.
all ready (completely prepared)
   We are all ready for the work ahead.

altogether (completely)
   My answer is altogether different from yours.
all together (in a group)
   The children were all together in the park.

anyone (any person at all)
   Anyone can count to a hundred.
any one (one person or thing in a specific group)
   Any one of these detergents will do the job.
Note: This also applies to: everyone—every one, someone—some one

maybe (perhaps)
   Maybe I will join the Peace Corps.
may be (the verb form meaning "might be")
   This may be his last public appearance.

278

II *Words that never split*:

another	downstairs	northeast
bathroom	everything	playroom
bedroom	granddaughter	roommate
bookkeeper	nearby	schoolteacher
cannot	nevertheless	yourself

III *Words that are always split*: The changeable nature of the English language makes it necessary for you to rely on an up-to-date dictionary for the current spelling of a word combination. Below are some of the common word combinations that are still written as two words.

a lot	high school	living room
all right	in fact	no one
dining room	in spite	per cent

IV *Words that are joined by a hyphen*: Because there are no rules to cover all the uses of the hyphen, you should rely on a dictionary whenever you are in doubt. There are, however, a few principles to guide you:

(a) Use a hyphen to join compound numbers from twenty-one to ninety-nine.

forty-seven   seventy-eight

(b) Use a hyphen (or hyphens) to join two or more words that are combined to refer to the same person or thing.

mother-in-law	passer-by	court-martial
cure-all	fighter-bomber	forget-me-not

(c) Use a hyphen (or hyphens) to join two or more words that form a single adjective before a noun.

ten-year-old boy	well-known poet	bluish-green eyes
absent-minded professor	first-rate performance	

(d) Use a hyphen to join certain prefixes and suffixes to the main word.

co-owner	ex-president	bell-like
self-sacrifice	re-elect	pro-American

EXERCISE 10D: Underline the correct word from the set of words in parentheses. If necessary, consult a dictionary.

Traveling in a trailer can be an (all together, altogether) unforgettable experience. Trouble (maybe, may be) (all ready, already) in sight if the trailer must be occupied by a family of ten which includes a (cocker-spaniel, cocker spaniel), a few (grandchildren, grand children), and a (motherinlaw, mother in law, mother-in-law). (Infact, In fact), the biggest problems can be created by so many people living (all together, altogether) in such close quarters. (Never-the-less, Nevertheless, Never the less), (every thing, everything) may be (alright, all right) if there is a good deal of patience, (selfsacrifice, self-sacrifice, self sacrifice), and a schedule for using the (bath room, bathroom)!

Before the travelers are (all ready, already) to leave on the trip, someone, some one) should check to see that the trailer hitch is secure. If the connection between the car and trailer were to break on a steep hill, the trailer could go on a trip of its own—in the wrong direction. For this reason, many states insist that (noone, no one) may ride in a moving trailer. (Anyone, Any one) of several other hazards may also occur. If (anyone, any one) is in bed when the moving trailer hits a big bump, he may instantly fly from the (bedroom, bed room) to the (livingroom, living room) floor. (An other, Another) problem may occur when the driver ignores a clearance sign at a tunnel entrance. Entering a low tunnel at (thirtyfive, thirty-five, thirty five) miles per hour may provide the trailer with instant (airconditioning, air conditioning). When the travelers stop (someplace, some place) for the night, they should make sure that the ground is firm and that a water supply is (near by, nearby). If the ground is soft, they may wake up to find the trailer slowly sinking so that it (can not, cannot) be moved. (Inspite, In spite) of these hazards, some people claim that traveling by trailer is a (first rate, first-rate) way of seeing all of the nation's (well-known, well known) sights.

Name: _____ Date: _____

EXERCISE 10E: Unscramble the letters in parentheses to form the missing words in each sentence. If necessary, check your spelling with the list of Demons in this chapter.

1. Many people need (RETHURF) _____ education in

   order to succeed in (SINSUBES) _____.

2. An (SAREDDS) _____ is often difficult to (BERREMEM)

   _____.

3. One sincere (YOGAPOL) _____ is worth a (DUNDHRE)

   _____ arguments.

4. The guests were having a (FERDULONW) _____

   time until their hostess (GABEN) _____ to sing "Stout-Hearted
   Men."

5. Meeting a stranger in a dark (LEYAL) _____ can be a very

   (ARWDAWK) _____ experience.

6. The (GHOUTHT) _____ process makes man

   (ENERFFDIT) _____ from the lower animals.

7. Frugal Freddie tried on quite a (TIEYARV) _____ of

   suits (REBOFE) _____ selecting the cheapest one in the
   store.

EXERCISE 10F: Using at least ten of the Spelling Demons listed in this chapter, on separate paper write a brief description of the poverty scene that is shown on page 268. Be sure to proofread your paragraph for any misspelled words.

Name: _____   *Date:* _____

USING THE RIGHT WORD

Errors in some words, more than in others, are often used as yardsticks to measure a person's maturity and level of education. While many such errors are made in everyday speech, formal written English never includes them. There are three major yardsticks.

(a) Comparisons
(b) Verbs
(c) Other yardsticks of mature writing

(a) Comparisons: When you are comparing two things, never use the superlative form. It is reserved for a comparison of three or more things. For example:

> Joe is the older of the two brothers.
> Joe is the oldest of the three brothers.

For most short words, form the comparative by adding an *-er* ending and form the superlative by adding an *-est* ending. For most longer words (of three syllables or more), form the comparative by using *more* and the superlative by using *most*.

Positive	Comparative	Superlative
old	older	oldest
green	greener	greenest
fast	faster	fastest
slow	slower	slowest
beautiful	more beautiful	most beautiful
optimistic	more optimistic	most optimistic
easily	more easily	most easily

Some words have irregular comparative and superlative forms:

Positive	Comparative	Superlative
good, well	better	best
bad	worse	worst
little	less	least
many, much	more	most

☞ YOU DO THIS:

In the following paragraph correct any errors in forming comparisons. Cross out the error and write the correct form directly above it. If necessary, check your answers in a dictionary.

A slum is probably the most bleakest sight in a city. Broken glass, old newspapers, and uncollected garbage make the streets look more dirty than a shantytown. The tenements, which are some of the oldest buildings in the area, have the most dark, narrow hallways imaginable. Most of the apartments have few furnishings, for it is importanter for the tenants to spend their money on food than on furniture. Although dirt is a major concern in these buildings, the hoards of rats are certainly a worser problem. These tiny rodents, the harmfulest creatures in the slum, spread the mostest amount of disease in the most short time. After viewing this gloomy scene, one might wonder which is the most serious problem facing America—civil rights or poverty.

(b) Commonly Confused Verbs: Certain verb forms may cause confusion because, while they look or sound very much alike, they are really quite different in meaning.

lay, lie
The verb *lay* means to place. (The action is in progress.)
The verb *lie* means to rest. (There is no action.)

lay	*lie*
Please *lay* the book on the table.	The children *lie* on mats.
The hen *laid* six eggs.	Yesterday I *lay* in bed all day.
	The dog *has lain* there for an hour.
Jack *has laid* out the map.	The deed *is lying* on the desk.
He *is laying* my coat on the chair.	

283

learn, teach

Learn means to gain knowledge.
Teach means to give knowledge.

Professor Higgins tried to teach me biology, but I must admit that I did not learn very much.

leave, let

Leave means to depart from.
Let means to permit or allow.

I will leave for Florida tomorrow if you will let me make the trip.

raise, rise

The verb *raise* means that the subject is making something move upward.
The verb *rise* means that the subject is moving.

raise	*rise*
Raise your hand if you want to speak.	The temperature *rises* during the summer months.
Helen *raised* carrots in her garden.	The sun *rose* through the morning mist.
The teacher *has raised* a provocative question.	The men *have risen* to greet the general.

sit, set

Sit means to be seated.
Set means to place or put.

If you will sit in this chair, I will set the cushion at your feet.

stay, stand

Stay means to remain.
Stand means to be be in an upright position.

He had to stay in bed for three days before he was allowed to stand up for a few minutes.

☞ YOU DO THIS:

In the following paragraph correct any verb errors. Cross out the error and write the correction directly above it.

Yesterday was certainly not my day. As I set down for breakfast, the chair broke and I was soon laying on the floor. Then when I rised from the floor, I bumped my head on the table. My troubles stayed with me in chemistry class where the professor was trying to learn me how to make acid. After he had demonstrated the process, I insisted, "Leave me do it now!" I mixed the chemicals, lay the stirring spoon on the counter, and then sat the test tube in a metal holder. Suddenly a loud explosion shook the laboratory, and a large black cloud raised from the counter. Yes, I really should have stood in bed yesterday!

(c) Other Yardsticks of Mature Writing:

among—between

Use *among* for three or more things, people, etc.
  The club treasury was divided among all ten members.
Use *between* for only two things, people, etc.
  What is the difference between an alligator and a crocodile?

amount—number

Use *amount* to refer to the total mass of something.
  A large amount of food is wasted every day.
Use *number* to refer to things that can be counted.
  A large number of people suffer from malnutrition.

bad—badly

Use *bad* with nouns and generally after verbs that refer to the senses: look, feel, smell, taste, and hear.
  I feel bad.
Use *badly* after most other verbs.
  Many people drive badly.

can—may

Use *can* to indicate the ability to do something.

My brother can stand on his head.

Use *may* to indicate permission or possibility.

May I leave the room?

can hardly (not: can't hardly)
can scarcely (not: can't scarcely)
could hardly (not: couldn't hardly)
could scarcely (not: couldn't scarcely)

I can hardly (not: can't hardly) see straight.

could have (not: could of)
would have (not: would of)
might have (not: might of)
should have (not: should of)

Tony could have (not: could of) done it better.

different from (not: different than)

The monastic life is different from (not: different than) ours.

fewer—less

Use *fewer* to refer to things that can be counted.

Fewer jobs are available for unskilled workers.

Use *less* to refer to quantity, value, or degree.

Many people have less education than they really need.

former—latter

Use *former* to refer to the first of two items that have been named.
Use *latter* to refer to the last of two items that have been named.

(If three or more items are referred to, do not use *former* and *latter*; instead use *first* and *last*.)

Haight-Ashbury and Greenwich Village are two places where many hippies live; the former is a section of San Francisco and the latter is a neighborhood in New York City.

good—well

Use *good* to describe a noun or pronoun only.

Muriel is a good swimmer.

Use *well* to describe a verb only.

She also bowls well.

In the following paragraph correct any errors in using the yardsticks. Cross out the error and write the correct form directly above it.

In America today, a surprisingly large amount of people are destitute; perhaps it can be a shock to people who live good to realize that many millions of fellow Americans live in extreme poverty. They can't hardly get enough food to eat and many suffer from malnutrition. In addition, most impoverished people have poor health which means that they feel badly and ill most of their lives. Although it is true that today less people are paupers than fifty years ago, public apathy to the nation's poor is little different than what it was in the past. Something should of been started years ago to completely eliminate such human deprivation and suffering. Surely, between the resources of the city, state, and federal governments, especially with the strong assistance of the latter, it is possible to institute swift and effective measures which would cure poverty conditions in America.

ought (not: had ought)

People ought (not "had ought") to be honest.

is when—is where, is that

Never use *when* or *where* to refer to a thing; use *that*.
  Awkward: A sonnet is when a poem has fourteen lines.
  Corrected: A sonnet is a poem that has fourteen lines.

kind—sort

Never mix singular and plural. Use *this* or *that* with *kind* and *sort*;
use *these* or *those* with *kinds* and *sorts*.
  This kind of flower is very rare, but those kinds are grown everywhere.

like—as (as if)

Use *like* when no verb appears in the section that follows.
Use *as* (or *as if*) when a verb does appear in the section that follows.

  If you do as I tell you, you will look like a movie star.

the reason is that (not: the reason is because, the reason is due to,
the reason is on account of)

  The reason is that (not: because) no one cares.

so—so that

Never use *so* to join two complete sentences; instead use *so that*
when you want to show purpose.
  The rocket increased its speed so that (not: so) it could with-
  stand the gravitational pull.

try to (not: try and)

  Please try to (not: try and) drive carefully.

used to—supposed to

Never leave out the final *d*; use *supposed to* and *used to*.
  Although Jeff was supposed to be a frugal man, he used to spend
  a great deal of money for clothes.

where, that

Never use *where* to refer to things; use *that*.
  I read in the newspaper that (not: where) Mr. Blowhard is
  running for mayor.

☞ **YOU DO THIS:**

In the following paragraph correct any errors in using the yardsticks. Cross out the error and write the correct form directly above it.

Television broadcasters had ought to stop presenting many of the unimaginative, hollow programs which are available hourly on television. After watching these sort of programs day after day, year after year, one finds it difficult not to become extremely angry with the broadcasters who have become use to unquestioned control over the video airwaves. Cretins do not comprise most of the viewing public, so why is it treated like it is? The reason is because by selling expensive time to advertisers, the broadcasters hope to try and make as much money as possible. Of course, sometimes one reads in the newspapers where a network is planning to present an original play. But this type of announcement is when the public should remind itself that, if the broadcasters made a determined effort, stimulating, imaginative programs could be a regular occurrence.

EXERCISE 10G: For each item below, write as many fully and interestingly developed sentences as are necessary to follow the directions.

1. Using comparison forms of *smart* correctly, compare three intelligent people you know.

_____

_____

2. Using forms of *raise* and *rise* correctly, tell about your getting up from your seat and opening the window yesterday in class.

_____

_____

289   Name: _____ Date: _____

3. Using *worst, bad, worse* correctly, tell about three days of poor weather.

_____

_____

4. Using *let* and *leave* correctly, tell someone that he should permit you to rest and that he should depart from your home.

_____

_____

5. Using *teach* and *learn* correctly, tell about a professor who has given you useful instructions in a subject.

_____

_____

6. Using the comparison form of *romantic* correctly, compare two songs that you enjoy.

_____

_____

7. Using *set* and *sit* correctly, tell where you will put your books before you will take a seat in class.

_____

_____

8. Using *little, less, least* correctly, tell the order in which you like swimming, hiking, and dancing.

_____

_____

9. Using forms of *lie* and *lay* correctly, tell what you put on the table before you got into bed last night.

_____

_____

Name: _____ Date: _____

10. Using comparison forms of *careful* correctly, compare three cautious drivers you know.

_____

_____

11. Using the comparison form of *sad* correctly, compare the unhappiness of two people who have just lost a one-hundred-yard dash.

_____

_____

12. Using comparison forms of *green*, compare three lawns you have seen.

_____

_____

13. Using the comparison forms of *large* correctly, compare an ant, an elephant, and a hunter.

_____

_____

14. Using *stand* and *stay* correctly, tell someone that he should not have left the house because his legs are still weak.

_____

_____

15. Using *good, better, best* correctly, compare three things which you like to eat.

_____

_____

Name: _____ *Date:* _____

EXERCISE 10H: Referring to "Other Yardsticks of Mature Writing" on page 285–288, select a word from the choices listed below and fill in the blanks.

Choices:	amount, number	like, as	former, latter
	good, well	bad, badly	can, may
	among, between	fewer, less	

1. Because no one has taken out the garbage in three days, the kitchen

   smells _____.

2. That is a large _____ of eggs to sell in one day.

3. _____ I call you up sometime?

4. With the temperature near zero, it is _____ that you brought along a warm sweater.

5. Now that I know how much preparation is necessary, I hope that we

   can invite _____ people to our next party.

6. Sid is kind _____ a good father should be.

7. For many people winter seems long and summer seems short; the

   _____ is cold and the _____ is hot.

8. Because the laundry was not washed today, you will have to choose

   _____ your red or your white socks when you get dressed for tonight's dance.

9. For the celebration, Belle made a large _____ of champagne punch.

10. From _____ all the friends he had, he would have to choose one in whom he could confide.

11. I suggest that you fire your chef because he cooks _____.

12. _____ you rapidly climb five steps without taking a breath?

13. His work is excellent; he draws quite _____ for a ten-year-old.

14. Gil works long hours _____ many businessmen.

15. There is _____ free food to hand out today than there was yesterday.

Name: _____ Date: _____

EXERCISE 10I: Referring to "Other Yardsticks of Mature Writing" on page 285–288, fill in the blanks.

1. The reason is _____ she wants to rebel against her parents.

2. Please try _____ be sure to turn off the lights.

3. Beings from outer space might not be different _____ us.

4. I _____ hardly wait to see his reaction when he opens the door.

5. She could _____ warned me _____ I would have known what to expect.

6. You really _____ to be more careful of the way you drive.

7. If they love each other, married people learn to get _____ to one another's unusual habits.

8. It is precisely this _____ of problem that calls for those

   _____ of solutions.

9. I heard on the radio _____ a severe storm is heading towards our village.

10. The team was _____ to rest today, but the coach called for a special practice session.

11. The protest should _____ been directed against the law, not against the president of the college.

12. The problems which young people face today are very different

    _____ those their parents faced twenty years ago.

13. _____ there will be no more misunderstandings, we had better decide on procedures right now.

14. Before she became a nurse, she _____ scarcely stand the sight of blood.

15. When I was a child, I _____ to have frightening dreams.

Name: _____ Date: _____

INFORMAL LANGUAGE

Different language is appropriate for different situations. It is necessary to fit your words to the occasion. You might tell a friend, "My old man is a head shrinker." However, when speaking to a possible employer, you had better say, "My father is a psychiatrist."

I How do you think someone who expects you to be formal would react to the following paragraph?

Within the next 30 years, you'll probably have more convenient shopping methods in the U.S. You may order everything over the phone using photos and newspaper ads as your guide. If you live in Wash., you'll be able to go shopping in a store in N.Y.; just turn on the TV and you'll be inside a shop on 5th Ave. Then you'll use your phone to tell the clerk, "I'll take that there hat and 3 of them red sweaters." Because supersonic jets will kind of speed up delivery, you should receive your order in a day or 2. Buying groceries will be just as easy. While you're looking at a couple of tomatoes on your TV screen, you can tell the grocer that they look sort of green and can argue with him 'til he finds some ripe ones. In a recent speech, the pres. of the Buy-Rite Co. stated that this here method will save the consumer about 25% of the time now spent on shopping.

Here are some of the basic yardsticks which will help you to correct this paragraph by writing the formal English that is required in an essay:

FORMAL WRITING CUSTOMS. Numbers under 100 should be written out in words. When your writing includes numbers both over and under 100, the numerals are generally used to maintain consistency. The % *sign* should be written out as *per cent* after numbers.

Because the pronoun *you* tends to give an informal tone to writing, it should be avoided when possible. "Person" or "people" can often be substituted. Other pronouns such as "he," "we," or "one" may also be used. But be careful not to overuse "one," for it can make your writing sound very stiff and pompous.

SHORTENED FORMS. You should avoid using *contractions* whenever possible. However, sometimes a contraction may be necessary to prevent a very awkward-sounding sentence. Are not the trees beautiful? would sound much better as: Aren't the trees beautiful?

Do not use most *abbreviations*. However, forms such as *Mr., Mrs., Ph.D., Dr.,* and *Jr.* are permissible when they are used with a person's name. The initials of various organizations may also be used if the organizations are usually referred to by their initials. FBI, UNESCO, NASA, VISTA, and GOP are some which are commonly used.

Shortened words such as phone, photo, TV, and ad are commonly used in everyday speech. However, when writing formal English, you should use the full words.

ADJECTIVES. You should avoid using certain informal adjectives in formal writing:

Instead of:	*Use*:
a couple of	a few
this here that there	this that
them (ex., them people)	those
kind of sort of (meaning somewhat)	somewhat, rather

☞ YOU DO THIS:

Referring to the yardsticks given, on separate paper rewrite the paragraph about future shopping methods using more formal English.

II How do you think someone who expects you to be formal would react to the following paragraph?

Sometimes folks just don't understand their kids. My old man is a real swell guy a lot of the time, and he usually lets me get away with murder. But last week he came home in a lousy mood because an awfully big business deal had gone sour. Well, he sure took it out on me! He said no the minute I asked him if I could use the car, a red job with lots of chrome. I explained that I figured on taking in a movie with Sally Swinger, a groovy chick with some shape. Because Sally is mighty popular, I wanted to impress her in the worst way. I banked on getting the wheels, but my old man went into all that jazz about how he had had to work plenty hard when he was a kid and I'm a lazy good-for-nothing. I had to take Sally to the movies on my old bike, and I'm so embarrassed that I ain't ever gonna see Sally again. I reckon my old man just don't understand me no how.

Here are more basic yardsticks which will help you to correct this paragraph by writing the more formal English that is required in an essay:

WORDS OF EMPHASIS. Everyday conversation is filled with many informal words that are used to add strength to a statement. However, formal English also has a wide selection of emphasis words. Use them when you write an essay.

Instead of:	Use:
awfully, mighty, so, plenty, real (used for emphasis)	very, extremely, exceedingly, acutely
in the worst way	very much, acutely, exceedingly
a lot, lots of	a great deal, many
sure (meaning "certainly")	certainly, surely, absolutely, truly
no how	not at all
lousy	bad, terrible, inferior
swell, super, some (used for emphasis)	good, excellent, outstanding, notable, distinguished

SLANG. Although slang is often colorful, it is to be avoided in situations which call for formal language. Words such as "guy," "chick," "groovy," and "kid" may be fine for a conversation with friends, but such slang expressions should not be used when you write formally. It is more accurate to use "agreement" or "transaction" instead of "deal" and to use "figure" instead of "shape" when you are referring to anatomy. When you are in doubt, use a dictionary to determine a word's acceptability.

VERBS. You should avoid using certain verb expressions in formal writing:

Instead of:	Use:
to figure to reckon	to suppose, to guess, to think
to bank on	to rely on
to take in a movie	to go to a movie
to take up with	to become friendly with
to take it out on	to release anger at

☞ YOU DO THIS:

Referring to the yardsticks given, on separate paper rewrite the paragraph about the generation gap using more formal English.

EXERCISE 10J: Each statement given below might be made by some people in an informal setting or might appear in an advertisement. Rewrite each statement as it would appear in the formal writing of an expository essay. Use normal formal English; do not use ludicrously stiff or pompous language.

1. One girl to another:
   "Gosh! He's one of my 9 favorite guys."

   _____

2. A student to his friend:
   "I don't like gym nohow."

   _____

3. A disc jockey to a listener:
   "If you don't like to swing, rattle, and shake, don't tune in to this here station."

   _____

   _____

4. A boy to his girl:
   "Just when we had time to take in a movie, this job had to go and get a flat."

   _____

   _____

5. An advertisement on the radio:
   "Want to look groovy in the worst way?"

   _____

6. One businessman to another:
   "That's a real swell deal you're offering."

   _____

Name: _____ *Date:* _____

7. A father to his son:
   "Want to make a couple of bucks?"

   _____

8. An advertisement on a highway billboard:
   "It's mighty comforting to know that you can bank on the Dr. being
   as close as your phone! ... but what do you do if he's out?"

   _____

   _____

   _____

9. One gambler to another:
   "Big deal! So I dropped a couple of smackers at the track."

   _____

   _____

10. Girl fan to football quarterback:
    "I'd sure like to give you my phone number."

    _____

11. Announcer on the air:
    "Stay tuned to your TV for the full scoop about the bank heist."

    _____

    _____

12. One worker to another:
    "I just got the sack because I fiddled around with that there new
    machine."

    _____

    _____

13. One woman to another:
    "Did you catch that hairy ad for soap on TV last night?"

    _____

Name: _____ Date: _____

14. One patient to another:
    "He's the best doc in these here parts."

    _____

15. A boy to his date:
    "Man! I dig you the most. I mean you really swing, baby."

    _____

16. Husband to wife:
    "The steak was lousy tonight."

    _____

17. Wife to husband:
    "Don't take it out on me. It's the butcher's fault."

    _____

18. Doctor to his patient:
    "You look a lot better today."

    _____

19. A waitress to a customer:
    "You won't like it so don't even taste it. I should know—I cooked the grub."

    _____

    _____

20. A guest to his host:
    "Your party was a gas."

    _____

Name: _____ Date: _____

EXERCISE 10K: Use only formal written language to follow each set of directions below. Avoid the use of *you* in all answers. Use normal formal English; do not use ludicrously stiff or pompous language.

1. Write an advertisement of eight words or more about a cigarette.

   _____

2. Write a group of sentences about rock music.

   _____

   _____

   _____

3. Write a group of sentences which tells how many courses you are taking and the name of each.

   _____

   _____

   _____

4. Write an advertisement of eight words or more for a bank. The advertisement must include the bank's rate of interest.

   _____

5. Write a sentence which strongly emphasizes how hungry you are after having missed breakfast and lunch.

   _____

   _____

6. Write a sentence which tells a friend exactly how he looks when a pretty girl walks by.

   _____

   _____

Name: _____ Date: _____

7. Write a group of sentences about a sports car. (It can be imaginary.) Include in your description its fastest speed.

_____

_____

_____

8. Using full sentences, write directions for your friend to get from your house to your school. Purposely avoid using the word _you_ in the directions.

_____

_____

_____

9. Write a group of sentences about anything that is very important to you. Use at least four words of emphasis and underline them.

_____

_____

_____

10. Write a group of sentences which discusses at least three things on which a person can hear music.

_____

_____

_____

Name: _____ Date: _____

1. Correct any errors in punctuation in the following paragraph.
2. Insert words of transition needed to help create unity.

Is it possible to turn a tenement into a clean well-ventilated building in just forty-eight working hours. Yes exclaims a famous architect. My new process can rehabilitate a slum area in less than a week. The architects plan has already been tried with great success in several large cities. A shaft is created by cutting an eight-foot hole through the roof and each floor of the tenement. After the walls ceilings and floors of the apartments are repaired the collected rubbish is thrown down the shaft. Workmen on the first floor shovel this material into dump trucks. A crane is used to lower an $8100 preassembled kitchen-bathroom unit through the hole in the roof and down into the apartments. The shaft is closed and the job is completed. Putting up a new building would take a few years of expensive planning demolition and construction. Instant rehabilitation can be done in six days at one third the cost.

Name: _____ Date: _____

SPRINGBOARDS TO WRITING

1. As a result of looking at the photograph and the political cartoon, reading the essay, or answering the questions that followed each, you might have some thoughts about the central theme—poverty. (Look back at those pages to refresh your memory.) For help in planning such an essay, refer to the Guide for Planning an Essay, which appears in Springboards to Writing, Chapter One on page 25.

2. Here are some topics which have not been directly mentioned in the questions asked so far. Perhaps one of them could be a writing springboard for you:

   (a) What Is Poverty?
   (b) My Plan for Combating Poverty in the United States.
   (c) Urban and Rural Poverty—A Comparison and Contrast.
   (d) Agree or disagree with this old saying:
       If you're born in poverty, you'll die in poverty.
   (e) Agree or disagree with this old saying:
       Nobody cares what a poor man thinks.
   (f) Should Government Money Be Used to Combat Poverty—Or Is It a Private Problem?
   (g) Malnutrition—Its Causes and Effects.
   (h) The Case for (against) a Guaranteed Minimum Wage.
   (i) The Case for (against) Welfare Payments.
   (j) My Plan to Improve Our Welfare System.
   (k) Some Causes of Slums.
   (l) Possible Cures for Slums.
   (m) Life in a Slum.
   (n) Why I Would Like to Work for VISTA.
   (o) The Plight of the American Indian Today.
   (p) The Plight of the Migrant Worker Today.

Dix, DANCE OF DEATH IN THE YEAR
'17. (DEAD MAN HILL.) *Collection, The
Museum of Modern Art, New York.*

eleven

Copyright © 1964 by Bill Mauldin.

SPRINGBOARDS TO THINKING

For informal, not written, response . . . to stimulate your thinking

1. What is the subject of the etching? What details, in addition to the slaughtered men, are shown?
2. Do you consider this etching to be a vivid illustration of the horror of war? Why or why not? Although the etching was done shortly after World War One, do you think it is still an accurate picture of war? Why or why not?
3. In the political cartoon, why is the "toy" being offered for sale of particular interest to the four people looking in the window?
4. Why has the cartoonist used children rather than grown people? Judging from their costumes, where do you think each child comes from?
5. If the situation shown in the cartoon is allowed to come about, do you think it will lead to scenes like the one depicted in the etching? Why or why not?
6. Should some nations be allowed to "play" with these deadly "toys"? Why or why not? How can we prevent the open sale of the "toys"?

305

Sabines, Shoes, and Sanity

NORMAN COUSINS

(1) It happened on an airplane shortly after the takeoff from Atlanta. A lady sitting towards the front of the plane pressed the release button on her seat and pushed back suddenly. This had the effect of knocking a book out of the hands of the lady seated in the row behind. For purposes of narrative flow we shall henceforth refer to the lady in front as Lady A and the lady in the rear as Lady B.

(2) Lady B, her book sent flying, forcibly asserted her sovereignty. She put both hands on the back of the seat of Lady A and gave it a powerful forward thrust. This produced a shock to the physical presence and psyche of Lady A, who forthwith denounced, in a high-decibel range, the action of Lady B. Lady A insisted she had paid for her seat and was entitled to do anything with it she wished. The response from Lady B to this line of reasoning was that no one had the right to push that seat in her face, whether paid for or not.

(3) Lady A could not accept the proposition. Once again, she pushed her seat back, her full weight pressed against it. This act of massive defiance thwarted Lady B's valiant efforts to shove the seat forward again. Lady B immediately transferred her attention and energies to the head of Lady A, detaching frighteningly large quantities of hair. Lady A, her head anchored, grabbed her large handbag and used it as a mallet over her shoulder for clouting Lady B.

(4) It had all happened so fast that the sky battle was in full force before most of the passengers and the stewardesses were aware of it. And then, to compound the problem, at least four other ladies of assorted convictions and sizes became emotionally and physically involved. Shrieks drowned out the roar of the engines. Arms flailed, fingernails flashed, and hairdos put together so painstakingly over hours came apart in seconds.

(5) A stewardess and a few male passengers tried to intervene but could not get through to the epicenter of combat. The pilot, however, summoned on the intercom, was able to penetrate through to the war zone by means of the forward access. As he separated the ladies, he sharply reminded them that their nonsense could jeopardize the lives of everyone on the plane. He put an end to the struggle, redistributed the ladies throughout the plane, strapped on their seat belts, then returned to the controls.

(6) It was a bizarre and ludicrous episode, redolent of Mack Sennett at his worst; it was also a stark and frightening reminder of the membrane-like thinness that separates grown people from their primitive beginnings.

These were well-groomed ladies, none of whom would be out of place at a reunion of university women, or a civic reception. What is most significant about the episode, however, is that it is not really isolated. All the elements of absurdity and potential tragedy were sharply focused because the setting was high above the clouds. We can smile even as we shake our heads at the image of the latter-day Sabines battling in the sky. But what makes the episode most painful of all is that it is not too far removed from a situation in which the full congeries of humans on earth is involved.

(7) We are all aboard the same flight. The plane is called the nuclear age. Some of the passengers seem to have no use for one another. But the situation in the cabin seems under reasonable control. What makes the problem immediately precarious is that there is audible snarling from the direction of the cockpit where the men at the controls are themselves engaged in ominous and ugly preliminaries to a brawl. One thing is certain. They cannot grapple with one another and keep their hands on the controls at the same time. If the plane goes down, all will go down with it.

(8) In a rational world, no man would be permitted to become the head of a government, or even a high official in it, unless his fitness for leadership, his basic emotional stability, his capacity to stand up under stress, his sense of responsibility, could be certified by highly qualified authorities. No airline would dream of hiring a pilot without checking thoroughly into all the factors of human personality that go into the making of mature, responsible behavior and the ability to maintain a sense of values under stress. If the safety of a few passengers is important, what about the safety of more than two billion? The picture of the head of a powerful government losing his temper and pounding his shoe on the table during a critical session of the U.N. is not merely a striking view of a man out of control. The man who swings the shoe can also pull the switch that can end the human journey. The fact of such power in temperamental hands is not the worst commentary on our times. The worst commentary is that the rest of us are going about our affairs as usual, apparently willing to assume that equal or greater power is a rational response to danger. The madness is not isolated. It holds a claim on everyone who thinks he himself is remote from danger, that he has no responsibility for what is happening, that he is helpless to change the course of events.

(9) Absolute power and absolute nonsense are being wedded to one another in the modern world. If it is to be changed, some nation will have to come forward with a prescription that fits the needs of a human society in quest of sanity. The prescription will have to look beyond unfettered national sovereignty to a condition of effective law applied to the states themselves. Offering such a prescription does not by itself provide acceptance. But it is barely possible, even at this late date, that the prescription might serve as a powerful rallying point for what may well be the last stand of the thinking free man in this corner of the universe.

READING SURVEY

1. Main Idea

What is the central theme of the essay?

2. Major Details

(a) What was the cause of the argument which resulted in a sky battle?

(b) This incident was a frightening reminder of what fact?

(c) According to Norman Cousins, what are some of the qualities that a head of government should have in a rational world?

3. Inference

(a) Read paragraph seven again. What are some of the "ominous and ugly preliminaries to a brawl" which go on between nations?

(b) In paragraph eight the "head of a powerful government losing his temper and pounding his shoe on the table during a critical session of the U.N." is a description of the behavior of Nikita Khrushchev, a former U.S.S.R. premier, at a United Nations Assembly meeting in 1960. In using this reference, Norman Cousins wants to emphasize that "the man who swings the shoe can also pull the switch that can end the human journey." How would the pulling of a switch end the human journey?

4. Opinion

(a) Do you agree that only a very thin membrane restrains grown people from primitive, irrational behavior? Explain.

(b) Have you ever lost your self-control and done something that you later regretted? Explain.

VOCABULARY BUILDING

Lesson One: The Vocabulary of War

Since the beginning of man's recorded history, never has there been a moment when a war was not going on somewhere in the world. Then, just as now, some wars were small—often in tiny, little-known places between primitive tribes; and some wars were huge—often pitting supposedly civilized nations against one another. Some of the words which are useful when discussing war appear in this essay:

Sabines	(title)
sovereignty	(paragraph 2)
valiant	(3)
intervene	(5)
jeopardize	(5)
tragedy	(6)
precarious	(7)
ominous	(7)
critical	(8)
temperamental	(8)

When an event
... is an unavoidable misfortune or disaster, ... it is a *tragedy*.
... is a decisive turning point, ... it is *critical*.
... is dangerous and its outcome uncertain, ... it is *precarious*.
... is overshadowed with the threat of evil or disaster, ... it is *ominous*.

When a man
... is like one of the primitive, often warring people who lived in the Apennines in 290 B.C., ... he is like one of the *Sabines*.
... is heroically brave in fighting, ... he is *valiant*.
... is excitable and unpredictable in his moods, ... he is *temperamental*.

When a country (or a man)
... is free from external control and maintains its own rights, ... it has *sovereignty*.
... is threatening to become involved in the internal affairs of another country, ... it wants to *intervene*.
... is, by its action, exposing people to dangerous peril of injury or death, ... it *jeopardizes* lives.

EXERCISE 11A: Fill in the blank with the appropriate word from the vocabulary list

1. For civilized men everywhere, the word "Nazi" will always evoke the

   _____ mood of cruel evil.

2. The sinking of the Titanic was a _____.

3. Frequently the U.S.S.R. tries to _____ in the internal affairs of other communist countries.

4. The contamination of the air by radioactive fallout will _____

   _____ the survival of all men.

5. When in battle, the Green Berets are known to be _____ soldiers.

6. Today most countries seem to be more eager to protect their national

   _____ than to try to insure a lasting peace among all the nations of the world.

7. The Battle of the Bulge was a _____ turning point in World War II.

8. Adolph Hitler was said to be an extremely high-strung and _____

   _____ man.

9. Modern man often seems little different from the ancient _____

   _____.

10. The safety of all is indeed _____ if a nuclear war can start by the pull of a switch.

Name: _____   Date: _____

Lesson Two: Vivid Words

A word is vivid when it adds power, color, and liveliness to what is being said. The use of a vivid word in the place of a plainer one can add strength and sparkle to your writing. Many vivid words appear in this essay:

massive	(paragraph 3)	**stark**	(6)
bizarre	(6)	**primitive**	(6)
ludicrous	(6)	**absurd**(ity)	(6)
redolent			

Plain	More vivid	For
large	massive	...something that is impressively huge, grand, monumental.
strange	bizarre	...something that is sensationally odd, weird, queer.
foolish	ludicrous	...something that is very obviously ridiculous and unbelievably improper.
brings back memories	redolent (of)	...something that is either sweet smelling or pleasantly reminiscent of the past.
bare	stark	...something that is harshly bare and sadly empty.
uncivilized	primitive	...something that is base, rough, or uneducated.
silly	absurd	...something that is nonsensical, foolish, ridiculous.

EXERCISE 11B: After each vivid word there is a set of five words. Circle three in each set that can be used with the vivid word.

Example: KEEN: ⟨mind⟩ carrot ⟨judgment⟩ ⟨eyesight⟩ mirror

1. STARK: room landscape peas look doorknob
2. MASSIVE: statue bird building law ship
3. REDOLENT: of scissors of roses of summer of ideas of childhood
4. LUDICROUS: behavior idea snake gasoline rumor
5. ABSURD: behavior tractor idea rumor gasoline
6. PRIMITIVE: wasps appearance tools water cabin
7. BIZARRE: nightclub sun stapler dress behavior

Name: _____ Date: _____

SPELLING

Lesson One: Spelling Demons

Here are some more words that are frequently misspelled. Using the helpful techniques given in Chapter One, you should make it a point to learn these new Demons, which were taken from "Sabines, Shoes, and Sanity."

acceptance	during	nuclear	safety
another	forward	official	shoulder
beginning	immediately	presence	temperamental
behavior	involve	primitive	themselves
capacity	maintain	problem	thoroughly
course	narrative	response	together

Lesson Two: Dropping the Final E

Many of the words in this essay can be learned easily with the help of this one simple spelling rule.

Words ending in silent *E*
usually drop the *E* before a suffix beginning with a vowel and keep the *E* before a suffix beginning with a consonant.

☞ YOU DO THIS:

Add the suffixes indicated to the following words.

	-ing	*-ment*	*-able*
move	_____	_____	_____
encourage	_____	_____	_____
manage	_____	_____	_____

Here are some examples:

guide + ance = guidance   complete + ness = completeness
care + less = careless   imagine + able = imaginable
decide + ing = deciding   grace + ful = graceful

☞ YOU DO THIS:

Apply the final *E* rule to the following words.

write + ing = _____   operate + ion = _____

amuse + ment = _____   sincere + ity = _____

love + able = _____   like + ly = _____

A SPECIAL NOTE: Here are some words that you see frequently which—if you look at them closely—are exceptions to the above rule.

true + ly = truly   agree + able = agreeable
argue + ment = argument   courage + ous = courageous
notice + able = noticeable   canoe + ing = canoeing

EXERCISE 11C: Apply the final *E* rule to these words.

1. expense + ive = _____

2. separate + ly = _____

3. create + ion = _____

4. argue + ment = _____

5. surprise + ing = _____

6. desire + able = _____

7. safe + ty = _____

8. insure + ance = _____

9. arrive + al = _____

10. immense + ity = _____

11. arrange + ment = _____

12. challenge + ing = _____

13. concentrate + ion = _____

14. true + ly = _____

15. response + ible = _____

16. peace + ful = _____

17. grieve + ance = _____

18. appropriate + ness = _____

19. recognize + able = _____

Name: _____ Date: _____

Down

1. the area between the neck and the arm
2. one more
3. a subject in school
4. a tale or story
5. to continue with
6. opposite of ending
7. This room is filled to _____.
8. having an excitable personality
9. freedom from danger
10. An atomic bomb uses _____ energy.
11. a person's conduct
12. completely

Across

13. answer
14. a person holding an office
15. opposite of rejection
16. dilemma
17. opposite of backward
18. at once
19. to include
20. opposite of apart
21. plural form of himself
22. The apeman lived in _____ times.
23. before, _____, after
24. Your _____ is requested at the wedding of . . .

Name: _____ Date: _____

SENTENCE LOGIC

Logic in thinking, as discussed in Chapter Seven, refers to clear and effective reasoning. Logic in sentences, the topic of this chapter, refers to the correct form and placement of words in a sentence. Three aspects of sentence logic are:

(a) parallelism
(b) logical word placement for precise meaning
(c) logical relationship between a "set-off" section and the sentence to which it is attached

(a) Parallelism:

In math ... parallel lines run in the same directions and are the same distance apart from each other so that they never meet. Thus, *they correspond or match.*

In English ... parallelism means that when words express equal or parallel ideas, *they must match or be parallel in form.*

We know that if a car tire goes flat and cannot be fixed, it must be replaced with a tire that is exactly the same size as the other three tires. If a different size is used, the car will sit awkwardly and drive poorly or not at all. Thus it is with sentences: equal (parallel) ideas must be expressed in matching (parallel) form so that all parts of the sentence work properly.

If you use words that are parallel in form, your writing style can improve a great deal. At times it will be necessary for you to rewrite a sentence so that your word order will be parallel; however, the result will be a more balanced and smooth product.

A SPECIAL NOTE: The spelling of the word *parallel* can be remembered from its meaning: *all* lines are par*all*el (and the double *l* looks like parallel lines!).

I WORDS IN A PAIR OR A SERIES MUST MATCH IN FORM.

Mike likes fishing
 and
 bowling.

Steve likes to swim,
 to fish,
 but not
 to hike.

Ed wants to be a programmer,
        an engineer,
        or
        a technician.

Bob never smokes,
        nor
        drinks.

Notice that the items in a pair or a series can be connected with *and, but, or, nor.*

☞ **YOU DO THIS:**

Fill in the blank with words that are logical and that match in form.

1. Jerry enjoys reading, _____, and dancing.

2. Stuart would like to be an assistant to a butcher, a baker, or _____

    _____.

3. Philip has never had a chance _____ nor to bowl.

II WORDS WHICH FOLLOW "SET-UP" WORDS MUST MATCH IN FORM

Some "set-up" words: if, that, who, which, that, could, a (an), the, so that, of, at.

If we stop trying to participate in government,
if we prefer not to feel pity for others,
and
if we refuse to take risks,
then we are headed for disaster.

☞ **YOU DO THIS:**

Fill in the blanks with words that are logical and that match in form.
1. Rita went into the city so that she could meet her friends and so that

_____.

2. Marco could speak six languages, could play the violin and could

_____.

Notice that the section that must match in form can start at a few different places. The number of words you decide to match should depend on
the emphasis and style you want to achieve.

Carol told me that   the plane   would be   delayed
       and [that] [the plane] [would be] crowded.

The second section of this sentence *may* include *that*, or *the plane*, or
would be; however, this section *must* include *crowded* because it is the
first word that is new for the section. Thus, each parallel section that follows the first does not have to repeat all the words in the first section;
however, each parallel section that follows the first must include any
words new for that section.

☞ YOU DO THIS:

Mark off the places where you could begin the matching form.

I told Carol that I hated to travel by plane
       but that I loved to travel by train.

III   WORDS THAT GO WITH PAIRS OF "SET-UP" WORDS MUST MATCH IN FORM.

Some pairs of "set-up" words: both . . . . . . and   not only . . . but also
                              either . . . . . or   which . . . . . and which
                              whether . . . or   that . . . . and that
                              neither . . . . nor   who . . . . and who

David is *both* strong   Bill is a man *who* likes responsibility
         and handsome.   *and who* enjoys a challenge.

☞ YOU DO THIS:

Fill in the blanks with words that are logical and that match in form.

1. If you are looking for Jeff, he is either playing baseball or _____

   _____.

2. Ray is not only an excellent cook but also _____

   _____.

317

EXERCISE 11E: In each of the sentences below, one parallel section does not match in form. Underline that section and rewrite the sentence making any changes necessary for correct parallelism. The goal is to make all parallel parts match; at times, no one possible form is more correct than another.

1. Mary tended to be fickle, to be pompous, and also she was frugal.

   _____

   _____

2. One year he preferred McCarthyism, and the next year he was telling people that he was studying mysticism.

   _____

   _____

3. My father used to tell us not only to work hard but also playing hard is important.

   _____

   _____

4. They debated whether to seek shelter in the barn or try running home in the rain.

   _____

   _____

5. He died in violence, for he was living in violence.

   _____

6. Even months later she would listen for his heavy breathing, or she expected to hear his frisky bark.

   _____

   _____

7. That man who is sitting at the table alone never uses a napkin and is eating with his fingers.

   _____

   _____

Name: _____ Date: _____

8. She expected neither to have her way nor that she would be lied to.

_____

_____

9. Brandishing his sword, he railed and was screaming at the Duke.

_____

_____

10. Stunned and crushed at the horror of it, he hoped that they would find the thief and that they were able to save the life of the woman who was stabbed.

_____

_____

_____

EXERCISE 11F: Fill in the blanks with words that are logical and that match in form. For effectiveness use more than one word in each of the matching parts.

1. If you do not find a job soon, you will not be able to pay the rent or

_____ .

2. Sue was pretty but _____ .

3. Howard is a man who enjoys reading and _____ .

4. In a melancholy mood, the student felt that _____ ,

   that _____ , and that _____ .

5. Scientists have discovered that man has many different cultures, but

_____ .

6. A fascist is someone who _____

   and who _____ .

Name: _____ Date: _____

7. This employer needs a stenographer who can _____,

_____, and _____.

8. When a person wants to try to help improve the world, he might ___

_____ or _____

_____.

9. People rationalize their actions when they feel guilty about their be-

havior, annoyed at their weakness, or _____

_____.

10. Malnutrition in children is both _____

_____ and _____.

EXERCISE 11G: Using parallelism, write a sentence about each of the following topics. Use as many types of parallelism with as many "set-up" words and pairs of "set-up" words as possible. Do this assignment on your own paper.

1. fascism	11. automation
2. morality	12. sickness
3. poverty	13. moon exploration
4. employment	14. rock music
5. unidentified flying object	15. hunger
6. pain	16. apathy
7. civil rights	17. logic
8. people	18. clothes
9. food	19. danger
10. cars	20. werewolf

Name: _____ Date: _____

(b) Logical Word Placement for Precise Meaning:

The position of a word or group of words can affect the meaning and logic of a sentence.

I   EACH WORD MUST BE PLACED AS CLOSE TO WHAT IT DESCRIBES AS POSSIBLE: Incorrect placement of one word can completely change the meaning of a sentence.

For example, the sentence: *He said that she was a wench.* When the word *only* is inserted in various places in the sentence, the meaning of the sentence changes completely:

ONLY	ONLY	ONLY	ONLY	ONLY	ONLY	
he	said	that	she	was		a wench.
No one else said it.	*He did not mean it.*	*He said nothing else.*	*There are no other wenches.*	*She was nothing else.*	*a low state to be sure!*	

☞ **YOU DO THIS:**

Insert the word *only* in as many places as possible. Explain the meaning that each placement creates.
Gary photographed Ann as she was modeling.

_____

_____

_____

A SPECIAL NOTE: Avoid putting a word between the two words in the infinitive form of the verb, such as *to run, to go, to be, to have, to think,* etc.

II   GROUPS OF WORDS MUST BE PLACED AS CLOSE TO WHAT THEY DESCRIBE AS POSSIBLE: Incorrect placement of groups of words can result in illogical —and unintentionally funny—sentences.

We took the broken chair to the carpenter with only three legs.
...a freak carpenter?
Ted kept a little black book with the telephone numbers of all the girls he had ever dated in his back pocket.
...that must have been a big pocket!

321

Explain the meaning of each sentence *as it stands*. Then underline the group of words which is incorrectly placed in the sentence. Finally, draw an arrow to where the group of words belongs.

1. Jerry gave some pieces of fudge to his friends with nuts in them. meaning:

_____

2. The astronomer sat long hours looking through the telescope without any food.   meaning:

_____

EXERCISE 11H: For each list of words or groups of words, record all the possible logical orders for a sentence. In some cases there is only one logical order; in other cases there is more than one. If the latter applies, explain any differences in meaning. Use separate paper.

1. all
   fell
   boys
   the
   nearly

2. in society
   the students
   the inequities
   want to protest

3. the bucolic life
   was
   what he wanted
   for himself

4. George put his
   before he went
   trunks on
   swimming
   in the pool

5. only
   a college student
   buys
   books

6. helped
   the man
   with a broken shoe
   the horse

7. can harm
   society
   most of the time
   apathy and indifference

8. at the age of two
   my mother
   for a vacation
   in the country
   took us

9. Edith gave
   in paper cups
   to the children
   ice cream

10. on the turnpike
    out of gas
    Lynn's firebird
    stopped

EXERCISE 11I: Find the word or group of words that are not as close to what they describe as possible. Rewrite the sentence with all words correctly placed.

1. Claire prefers to usually read rather than to watch television.

   _____

2. Because he did not pass one test, the teacher failed the student.

   _____

   _____

3. Elliott helped Jerry to repair the boat's motor quickly.

   _____

4. She fidgeted thinking of how she could escape the hot classroom in her seat.

   _____

   _____

5. It is a generalization to always say that girls are fickle.

   _____

6. At the age of four, Ben took his children fishing.

   _____

7. The operation was performed before too much serious damage was done by the surgeon.

   _____

   _____

8. He just works during his vacation.

   _____

9. Barbara looked up at the huge skyscraper with sunglasses on.

   _____

   _____

10. The composer gave the piano to the opera singer which was a family heirloom.

   _____

   _____

Name: _____ *Date:* _____

(c) Logical Relationship Between a "set-off" Section:

(usually with commas) and the sentence to which it is attached: A section which adds material to the main sentence is often "set-off" either by a single comma (if the added section comes at the beginning or end of the sentence) or by a set of commas (if the added section comes in the middle of a sentence).

If there is no subject in the "set-off" section, its subject must be given in the main sentence. Thus, the "set-off" section must logically and clearly connect with the subject of the main sentence. If the relationship is not logically clear, the result can be illogical—and unintentionally funny.

Climbing a ladder, my head struck a branch.
... a head that climbs a ladder?
Crossing the street, the Empire State Building came into view.
... the Empire State Building walks?

A SPECIAL HINT: To find the subject of a "set-off" section, ask of its verb, "Who?" or "What?" The answer is the subject; it is this subject that *must* be clearly given either in the "set-off" section or in the main sentence.

☞ YOU DO THIS:

Explain why each of the following is illogical.
1. Falling in the river, my clothes got wet.

_____

2. Taught to study hard from an early age, the good grade came as no surprise.

_____

3. After eating dinner, sitting in a tub, the food began to give me stomach pains.

_____

4. The moon set in the west, while wondering about this misleading visual experience.

_____

This error can be corrected either (1) by using the logical subject in the main sentence or (2) by inserting the logical subject into the "set-off" section.

(1) Climbing the ladder, *I* struck my head against a branch.
(2) As *I* was climbing a ladder, my head struck a branch.

☞ YOU DO THIS:

Correct each of the four sentences in the exercise above.

1. _____

_____

2. _____

_____

3. _____

_____

4. _____

_____

A SPECIAL NOTE: Errors in sentence logic can be slippery—when reading your own writing, you often tend to subconsciously add what is missing. Because it is more difficult to see what is illogical in your writing when you are too involved with it, plan your study time so that you can write, correct, *and then leave the product alone for a while.* Do not look at it for a day or two. When you come back to it, you will be more objective and, therefore, more able to recognize your errors.

EXERCISE 11J: Read each sentence below to see if the subject of the "set-off" section is clearly stated. If not, rewrite the sentence employing one of the two correction methods given on page 325.

1. Having been overwhelmed by curiosity, the "X" rated movie was a disappointment.

_____

_____

2. Weary from the difficult climb, the food tasted good.

_____

_____

3. Feeling estranged from society, drugs became tempting to the rebel.

_____

_____

4. Being undernourished and sick, the child did not have long to live.

_____

_____

5. Making an ambiguous statement, the argument was unclear.

_____

_____

6. To learn vocabulary, some memorization is necessary.

_____

_____

Name: _____ Date: _____

7. In favor of desegregation, the school opened its doors to all.

_____

_____

8. Although knowing that the tenement had rats, the landlord refused to plaster the walls.

_____

_____

_____

9. Being deprived of many things, the lottery money came in handy.

_____

_____

10. Enjoying the study of geology, the moon rock samples provided fascinating clues to the origin of the Earth.

_____

_____

_____

Name: _____ Date: _____

EXERCISE 11K REFRESHER:

1. On separate paper, rewrite the following paragraph, correcting any errors in usage and informal language.
2. Correct any errors in parallelism, in logical word placement, and in logical relationship between introductory sections and the sentence to which it is attached.

Darwin's theory of evolution sure did make a lot of folks feel badly. The reason is because they discovered that they are related to the monkeys. But did you ever see a monkey try and steal a couple of bananas by clobbering another monkey with a club who was just minding his own business? Have you ever seen a monkey throw a bomb at a monkey that looked different than him? During an argument, have you ever seen a monkey belt another monkey? Have you ever seen a monkey that liked destroying private property and to kill just other animals for kicks? Have you ever seen 2 groups of monkeys wipe each other out by the thousands? If lots of people are kind of embarrassed because they're suppose to be related to the monkeys, can you imagine how embarrassed the monkeys must be!

Name: _____ Date: _____

SPRINGBOARDS TO WRITING

1. As a result of looking at the etching and the political cartoon, reading the essay, or answering the questions which follow each, you might have some thoughts about the central theme—war in the nuclear age. (Look back at those pages to refresh your memory.) For help in planning such an essay, refer to the Guide for Planning an Essay, which appears in Springboards to Writing, Chapter One on page 25.

2. Here are some topics which have not been directly mentioned in the questions asked so far. Perhaps one of them could be a writing springboard for you:

   (a) War Is Sometimes (Never) Necessary.
   (b) Not Everyone Hates War.
   (c) War Is (Is Not) Glorified by Movies, Television, Books, etc.
   (d) One Individual Is (Is Not) Helpless to Change the Course of World Events.
   (e) A Prescription for World Peace.
   (f) Our Process of Selecting a President Is (Is Not) Outdated.
   (g) How to Protest without Being Violent.
   (h) How Overpopulation Can Lead to War.
   (i) The Effectiveness of the U.N.
   (j) Nuclear Energy—A Mixed Blessing.
   (k) Qualities Necessary to Be a World Leader.
   (l) The Case for (against) a World Government.

Luoma from Monkmeyer.

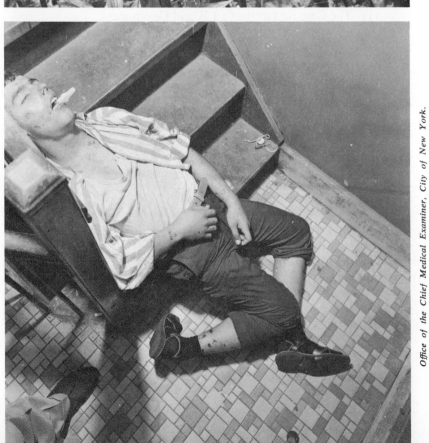

Office of the Chief Medical Examiner, City of New York.

twelve

SPRINGBOARDS TO THINKING

For informal, not written, response ... to stimulate your thinking

1. Before the young addict shown in the photograph died, what do you think took place?
2. If you happened to walk through a field of poppies such as the one shown, might you admire its beauty?
3. What do you think might be the connection between this field and the dead youth? Would you think that the flowers could be an indirect cause of a youth's death? Why or why not?
4. These flowers are opium poppies which are the source of morphine and codeine, two pain-killing drugs extremely valued in medical science. Heroin, in turn, is refined from morphine. Thus, something of use and benefit for mankind is adapted for destructive purposes. What other useful, beneficial things are adapted by man for destructive purposes?
5. In what other ways does man hurt himself by misusing and abusing his planet Earth?

Give Drugs to Addicts So We Can Be Safe

JONAH J. GOLDSTEIN

(1) Not long ago an office building in New York's Rockefeller Center area hired private detectives to catch the thieves who were stealing everything movable and salable from the offices in the buildings, night after night. The detectives caught forty-nine men; forty-three of them were narcotics addicts.

(2) Half the crimes in New York City today—the robberies, the muggings, the burglaries—are committed by drug addicts, and other cities are beginning to share New York's dangers. A while back, one of our newspapers carried a banner headline: NEW CRIME WAVE EXPECTED. Because federal narcotics agents had seized a big heroin shipment in the port, the story explained, heroin prices would go up, and the addicts would have to rob more people to buy their shots.

(3) What kind of police protection is it—what kind of law is it—that turns a great triumph of law enforcement into the cause of a crime wave?

(4) Discussions of drug addiction always seem to turn on the question of what happens to the addict. Instead of worrying so much about the one tenth of one percent of the population who are hooked on drugs, let's worry about the 99.9 per cent who aren't and whose homes and loves are are less secure because we drive sick people to crime with our narcotics laws.

(5) Mind you, the drug addict is almost never dangerous when he's under the influence of drugs—narcotics are sedatives. What makes him dangerous is the desperate need for the money to buy the next dose. And the costs are stupendous. The $50 a day addict must steal $250 to $300 in merchandise daily to support his habit; and when you catch him it costs $15 a day of tax revenues to keep him alive in jail.

(6) I don't want the kind of system where people have to register to get their narcotics. Some addicts are wanted by the police: they wouldn't register. All we need is a simple arrangement by which the addict who can pay for the shot can go to the doctor and get it—and the poor addict can go to the clinic, just as the poor diabetic goes to the clinic for a shot of insulin.

(7) "You don't have to worry about giving him too much and killing him," says Dr. Herbert Berger, formerly head of the committee on addiction of the Medical Society of the State of New York. "His problem is that his tolerance for the stuff increases. You have to give him enough to keep him comfortable, the way you give the diabetic enough insulin to maintain his bloodsugar level."

From *The Saturday Evening Post*, July 30, 1966. Reprinted by permission.

(8) Nobody would have to sign up for "treatment" unless he wanted it; nobody would even have to give a name or sign a receipt—just walk in the front door, get the shot and walk out the back door. Any nurse could do the job. The single dose, of course, would have to be moderately light. If a man's condition is such that he needs another dose, he can come around to the front door again.

(9) A simple test could guarantee that nobody gets narcotics at the clinic unless he is already addicted. Another test, perhaps an invisible ink time stamp that comes out under an ultraviolet lamp, could give enough control on the number of doses to make sure nobody used the clinic's narcotics to the point of killing himself.

(10) Under today's rules, we can't even prevent the use of narcotics for murder. I once proposed my version of the perfect crime to the inspector in charge of New York's narcotics bureau. The mob suspects that one of the boys, an addict, is a stool for the police. So the next time he makes his connection, his little packet contains much more than his usual dose. He puts it in his arm, and goes out like a light. In New York you would hear about it because our Chief Medical Examiner finds everything and tells everything he finds—but there are lots of places in this country where that kind of murder would go into the books as heart failure. I wonder how many police informers died of such "heart failure." My inspector friend heard me out, then said sourly, "Do you know any more jokes?"

(11) One night at dinner at the Grand Street Boys Association I was talking about narcotics with a monsignor of the Catholic Church. He asked me if I'd give a man five dollars to buy a shot of heroin. I said, "Of course I would."

"Wouldn't you be concerned that you might be shortening his life?" the Monsignor said.

"That's his business," I said.

(12) I smoke cigars. Now that I'm eighty I've cut down, by smoking only one at a time. I know it's bad for me. And if you don't smoke, are you going to live forever? What are they going to do about smoking—make it a crime?

(13) I think there'd be a good case for giving the addict his drugs even if it did help him harm himself. There are a thousand times as many people who are not addicts as there are addicts, and the important thing is to help them. And I can't see how an addict can harm himself more by going to a clinic than he does now by roaming the streets and robbing people to get the money to buy adulterated stuff from a vicious pusher. Is the female addict any better off as a prostitute? Anyway, why do you think the addict is so sure to be harmed?

(14) When I was on the bench and the cops brought in a working man who was an addict, I'd call him and his wife into my chambers and I'd show them a map of Texas. I'd say, "Pick a town near the Mexican border,

and go down there and get yourself a job. When you need the drugs, just walk across the border—you can buy the stuff there for the price of a pack of cigarettes. So you don't work eight hours a day, you only work six— you're still a lot better off than you will be up here, going in and out of jails and hospitals."

(15) The son of one of my best friends got hooked while he was at college. He and his father fought it for years—all the treatments they could buy, federal hospital in Lexington, Ky., and all the rest. Finally they came to me for advice. I said, "Pick a country where you can get the the drugs, and go live there." I saw that young man not long ago in his new country: he's married, he's got children, he's living a useful life. Here he'd be in hiding all the time.

(16) In my twenty-five years as a judge, I never had a rich user brought before me. I said that while I was still on the bench, and the newspapers picked it up. The next day I got a call from the Government's chief New York narcotics agent, who said he wanted to see me. He came up to my chambers and said, "It's not true we don't go after the rich addicts. We've been following one for five years, and one of these days we're going to get him."

(17) I asked for the name, and he mentioned one of the most famous and best-loved men in America, a man who's given away fortunes to charity, especially charity to help kids. I asked the federal chief what good he thought it would do to take a man like that and throw him in jail and ruin him, just because he uses drugs. And then—as a citizen, not as a judge— I called the man and warned him. He said sadly, "I know about it."

(18) Some say that giving shots to addicts will increase addiction. I doubt it. I don't think the end of prohibition increased the consumption of alcohol, or the number of alcoholics.

(19) At football games in the 1920's you saw lots of people carrying flasks; you don't see as much of that today. Before I was judge I was Al Smith's assistant. He used to carry a cane with a tube inside, all through prohibition. At banquets when he was governor, Franklin Roosevelt would have a coffee cup with bourbon in it. I remember once he told the leader of the State Assembly to pick up some Pikesville whiskey for him on a trip to New York. That was his favorite—Pikesville whiskey. That whiskey had a New York City motorcycle escort to the city line, then state troopers all the way to Albany, to make sure the prohibition agents wouldn't interfere. Later the man who delivered it to the governor told me Roosevelt immediately opened one of the jugs and slung it over his arm, country style, to take a drink. My friend said, "That man'll never amount to anything!"

(20) During prohibition important people never had any trouble getting whiskey. And there are some important people who have no trouble getting drugs today. Harry Anslinger, who was federal Commissioner of Narcotics, once testified to supplying a congressman with drugs out of the Government's own stock, because it would be dangerous to let somebody

outside get that kind of hold on a congressman. Everybody knows about doctors and anesthetists who have the habit. Narcotics agents don't want to let the doctors handle the problem because the police know that many doctors are addicts themselves. Men work as orderlies in hospitals for less money than they could make washing dishes in a cafeteria, because the job brings them near the source of their drugs. But why touch them—if they can live with their habit and do their work?

(21) For years I have been receiving letters from people who are addicts, but nobody knows it except themselves and their doctors. They were in an accident or a fire once, or badly wounded in the war (I once had a man before me who got the habit as a prisoner of war in North Korea) The doses that then kept them from agony later became the curse of their lives. Some of them became substantial businessmen and professional men, but they had to live with the knowledge that they and their doctors were breaking the law every day.

(22) Though many of the addicts we now make criminals could live useful lives with their habit, many others are hopeless derelicts. Nobody who has served as a judge in a criminal court could ever deny that addiction is a terrible thing. If we had a cure for addiction, there might even be an argument for the sort of program Governor Rockefeller has been advocating—ordering users to hospitals for treatment as soon as their addiction is discovered. But the hospitals don't help. We've had federal narcotics hospitals for more than thirty years in Lexington and Fort Worth, and the biggest claim I've ever seen for cures is ten per cent. Most doctors I know think two per cent as optimistic.

(23) In planning what to do right now, we have to start with the fact that addicts as a rule can't shake the habit, and that nothing we know how to do is much help to most of them. The psychiatrists have quit on the problem. One of them, Dr. Joost A. M. Meerloo, recently put their belief in his own kind of language: "Drug addiction is much more related to the pusher and the existence of criminal seduction and the hypocritical laws than to circumscribed pathology within the individual." Do you eliminate the pushers and criminal seduction and hypocritical laws by ordering people into hospitals?

(24) All the police and the courts can do with today's laws is increase the risk to the pusher. The greater the risk to the pusher, the higher the profits from pushing, and the stronger the temptation to push. The mob opposes reform of the narcotics laws now, just as the bootleggers always backed the drys in the fight on prohibition.

(25) Make the drugs easily available to the addicts, and you take the profits out of pushing. Then if you find anybody pushing drugs, especially to kids, you can slap him in jail and throw away the key—let him rot. The law can do its job. Without the profits, there won't be new pushers to come up and replace the jailbirds.

(26) Giving away the drugs doesn't solve the problem—we'll still need a cure for the addiction as much as we ever did. Today's stupid laws

335

make it nearly impossible to launch a research project big enough to get near the problem. Dr. Berger estimates that in New York, the worst-afflicted city, there are now only five or six doctors interested in the addiction problem. Take the stigma off the subject and provide money, and maybe we can have doctors instead of pushers and police determining what happens to sick people in our country.

(27) But let's keep our eyes on what our criminal laws are supposed to do. We don't write them to protect or to rehabilitate the addict or the criminal, to mete out exact Solomon-like justice to the pusher. We write them to protect the society, all the ordinary people who obey the law without even knowing that's what they're doing. Our laws on narcotics should benefit the 190-odd million who don't take drugs, not the 200,000 who do. I think it would turn out that we'd help them, too, but that's not what's important. The significant victim of the present law is not the derelict half-crazed addict with the need for drugs who mugs the old lady on the street, but the old lady herself.

(28) Let's forget some of the fancy theories and make our cities safer by giving the addict the narcotics he needs.

READING SURVEY

1. Main Idea
What is the central theme of the essay?

2. Major Details
(a) Why is there a big crime wave each time that narcotics agents seize a heroin shipment?
(b) What is Jonah Goldstein's plan for giving drugs to addicts?
(c) How have some people been led into drug addiction unintentionally?
(d) According to the author how successful have federal narcotics hospitals and psychiatrists been in curing drug addicts?

3. Inference
(a) Read paragraph sixteen again. Why are most rich addicts not brought to court for using drugs?
(b) Read paragraph twenty again. What kind of hold can a drug supplier get on a congressman?

4. Opinion
(a) What do you think of Jonah Goldstein's plan for giving drugs to addicts? Explain.
(b) Read paragraph fifteen again. Do you think Judge Goldstein gave the young man good advice? Why or why not?

VOCABULARY BUILDING

● **Lesson One: The Vocabulary of Addiction, Part I**

Life is not always what one wishes it could be. But most people learn to accept disappointments without feeling unusually sorry for themselves. However, those people who cannot tolerate disappointment sometimes retreat into a private world distorted by sense-dulling drugs. Some of the words which are useful when discussing addiction appear in this essay:

addicts	(paragraph 1)
narcotics	(1)
heroin	(2)
sedatives	(5)
adulterated	(13)
consumption	(18)
derelicts	(22)
stigma	(26)
rehabilitate	(27)
half-crazed	(27)

Today, most *addicts*, people who have become accustomed to something which is habit-forming, are dependent either on alcohol or sense-dulling drugs known as *narcotics*. Of course, most normal people have to take medication at one time or another. Such drugs, properly prescribed by a doctor, are not a problem; it is their overuse and heavy *consumption* that is dangerous. At times, a normal person might take a *sedative* to help subdue pain, induce sleep, or tranquilize nerves. Many sedatives contain small amounts of narcotics which are not dangerous because a very tiny dose is mixed with milder medicines. However, a narcotic can be extremely destructive if not mixed with other substances to *adulterate* it from its pure state. *Heroin*, a by-product of morphine extracted from the opium poppy, is one of the most widely used narcotics in America.

If a drug addict does not get what he is used to, he will become desperate and hysterical, thus behaving in a *half-crazed manner*. If an alcoholic or drug addict is no longer able to support himself, he becomes a run-down bum or *derelict* who must hang out in doorways and stairwells. There are a number of organizations which have *rehabilitation* programs designed to help restore those addicts who truly want to *rehabilitate* themselves to their former condition of health and usefulness. Nevertheless, even if this works, a former addict always carries an invisible, emotional scar—the *stigma* of knowing that he was once an addict.

EXERCISE 12A: Match each quotation with a word from the vocabulary list.

1. "Sometimes my doctor prescribes a medicine which induces sleep." _____

2. "They are people habituated to taking drugs." _____

3. "He's a debased man who roams the street like a decaying bum." _____

4. "Wherever I go I carry my invisible scar of shame." _____

5. "To maintain my habit, I must frequently increase the amount of my drug feeding." _____

6. "I am half out of my mind." _____

7. "I want to return to a normal life. I need treatment which will rebuild me." _____

8. "That man is selling habit-forming drugs." _____

9. "Some addicts I know have died because the narcotics sold to them were spoiled by being mixed with foreign substances." _____

10. "A frequently used narcotic, a derivative of morphine, is $C_{21}H_{23}NO_5$." _____

Name: _____ Date: _____

Lesson Two: The Vocabulary of Addiction, Part II

Here are words which do not appear in this essay but which are useful when discussing addiction:

alienation
alienated
reality
fantasy
hallucination
psychedelic
perception
euphoria
degenerate
depravity

Alienation, the state of feeling estranged and withdrawn from society, is common to most addicts. *Alienated* people often dislike the real events and things of the world. Instead of this *reality,* alienated people often prefer the *fantasy* world of daydreams, fancy, and imagination. Visions which are imaginary, called *hallucinations,* are caused by a nervous system disorder that is usually brought on by heavy alcohol or drug consumption. Some drugs, especially LSD, create *psychedelic hallucinations.* Although *psychedelic* once meant "the showing of the soul," today it refers to colorful designs and visions.

Naturally, all normal people are aware of their surroundings and make observations of the world. Such normal *perception* is usually fairly accurate and dependable. But addicts seek to distort their *perception* and to maintain a constant feeling of well-being and intense happiness. In order to achieve this state of *euphoria,* the addict takes narcotics or consumes large amounts of alcohol. Yet, along with an inner state of *euphoria,* the the addict lives an external life of decay. He can become a *degenerate* who has fallen to a low and degraded existence, often as a sexual pervert. Such *depravity* and degeneracy often leads to total downfall—and death.

EXERCISE 12B: Match each quotation with a word from the vocabulary list.

1. "I prefer the feeling of heightened well-being and happiness." _____

2. "He is a degraded, perverted person." _____

3. "I feel estranged from the world." _____

4. "This poster is one of splashy, colorful designs." _____

5. "Sometimes I find it difficult to accept the real world." _____

6. "When I take drugs, they distort the way I see things." _____

7. "Bizarre monsters appear in my imaginary visions." _____

8. "Some of my friends prefer to live in an imaginary world of fancy and and daydreams." _____

9. "His condition is one of personal corruption and low moral standards." _____

10. "I live in a state of unfriendliness and distance from society." _____

Name: _____ Date: _____

SPELLING

Lesson One: Spelling Demons

Here are some more words that are frequently misspelled. Using the helpful techniques given in Chapter One, you should make it a point to learn these new Demons, which were taken from "Give Drugs to Addicts So We Can Be Safe."

across	cigarette	eliminate	mention
alcohol	comfortable	estimate	merchandise
amount	committee	favorite	prisoner
association	desperate	finally	simple
available	discussion	governor	substantial
biggest	easily	increase	write

Lesson Two: Spelling Rule—Doubling

Many of the words in Jonah Goldstein's essay can be learned easily with the help of this one spelling rule.

When a suffix is added to a word, the final consonant of the word is doubled if it meets all of these three tests:

(a) the suffix begins with a vowel
(b) the word ends with a vowel followed by a consonant
(c) the word is one syllable or has its accent on the last syllable.

☞ YOU DO THIS:

Add the suffixes indicated to the following words.

	-ing	*-ed*	*-ment*
ship	_____	_____	_____
prefer	_____	_____	_____
equip	_____	_____	_____

Here are some examples:

begin + ing = beginning   drop + ed = dropped
hot + est = hottest   forget + ful = forgetful
cost + ing = costing   happen + ed = happened

☞ YOU DO THIS:

Apply the doubling rule to the following words.

occur + ence = _____   commit + ment = _____

cold + er =   _____   admit + ance =   _____

forget + ing = _____   benefit + ed =   _____

EXERCISE 12C: Apply the doubling rule to these words.

1. occur + ing =   _____

2. transfer + ed =   _____

3. differ + ent =   _____

4. win + er =   _____

5. swim + ing =   _____

6. wrap + ed =   _____

7. regret + able =   _____

8. old + est =   _____

9. plot + ed =   _____

10. plan + ing =   _____

11. defer + ment =   _____

12. skip + ed =   _____

13. forbid + en =   _____

14. appear + ance =   _____

15. control + able =   _____

16. stop + ed =   _____

     Name: _____ *Date:* _____

17. beg + ing = _____

18. listen + ing = _____

19. acquit + al = _____

20. wet + est = _____

EXERCISE 12D: Fill in the blanks with any missing letters.

A Congressional com__t____e has f__n____ly released its report on the prisons a__r____s the nation. The rather s__mp__e life of a pr__s-__n__r is usually centered around his work in a shop that manufactures goods used in the prison or other m_____ch__nd____e used by the state. A convict spends the big__st am____nt of time in a cell that is anything but c__mf____t__ble. Naturally, drinks containing al____h__l are forbidden and only a limited number of c__g__r__t____s are av____l-____le. Because most p__i__o__e__s are d__sp__r__te for news about the outside world, they __r__te many letters. Of course, their f__v__r-__t__ news concerns their parole. The Congressional report also m__n-t____ns that little is being done to el__m_____te the criminal's antisocial behavior. At a recent civic as__c____t____n meeting, a well-known g__v____n__r est_____t__d that only seventeen cents a day is given for a prisoner's rehabilitation in some states. The g____er____r ended the d__s____s____n by insisting that, although rehabilitation will never be accomplished e__s____y, there must be a s__b__t__n_____l inc_____se in funds for this purpose.

Name: _____   Date: _____

THE ESSAY: EXPLAINING A PROCESS
CONSTRUCTING A DEFINITION
ARGUING AN OPINION

There are many types of expository essays. In this chapter, three of the most frequently assigned types will be discussed. They are:

(a) Explaining a Process
(b) Constructing a Definition
(c) Arguing an Opinion

If you refer to Chapter Six of this book, you will be reminded that an expository essay is written for the purpose of conveying information. Thus, any of the specific types of expository essays listed above are merely alternate approaches to the main purpose—to convey information. In addition, you will also be reminded that in many ways an expository essay has the same structure as a paragraph, except that the essay has more extended discussion and uses additional specific examples.

This chart summarizes the connections between the paragraph and the essay:

The Paragraph	Purpose	The Essay
the topic sentence	to state, limit, and control the main idea	the introductory paragraph
development with use of facts, examples, incident, definition, or comparison and contrast	to develop the main idea with specific points	the main body paragraphs (There should be at least three of them.)
(in certain cases: the concluding sentence)	to conclude by coming back to the general main idea	the concluding paragraph

Explaining a Process

Curiosity to explore and understand the unknown is typical of the human mind. Expository essays which explain a process should encourage the reader's natural curiosity. There are three basic types of process essays:

(a) The most familiar is the *How to* . . . type of process essay. It gives directions which should be clearly stated step by step so that the reader can learn, for example, how to make pizza or how to clean a bolt-action rifle.

344

(b) A favorite of many people is the *How . . . Was Done* type of process essay. It describes how something unusual and complicated was achieved so that the reader can learn, for example, how the U.S. won the race to the moon or how I lost ninety pounds in six months.

(c) Of particular interest to many people is the *How . . . Works* type of process essay. It explains, in non-technical language, how scientific and other complex processes work so that the reader can learn, for example, how the atomic bomb is detonated or how the LEM was tested and perfected.

In all process essays, the introduction should state what the process is and why it is important. Then, the main body paragraphs should clearly and logically describe the steps in the process.

☞ YOU DO THIS:

For each process given, tell why it is important.

1. How to Drive a Car: Why important? _____

_____

_____

2. How My Parents First Met: Why Important? _____

_____

_____

In explaining a process, you should also make your essay lively so that it encourages curiosity and entertains as it teaches. To do more than merely recite a recipe or give a dry list of facts and dates, you can try to include one or more of the following—if they clearly relate to the process: (1) an amusing or dramatic incident, (2) an unusually surprising fact, (3) a conclusion which challenges the reader to think and explore further.

Specifically, how would you make the following process essays lively and interesting?

1. Think of how you either passed or failed a recent test. If you had to write an essay which tells how this process was done, what might you include to make it more lively and interesting?

   A surprising fact: _____

   _____

   An amusing or dramatic incident: _____

   _____

   _____

   A challenge to think and explore further: _____

   _____

2. Assume that you must write a process essay which tells how the telephone system in the U.S. works. (Consult your telephone directory for direct-dialing information, charge rates, etc.) What might you include to make it more lively and interesting?

   A surprising fact: _____

   _____

   An amusing or dramatic incident: _____

   _____

   _____

   A challenge to think and explore further: _____

   _____

(a) The *introduction* should always tell what the process is and why it is important.

(b) The *main body paragraphs* should give the parts of the process in an order that is appropriate for the clear and logical presentation of a topic. Time is the most common type of order; it presents what happened first, second, third, etc.

Here are the most useful types of order:

The order (or its reverse!)   For example

By IMPORTANCE:

How I Lost Ninety Pounds in Six Months
Introductory paragraph
   I. will power
  II. dietetic foods
 III. doctors and drugs
Concluding paragraph

By LOCATION:

How to Clean a Bolt-Action Rifle
Introductory paragraph
   I. the bore
  II. the breech
 III. the stock
Concluding paragraph

From SIMPLE TO COMPLEX:

How the Atomic Bomb Is Detonated
Introductory paragraph
   I. bomb design
  II. Uranium-235
 III. the implosion chamber
Concluding paragraph

From KNOWN TO UNKNOWN:

How the U.S. Won the Race to the Moon
Introductory paragraph
   I. billions of dollars
  II. dedicated specialists
 III. scientific breakthroughs
Concluding paragraph

Of TIME:

How to Make Pizza
Introductory paragraph
   I. the proper ingredients
  II. hands, utensils, and oven
 III. the masterful combining of
     ingredients
Concluding paragraph

(c) To avoid being dull, tease the reader's curiosity with a particularly interesting piece of information or arouse the reader's interest with an amusing or dramatic incident.

(d) In order to achieve a unified essay, use words of transition and the deliberate repetition of key words which will tie the parts together.

(e) The *conclusion* can challenge the reader to think and explore thoroughly.

EXERCISE 12E: For each process essay title given, select the order which would be most effective. Then list three major parts of the process by indicating the main idea of each paragraph.

1. How to Make a Banana Split   Order: _____
   Introductory paragraph

   I. _____

   II. _____

   III. _____
   Concluding paragraph

2. How Computerized Dating Works   Order: _____
   Introductory paragraph

   I. _____

   II. _____

   III. _____
   Concluding paragraph

3. How I Lived through My Two Years
   in the Army   Order: _____
   Introductory paragraph

   I. _____

   II. _____

   III. _____
   Concluding paragraph

Name: _____ *Date:* _____

4. How the Assembly-Line Principle
   Works   Order: _____
   Introductory paragraph

   I. _____

  II. _____

 III. _____
   Concluding paragraph

5. How Poverty Can Cripple the
   Minds of Children   Order: _____
   Introductory paragraph

   I. _____

  II. _____

 III. _____
   Concluding paragraph

6. How to Write a Good Expository
   Essay   Order: _____
   Introductory paragraph

   I. _____

  II. _____

 III. _____
   Concluding paragraph

7. How Smoking Can Cause Death   Order: _____
   Introductory paragraph

   I. _____

  II. _____

 III. _____
   Concluding paragraph

        Name: _____   *Date:* _____

8. How to Impress the Opposite Sex   Order: _____
   Introductory paragraph

   I. _____

   II. _____

   III. _____
   Concluding paragraph

9. How Columbus Discovered America   Order: _____
   Introductory paragraph

   I. _____

   II. _____

   III. _____
   Concluding paragraph

10. How to Prevent Wars   Order: _____
    Introductory paragraph

   I. _____

   II. _____

   III. _____
   Concluding paragraph

11. How to Prevent the Population
    Explosion   Order: _____
    Introductory paragraph

   I. _____

   II. _____

   III. _____
   Concluding paragraph

Name: _____ Date: _____

EXERCISE 12F: Are these introductions to process essays appropriate? Why or why not? As you evaluate them, refer to (1) the pointers to remember when explaining a process, page 347, and (2) in Chapter Six, page 162–163, the list of Common Errors to Avoid in Introductions and Conclusions.

1. *Title*: How the Jet Engine Works
   Introduction:
      In this essay I will tell you how the jet engine works. It is very complicated, but I will try, with my limited knowledge, to explain it.
   Question: Appropriate? Why or why not?

   _____

   _____

   _____

2. *Title*: How to Analyze Handwriting
   Introduction:
      Does your handwriting, when you use unlined paper, often run downhill—or uphill? If the former, you are probably sour and pessimistic; if the latter, you are probably cheerful and optimistic. It is possible to discover a great deal about a person by analyzing his handwriting. It is also an amusing pastime with which you can entertain your friends.
   Question: Appropriate? Why or why not?

   _____

   _____

   _____

3. *Title*: How America Entered World War II
   Introduction:
      America is a country dedicated to the proposition that all men are created equal. This great country will defend to the death the rights of all men—of all races, all colors, and all creeds. It was Voltaire who said, "I disapprove of what you say, but I will defend to the death your right to say it."
   Question: Appropriate? Why or why not?

   _____

   _____

   _____

Name: _____ Date: _____

(b) written *to illustrate and comment on an aspect of human nature, society, etc.* Often this is done by the construction of a definition of an event, a person, or a place.

☞ **YOU DO THIS:**

Refer to the essay "Bull Connor's Birmingham" by Dr. Martin Luther King, which appears at the beginning of Chapter Three.

1. Is Birmingham's geographical location given? _____

   Why or why not? _____

2. Is the number of people registered to vote in Birmingham given?

   _____ Why or why not? _____

   _____

3. What people are especially affected by the city? _____

   _____

4. What word can describe the mood of the city? _____

5. Give a brief description of Bull Connor's Birmingham: _____

   _____

   _____

6. About what aspect of society is the author commenting? _____

   _____

(c) written *to clarify an existing practice and perhaps to present a new plan of action.* Often this type can persuade the reader.

● ☞ YOU DO THIS:

Refer to the essay "The Case for Drafting All Boys—and Girls" by Margaret Mead, which appears at the beginning of Chapter Five.

1. In paragraphs two and three, Margaret Mead defines "young American today." Briefly summarize her definition: _____

_____

_____

2. In paragraphs four through seven, the draft as the "focus of protest" is defined. Briefly summarize it: _____

_____

_____

3. In paragraphs ten through fifteen, the author presents her new plan of action by defining "universal military service." Briefly summarize that definition: _____

_____

_____

_____

4. What is the purpose of the definitions which Margaret Mead has presented? _____

_____

_____

... A FEW GOOD POINTERS TO REMEMBER WHEN CONSTRUCTING A DEFINITION:

(a) The *introduction* should state what is being defined. You should avoid using a dictionary definition because it provides too narrow a start (as well as being a technique vastly overused by students). The introduction might, when appropriate for the subject being defined, consider such questions as: What or whom does it effect? Why is it significant? When did it take place?

(b) The *main body paragraphs* should break what is being defined into its major parts. A separate paragraph should be devoted to each of these major parts. If what you are defining is:

    ... *an object*, such as an automobile, the parts are concrete.

    ... *an idea, person, or place*, such as love, President Lincoln, or Cape Kennedy, the parts can be things which are not concrete because they concern abstract ideas such as spirit and feelings.

(c) The *parts which you select* will reflect your judgment and point of view; the parts selected should reflect your major purpose, such as:

    (1) to suggest a new or enlarged way of looking at something.

    (2) to illustrate and comment on an aspect of human nature, society, etc.

    (3) to clarify an existing practice and perhaps present a new plan of action.

(d) The *order* in which the selected parts are presented should be clear and logical. Look back at the "Pointers to Remember When Explaining a Process" in Chapter Twelve for a more complete explanation of these orders: by importance, by location, from simple to complex, from known to unknown, and of time.

(e) If your definition seems too shallow, try to enrich your perception of the subject. Try thinking about your subject in terms of:

    (1) its physical properties (through all five senses: sight, touch, hearing, smell, taste).

    (2) its uses—and dangers.

    (3) its effect on: people, history, attitudes, etc.

    (4) what it is not.

(f) Whenever possible, illustrate with specific examples, facts, or incidents. A definition which merely recites synonyms goes around in circles because it avoids being specific.

EXERCISE 12G: The parts listed for each of the definition essays below are too shallow for the scope and purpose of the title given. Referring to the Pointers to Remember When Constructing a Definition, tell why the definition is shallow and then list parts which would be more appropriate for the title.

1. The Opium Poppy—Deceptive Beauty
   Introduction

   I. what it looks like

   II. what its uses are

   III. where it grows
   Conclusion

   Revised Parts

   Introduction

   I. _____

   II. _____

   III. _____
   Conclusion

   Why shallow? _____

   _____

2. There Are Many Kinds of Poverty
   Introduction

   I. a pauper has no job

   II. a pauper has no decent housing

   III. a pauper has no goal in life
   Conclusion

   Revised Parts

   Introduction

   I. _____

   II. _____

   III. _____

   Conclusion

   Why shallow? _____

   _____

3. The Fabulous Cape Kennedy
   Introduction

   I. where it is located

   II. who works there

   III. its night life
   Conclusion

   Revised Parts
   Introduction

   I. _____

   II. _____

   III. _____
   Conclusion

   Why shallow? _____

   _____

Name: _____ Date: _____

4. What Is Dishonesty?
   Introduction

   I. stealing a car

   II. stealing clothes

   III. stealing money
   Conclusion

   Why shallow? _____

Revised Parts
Introduction

I. _____

II. _____

III. _____
Conclusion

---

5. What Was McCarthyism?
   Introduction

   I. the childhood of Senator Joseph McCarthy
   II. his marriage

   III. who worked with him
   Conclusion

   Why shallow? _____

Revised Parts
Introduction

I. _____

II. _____

III. _____
Conclusion

---

6. Football Is a Rugged Sport
   Introduction

   I. types of stadiums

   II. numbers of tickets sold

   III. habits of fans
   Conclusion

   Why shallow? _____

Revised Parts
Introduction

I. _____

II. _____

III. _____
Conclusion

---

7. The Old City of Jerusalem—
   A Step into History
   Introduction

   I. location

   II. population

   III. appearance
   Conclusion

Revised Parts

Introduction

I. _____

II. _____

III. _____
Conclusion

Name: _____ Date: _____

Why shallow? _____

_____

8. Perfume—for the Romanticist   *Revised Parts*
   Introduction   Introduction

     I. the manufacturing   I. _____
   process
      II. its look and smell   II. _____

   III. the types of bottles   III. _____
   and prices
   Conclusion   Conclusion

Why shallow? _____

_____

9. Some Sabines of Today   *Revised Parts*
   Introduction   Introduction

    I. who the Sabines were   I. _____

   II. where the Sabines   II. _____
   lived
     III. what the Sabines did   III. _____
   Conclusion   Conclusion

Why shallow? _____

_____

10. What Is a Definition Essay?   *Revised Parts*
    Introduction   Introduction

    I. its length   I. _____

   II. its neatness   II. _____

  III. its introduction   III. _____
    Conclusion   Conclusion

Why shallow? _____

_____

    Name: _____ Date: _____

EXERCISE 12H: Construct a definition for each topic below. First, decide on a purpose for your definition. Next, select the parts which should be discussed in order to achieve your purpose.

1. Topic: success

   Your purpose: _____

   _____

   Parts selected: I. _____

                      II. _____

                      III. _____

2. Topic: a penny

   Your purpose: _____

   _____

   Parts selected: I. _____

                      II. _____

                      III. _____

3. Topic: your block or neighborhood

   Your purpose: _____

   _____

   Parts selected: I. _____

                      II. _____

                      III. _____

4. Topic: violence

   Your purpose: _____

   _____

   Parts selected: I. _____

                      II. _____

                      III. _____

Name: _____ Date: _____

5. Topic: the revolutionary

   Your purpose: _____

   _____

   Parts selected: I. _____

                         II. _____

                        III. _____

6. Topic: the radio

   Your purpose: _____

   _____

   Parts selected: I. _____

                         II. _____

                        III. _____

7. Topic: Disneyland

   Your purpose: _____

   _____

   Parts selected: I. _____

                         II. _____

                        III. _____

8. Topic: voting rights

   Your purpose: _____

   _____

   Parts selected: I. _____

                         II. _____

                        III. _____

Name: _____ Date: _____

9. Topic: the educated man

Your purpose: _____

_____

Parts selected: I. _____

II. _____

III. _____

10. Topic: God

Your purpose: _____

_____

Parts selected: I. _____

II. _____

III. _____

Name: _____ Date: _____

Arguing an Opinion

Most people like to have reasonable, well thought-out opinions on many of the subjects which are of major concern in life. Intelligent opinions should be based on evidence which is factual and logical. Such opinions, however, should not be rigidly unchangeable; if an argument presents either new evidence or a new approach to already known evidence, people should be openminded enough to alter their opinion.

In arguing an opinion your purpose is to tell the reader *why* you have your opinion and to persuade him to agree with you. By the use of facts, reasons, examples, authorities, and other evidence, you should build a forceful and convincing argument.

To evaluate the effectiveness of an essay which argues an opinion, you should ask two questions:

(a) IS THE OPINION BASED ON FACTS AND SPECIFIC EVIDENCE RATHER THAN ON PERSONAL JUDGMENTS AND EMOTIONAL REACTIONS? A fact is something which can be clearly measured or observed; specific evidence is something which comes from a recognized authority, such as an encyclopedia, book, or person who is an expert.

☞ YOU DO THIS:

Select which of each set is a fact:

1. _____ Randi is a lovely girl.
   _____ Randi has smooth skin, liquid brown eyes, and flashing, white teeth.

2. _____ According to Judge Jonah Goldstein, author of the essay "Give Drugs to Addicts So We Can Be Safe," between two per cent and ten per cent of all drug addicts are permanently cured.
   _____ Drug addicts are hopeless derelicts who refuse to try to help themselves.

3. _____ Mach 1, the speed of sound, is usually given as 1088 feet per second at sea level when the temperature is 32 degrees.
   _____ There is power in speed.

(b) DOES THE METHOD OF PRESENTING THE OPINION HAVE ENOUGH IM-PACT TO PERSUADE THE READER TO AGREE? Some of the devices useful when planning an effective argument can be borrowed from the three other types of expository essays discussed in this and the preceding chapter:

(1) To support an opinion, include a dramatic incident which illustrates the main point.

(2) To explain an opinion, describe the process of how something is, was, or might be.

(3) To clarify an opinion, construct a clear definition of a key term or concept.

☞ YOU DO THIS:

Refer to the essay "Give Drugs to Addicts So We Can Be Safe," which appears at the beginning of this chapter.

1. What incident does the author use at the beginning of the essay?

_____

_____

2. In paragraphs six through nine, the author describes a process. What

is it? _____

_____

_____

3. In paragraph five the author briefly defines what makes a drug addict

dangerous. Summarize the definition: _____

_____

_____

(a) The *introduction* should lead into the reasons for your opinion. This can be done by:

    (1) stating your opinion at the outset;

    (2) giving an appropriate incident which will clearly illustrate and give impact to your opinion;

    (3) asking a provocative question which will stimulate thought on the subject of your opinion.

(b) The *full statement of your opinion* should appear where it has the most impact. This can be done in the introduction, main body, or conclusion.

    (1) If your opinion is in the introduction, all reasons given must relate directly back to your basic position and the conclusion should include a restatement of your opinion.

    (2) If your opinion is in the main body, it should smoothly follow the device used in the introduction.

    (3) If your opinion is in the conclusion, it should not come as a surprise. All reasons which are presented must build to the inevitable climax or conclusion.

(c) The *support for your opinion* should be based on facts, examples, authorities, and other specific evidence. This support must be strong enough to stand on its own. The reader should be able to form an intelligent opinion from the evidence you have presented; you should not have to insist that you are correct.

(d) Your argument should be logical. Refer to Chapter Seven for a more complete discussion of logic so that you will be reminded not to make errors such as oversimplification, generalization, attacking the man, etc.

(e) For impact try these argument techniques:

    (1) To illustrate:

        . . . use a dramatic incident.

        . . . explain the process of how something was, is, or might be.

    (2) To clarify:

        . . . give a clear definition of a key term.

        . . . ask an organizing question to give focus.

        . . . anticipate an objection by stating it and then answering it.

    (3) To dramatize:

        . . . give the dangers of the present system.

        . . . make a comparison to something else.

EXERCISE 12I: Read each of the following statements carefully. Label each either *fact* or *opinion*.

1. Babe Ruth hit 714 home runs, which is the record number of home runs in baseball history. _____

2. The sun is a majestic phenomenon of nature. _____

3. The sonic booms made by jets breaking the sound barrier are a terrible nuisance. _____

4. The word "Mach," which precedes a number to describe supersonic speeds, comes from the name of the German physicist Ernest Mach, who specialized in the study of sound. _____

5. We say that it is hot when the temperature reaches ninety degrees. But consider the sun: its surface temperature is estimated to be 10,000 degrees Farenheit, and its inner temperature is estimated to be 35,000,000 degrees Farenheit! _____

6. The flag of Canada is very beautiful. _____

7. Alcoholics are addicted to alcohol. _____

8. Babe Ruth was a fantastic baseball player. _____

9. When a plane moves at the speed of sound, it is at Mach 1. _____

10. The Mason-Dixon line, the symbolic division between the North and South, is useless. _____

11. The effects of LSD are wonderful. _____

12. The effects of LSD are awful. _____

13. Recent scientific studies have revealed that LSD can, among other things, affect the genes and cause birth defects. _____

14. There are estimated to be 6,000,000 alcoholics in America _____

15. When a plane flies at Mach 1 or more, people on the ground can hear the thunderclap boom as the plane breaks the sound barrier; however, the pilot in the plane does not hear it. _____

Name: _____ Date: _____

EXERCISE 12J: Many essays in this book are excellent examples of arguing an opinion. It can help your writing to notice the methods of other writers. Use your own paper for the answers to the following.

1. Refer to "The New Case for Chastity" by Ernest Gordon, which appears at the beginning of Chapter Three.

    (a) Read paragraph one. What is the author's opinion?
    (b) What argument technique does the author use in paragraph three?... paragraph seven?... paragraphs fifteen through eighteen?
    (c) Read paragraph ten. How does the author support his opinion?
    (d) Read paragraph twenty-one. Summarize the definition which is developed.
    (e) *Your Reaction:*
        ...Do you think that the author gives enough support for his opinion? Why or why not?
        ...Do you think that this is an effective argument? Why or why not?

2. Refer to "Four Choices for Young People" by John Fischer, which appears at the beginning of Chapter Eight.
    (a) Read paragraphs one and two. With what technique does the author begin his argument?
    (b) In what paragraph does the author first present his opinion? Summarize that opinion.
    (c) What argument techniques the author does use in paragraph six? ... paragraphs eight through twenty-one?
    (d) Does the author restate his opinion at the end of the essay? In what paragraph?
    (e) *Your Reaction:*
        ...Do you think that the author gives enough support for his argument? Why or why not?

3. Refer to "Give Drugs to Addicts So We Can Be Safe" by Jonah Goldstein, which appears at the beginning of Chapter Thirteen.
    (a) In what paragraph is the author's opinion first given? Briefly summarize that opinion.
    (b) What argument technique does the author use in paragraph two? ... paragraph three? ... paragraph ten? ... paragraph sixteen? ... paragraphs eighteen and nineteen? ... paragraph twenty-two? ... paragraph twenty-six?
    (c) In what paragraphs does the author restate his opinion?
    (d) *Your Reaction:*
        ...Do you think that the author gives enough support for his opinion? Why or why not?
        ...Do you think that this is an effective argument? Why or why not?

367

EXERCISE 12K REFRESHER:

1. Correct any errors in parallelism, in logical word placement, and in logical relationship between "set-off" sections and the sentences to which they are attached.
2. On separate paper rewrite the paragraph, rearranging the sentences in a more logical order for a process.

Several community-sponsored drug rehabilitation programs have been formed in the large American cities which are highly successful. Because they are sometimes asked to lecture on drug addiction, the addicts attend an afternoon seminar on public speaking. Each addict ends the day at a private meeting with a counselor, who discusses the addict's progress and offers advice about the future. If the addict is still taking drugs when he comes to the organization, he is first sent to a local hospital. Although these programs may vary in some ways, each uses a similar process. Later in the day the topic of conversation moves from public speaking to current news items. After having talked about such varied subjects as the World Series, the stock market, and popular music, the discussion becomes much more serious as the addicts begin to tell about their problems When the addict is finally cured mentally, the organization helps to find him a job and gives him the encouragement he needs to resist the temptation of drugs. After three weeks of "kicking" the habit phy-

Name: _____ Date: _____

sically, he leaves the hospital and joins the daily schedule of the program. In the morning the addicts usually visit a museum, go to a ball game, or they may take a boat ride.

SPRINGBOARDS TO WRITING

1. As a result of looking at the photographs, reading the essay, or answering the questions which followed each, you might have some thoughts about the central theme—drug addiction. (Look back at those pages to refresh your memory.) For help in planning such an essay, refer to the Guide for Planning an Essay, which appears in Springboards to Writing, Chapter One on page 25.

2. Here are some topics which have not been directly mentioned in the questions asked so far. Perhaps one of them could be a springboard for you:

In planning one of the following, try to use the technique of explaining a process. Remember to select the order that will be most effective for your purpose.

    (a) How to Curb Drug Addiction.
    (b) How to Educate Young People to the Dangers of Drug Addiction.
    (c) How to Prevent Your Child from Becoming a Drug Addict.
    (d) A Plan for Rehabilitating Drug Addicts.

In planning one of the following try to use the technique of constructing a definition. Remember to first decide on a purpose for your definition, then select the parts which will reflect your purpose.

    (e) Drug Addiction—An Illness or a Crime?
    (f) Narcotics—A Personal or a Public Problem?
    (g) What Is Heroin?
    (h) "Cop Outs" of the Older Generation.
    (i) What Does It Mean to Be Alienated?
    (j) What Is Justice?

In planning one of the following try to use the technique of arguing an opinion. Remember to support your opinion with specific facts and evidence and to include devices which have enough impact to persuade the reader to agree with you.

    (k) The Case for (against) Legalizing the Sale of Marijuana.
    (l) LSD—To Expand the Mind or Destroy It?
    (m) Drugs as a "Cop Out" for Young People.
    (n) The Effectiveness of Synanon, Daytop Village, Federal Hospitals for Addicts, etc.
    (o) We Can (Cannot) Legislate Morality.

APPENDIX I: PRINCIPAL PARTS OF VERBS

The principal parts of a verb are its

1. Present	This part is formed from the infinitive by dropping the word *to* and using the stem that remains.
	    For example:
	    infinitive: *to walk*
	    present: *walk*

2. Past	
3. Past participle	This part is used only with a helping verb such as: **am, is, was, were, have, has, had,** etc. For example: He *has built* his own car.

Many verbs can be put into the past form and the past participle form merely by adding *-d* or *-ed* to the present stem. For example:

Present	*Past*	*Past participle*
walk	walked	walked
live	lived	lived
use	used	used

Many other verbs are unusual in their past form and/or their past participle form. Here is a list of the principal parts of such verbs:

Present	*Past*	*Past participle*
am	was	been
arise	arose	arisen
awake	awoke or awaked	awaked
bear	bore	borne
beat	beat	beaten
become	became	become
begin	began	begun
bend	bent	bent
bet	bet	bet
bid (offer)	bid	bid
bid (command)	bade	bidden
bind	bound	bound
bite	bit	bitten or bit
blow	blew	blown
break	broke	broken
bring	brought	brought

Present	Past	Past participle
build	built	built
burst	burst	burst
buy	bought	bought
cast	cast	cast
catch	caught	caught
choose	chose	chosen
cling	clung	clung
come	came	come
cost	cost	cost
creep	crept	crept
deal	dealt	dealt
dig	dug	dug
dive	dived or dove	dived
do	did	done
drag	dragged	dragged
draw	drew	drawn
drink	drank	drunk
drive	drove	driven
drown	drowned	drowned
eat	ate	eaten
fall	fell	fallen
feed	fed	fed
fight	fought	fought
find	found	found
flee	fled	fled
fling	flung	flung
fly	flew	flown
forbid	forbade or forbad	forbidden
forget	forgot	forgotten or forgot
forsake	forsook	forsaken
freeze	froze	frozen
get	got	got or gotten
give	gave	given
go	went	gone
grow	grew	grown
hang (suspend)	hung	hung
hang (execute)	hanged	hanged
hide	hid	hidden
hold	held	held
keep	kept	kept
know	knew	known
lay	laid	laid
lead	led	led
leave	left	left

Present	Past	Past participle
lend	lent	lent
lie	lay	lain
light	lighted or lit	lighted or lit
lose	lost	lost
make	made	made
mean	meant	meant
pay	paid	paid
prove	proved	proved or proven
raise	raised	raised
read	read	read
rid	rid	rid
ride	rode	ridden
ring	rang	rung
rise	rose	risen
run	ran	run
say	said	said
see	saw	seen
seek	sought	sought
sell	sold	sold
set	set	set
shake	shook	shaken
shine (glow)	shone	shone
shine (polish)	shined	shined
show	showed	shown or showed
shrink	shrank	shrunk
sing	sang	sung
sink	sank	sunk
sit	sat	sat
slay	slew	slain
sling	slung	slung
speak	spoke	spoken
spend	spent	spent
spin	spun	spun
spring	sprang or sprung	sprung
stand	stood	stood
steal	stole	stolen
sting	stung	stung
stink	stank	stunk
stride	strode	stridden
strike	struck	struck
strive	strove	striven
swear	swore	sworn
swim	swam	swum
swing	swung	swung

Present	Past	Past participle
take	took	taken
teach	taught	taught
tear	tore	torn
think	thought	thought
throw	threw	thrown
wake	woke or waked	waked
wear	wore	worn
wring	wrung	wrung
write	wrote	written

VERB EXERCISE: Using the verb given in front of each sentence, fill in the correct form of the verb in the blank space provided. For unusual forms consult the list of principal parts of the verb.

1. *to catch*: Peter was the one who _____ the fish that they are eating for dinner.

2. *to give*: Your fraternity has _____ a great deal of money to charity.

3. *to seek*: We _____ to uncover the riddle in her words.

4. *to know*: Mitchell should have _____ that we would tease him.

5. *to prove*: Dr. Bork has _____ that calories do count.

6. *to fall*: Because of the blast all of the books have _____ off of the library shelves.

7. *to swim*: Yesterday Allen _____ two miles in an hour.

8. *to break*: You have _____ your promise to me for the last time.

9. *to awake*: Tom _____ at four-thirty in the morning.

10. *to join*: We have _____ the gym club in order to get in shape.

11. *to teach*: John's father has _____ him how to drive.

12. *to write*: Have you _____ your term report for history?

13. *to drown*: Because he was knocked unconscious by the rock, the boy _____ in four feet of water.

14. *to become*: His mother thinks that he has _____ too independent.

15. *to strike*: Casey _____ out with three on base.

16. *to drink*: Ed has _____ more beer than any of us.

17. *to begin*: I have _____ to understand what hard work means.

18. *to creep*: He _____ through the jungle as quietly as possible.

19. *to eat*: Carmen has _____ more than anyone else.

20. *to cry*: The baby _____ all day long.

APPENDIX II: COMMON PREFIXES AND SUFFIXES

A *prefix* is a syllable which, when added to the beginning of a word, affects its meaning.

A *suffix* is a syllable which, when added to the end of a word, affects its meaning.

Being familiar with the most common prefixes and suffixes can help you to increase your vocabulary and improve your spelling.

Common Prefixes

meaning AGINST

anti-	antiballistic
contra-	contrary

meaning MORE THAN

extra-	extraordinary
hyper-	hypersensitive
super-	superman
ultra-	ultraconservative

meaning THE NEGATIVE

dis-	disagree
il-	illegal
im-	immoral
in-	inadequate
ir-	irresponsible
mal-	malnutrition
mis-	mistake
non-	noninvolvement
un-	unhappy

concerning numbers: meaning . . .

HALF:	semi-	semicircle
ONE:	uni-	uniform
ONE:	mono-	monologue
MANY:	poly-	polysyllable

concerning place: meaning . . .

BEFORE:	ante-	anteroom
BEFORE:	pre-	predate
AFTER:	post-	postscript
BACK:	re-	return
BACK:	retro-	retrofire
UNDER:	sub-	submarine
ACROSS:	trans-	transplant
BETWEEN:	inter-	interpersonal
INSIDE:	intra-	intravenous

meaning SELF:

auto-	automobile

Common Suffixes

noun *meaning* ACTION

-tion   segregation

noun *meaning* STATE OF

-hood   manhood
-ment   estrangement
-ness   kindness
-ship   friendship
-tude   gratitude
-dom   freedom

adjective *meaning* ABLE TO BE

-able   comfortable
-ible   compatible

adjective *meaning* FULL OF

-ate   passionate
-ful   tactful
-ous   pompous
-y   gloomy

adjective *meaning* NONE

-less   penniless

verb *meaning* TO MAKE, TO PERFORM

-ate   integrate
-ify   unify
-ize   computerize

EXERCISE PS1: To determine the correct prefix for a word, you will often have to consult the dictionary. In this exercise, however, the correct prefix is supplied. Form the following words:

	Using the prefix:	*Form:*	
1.	un	not truthful	_____
2.	il	not logical	_____
3.	semi	half civilized	_____
4.	post	date it after	_____
5.	non	not athletic	_____
6.	in	not decent	_____
7.	anti	against the freeze	_____
8.	uni	one sphere	_____
9.	im	not possible	_____
10.	dis	not appear	_____
11.	hyper	excessively active	_____
12.	sub	below the conscious	_____
13.	ir	not rational	_____
14.	mal	not functioning	_____
15.	mis	not understood	_____

EXERCISE PS2: For each word below, give a general definition. (If you are unsure of a meaning, consult your dictionary.) Next, briefly explain how the prefix influenced the word's meaning.

1. autobiography: _____

2. retrorocket: _____

3. supernatural: _____

4. prehistoric _____

5. transform: _____

6. monogamy: _____

7. polygamy: _____

8. reconcile: _____

9. ultrahigh (frequency): _____

10. intrastate (highway): _____

11. interstate (highway): _____

12. extrasensory: _____

13. contradiction: _____

14. antechamber: _____

EXERCISE PS3: Construct each word by referring to the list of common suffixes and, if necessary, to the dictionary.

1. noun: state of being happy _____

2. noun: act of flirting _____

3. noun: state of being a child _____

4. adjective: full of fortune _____

5. adjective: able to agree _____

6. adjective: having no worth _____

7. verb: to make ideal _____

8. verb: to make beautiful _____

9. noun: state of being an apprentice _____

10. noun: state of being contented _____

11. adjective: full of wind   _____

12. adjective: able to deduct   _____

13. noun: state of being solitary   _____

14. noun: state of being a serf   _____

15. adjective: full of thanks   _____

16. adjective: full of courage   _____

17. verb: to make originally   _____

A PREFIX-SUFFIX SPELLING NOTE. Are you ever unsure of whether to use one or two "l's" in "generally" or one or two "s's" in "misspell"? The following principle concerning prefixes and suffixes will help you to avoid this type of confusion.

When the prefix ends with the same letter that begins the main part of the word, be sure to include both letters.

When the suffix begins with the same letter that ends the main part of the word, be sure to include both letters.

☞ YOU DO THIS:

Create a new word by joining each prefix or suffix with its main word.

ideal + ly = _____   mean + ness = _____

ir + regular = _____   il + legal = _____

un + necessary = _____   over + run = _____

Here are some examples:

dis + satisfied = dis*s*atisfied   im + moral = im*m*oral

inter + racial = inter*r*acial   ir + relevant = ir*r*elevant

mis + state = mis*s*tate   il + logical = il*l*ogical

☞ YOU DO THIS:

Create a new word by joining each prefix or suffix with its main word.

cruel + ly = _____   un + natural = _____

ir + resistible = _____   definite + ly = _____

dis + appoint = _____   over + ripe = _____

EXERCISE PS4: Fill in the missing letters in each word using either one or two of the letters indicated. If necessary, refer back to the list of common prefixes and suffixes.

1. *r*   i___esponsible
2. *n*   drunke___ess
3. *r*   i___eplaceable
4. *s*   mi___pelling
5. *s*   di___appear
6. *l*   accidenta___y
7. *n*   u___eighborly
8. *r*   inte___action
9. *s*   di___illusioned
10. *r*   inte___eaction

11. *r*   ove___ated
12. *n*   u___acceptable
13. *l*   i___igitimate
14. *n*   kee___ess
15. *s*   mi___inform
16. *r*   inte___elationship
17. *m*   i___ature
18. *s*   di___agreeable
19. *r*   ove___ule
20. *l*   i___iterate

INDEX OF VOCABULARY WORDS

oppressed, 32
optimistic, 9
ostracism, 32
output, 144
overwhelmed, 275

p

parasitic, 205, 206
pastoral, 205, 206
pauper, 276
peers, 116
perception, 339
persistent, 181, 182
perspicacious, 181, 182
plethora, 89
pompous, 9
pragmatic, 205, 206
precarious, 309
premise, 179, 180
primitive, 311
probe, 88
program, 144
promiscuity, 55
propels, 247
propulsion, 86, 87
protest, 114
provocative, 55
psychedelic, 339

r

racist, 32
railed, 247
rationalization, 179, 180
razed, 247
reality, 339
reconcile, 116
reconnaissance, 86, 87
redolent, 311
rehabilitate, 337
relevant, 179, 180
reluctance, 245, 246
rendezvous, 88
resentment, 145
restive, 114
retaliation, 245, 246
revolutionary, 205, 206
rift, 114
righteous, 56

romanticist, 8
Rousseau, 209, 210
routine, 145

s

Sabines, 309
satellite, 88
sedatives, 337
segregation, 32
shanty, 276
skepticism, 205, 206
slum, 275
sovereignty, 309
stake, 114
stark, 311
status, 114
stigma, 337
stunned, 245, 246
suave, 9
subsistence, 276

t

tactful, 9, 10
technological, 143
temperamental, 309
tenement, 275
tension, 145
tragedy, 309
transform, 116
Trotsky, Leon, 209

u

undernourished, 276
unify, 89
universal, 114
unscrupulous, 56
upgrades, 145

v

valiant, 309
Vergil, 209, 210
violation, 34

w

weary, 275
wench, 8
werewolf, 9, 10

INDEX OF SPELLING DEMONS

d

decision, 35
defense, 249
definitely, 91
definition, 211
dependent, 278
describe, 91
description, 146
desire, 183
despair, 211
desperate, 341
determine, 57
different, 278
difficult, 11
dilemma, 117
dimension, 183
disastrous, 146
discussion, 341
disease, 146
disgust, 249
disillusioned, 35
dissolve, 91
distinguish, 57
due, 278
during, 312

e

eager, 11
easily, 341
efficient, 11
eliminate, 341
embarrassing, 57
emphasize, 183
endeavor, 146
enjoy, 57
enough, 278
environment, 117
escape, 211
especially, 117
estimate, 341
evidently, 91
exactly, 183
examine, 183
exclaim, 183
exercise, 117
existence, 117

expense, 11
experience, 57
explanation, 249
exquisite, 183
extremely, 146

f

familiar, 11
fantasy, 11
fashion, 183
favorite, 341
finally, 341
fortunately, 211
forty, 91
forward, 312
fourth, 211
fulfill, 117
fundamental, 249
further, 278

g

genuine, 57
government, 35
governor, 341
group, 249
guarantee, 11
guard, 211
guess, 183

h

height, 91
huge, 183
hundred, 278

i

imagination, 35
immediately, 312
immense, 183
importance, 183
increase, 341
individually, 117
inevitable, 211
influence, 57
instance, 183
intelligence, 183
interest, 11

interrupt, 146
involve, 312
irresistible, 183

k

knowledge, 117

l

laborer, 146
library, 183
lonely, 11

m

machinery, 146
magazine, 91
maintain, 312
majority, 211
management, 211
manner, 183
manufacturer, 146
marriage, 57
matter, 249
meant, 57
medical, 146
melancholy, 278
mention, 341
merchandise, 341
methods, 57
minutes, 249
muscle, 146
mysterious, 91

n

narrative, 312
naturally, 91
necessary, 117
nervous, 146
noble, 211
nuclear, 312
numerous, 146

o

obstacle, 35
official, 312

operate, 91
opponent, 183
opportunity, 249
opposite, 183
organization, 117
original, 57
originate, 91

p

particular, 57
peculiar, 146
performance, 146
permanent, 57
persistent, 183
personal, 11
persuade, 211
phenomenon, 249
physical, 35
pleasant, 249
political, 211
population, 211
possible, 117
practical, 57
practice, 91
preparation, 11
presence, 312
prevalent, 35
primitive, 312
prisoner, 341
privilege, 35
probably, 249
problem, 312
professor, 249
prominent, 249
psychology, 11

q

quarter, 211

r

realize, 57
really, 278
recognize, 57
recommend, 211
region, 211
religion, 249

remember, 278
representative, 91
response, 312
responsible, 211
restaurant, 183
reveal, 91
rough, 211

s

safety, 312
salary, 146
schedule, 35
separate, 35
several, 249
shoulder, 312
significance, 57
similar, 11
simple, 341
simply, 57
since, 35
sophomore, 11
source, 249
speech, 35
strength, 35
substantial, 341
substitute, 146
succeed, 211
suggestion, 249
suppose, 117
surprise, 11
symbol, 57

t

technique, 146
temperamental, 312
tendency, 249
themselves, 312
theory, 11
therefore, 57
thoroughly, 312
thought, 278
together, 312
tomorrow, 211
tragedy, 35
tremendous, 91
tyranny, 35

v

variety, 278
various, 91

w

warrant, 91
welfare, 278
woman, 278
wonderful, 278
write, 341

GENERAL INDEX

Collective noun:
  agreement with pronouns, 128
  agreement with verbs, 124
Collective subject:
  agreement with pronouns, 128
  agreement with verbs, 124
Colloquial language, 294–296
Colon:
  after opening in letter, 220
  basic uses, 228
Comma, 216–220
  with conventional material, 220
  with coordinate adjectives, 217–218
  in coordinate sentences, 96, 217
  with interrupters, 219–220
  with interrupting subordinate section,
    104–105
  with introductory material, 218
  with introductory subordinate section,
    99
  with nonrestrictive clauses, and
    phrases, 104–105
  in series, 216
Comma fault, 69–70
Commands, 62–63
Comma splice:
  correction of, 70
  identification of, 69–70
Commonly confused verbs:
  lay, lie, 283
  learn, teach, 284
  leave, let, 284
  raise, rise, 284
  sit, set, 284
  stay, stand, 284
Commonly confused words:
  list of 147–148
  memory tricks for, 148
Comparative form for comparisons, 282
Comparison and contrast, in paragraph
    development, 40
Comparisons:
  of adjectives and adverbs, 282
  false, 189
Complimentary close of letter, comma
    with, 220
Compound nouns:
  formation of plurals, 249
  formation of possessives, 213

Compound nouns (*cont.*)
  hyphenated, 279
Concluding paragraph:
  common errors to avoid in, 162–163
  types of, 161–162
Conclusions, 161–163
Conjugated verb, defined, 61
Conjunctions:
  coordinating, 95–96, 217
  subordinating, 64, 98
Connectors, 95
Constructing a definition, the essay,
    353–356
Contractions:
  avoided in formal writing, 294
  formation of, 212
Contrast, in paragraph development, 40
Conventional material, commas with, 220
Coordinate adjectives, comma to separate,
    217–218
Coordinate sentences:
  formation of, 95–96
  use of comma to separate, 96, 217
Coordinating conjunctions:
  use in coordination, 95–96
  use of comma before, 96, 217
Coordination:
  excessive, 96, 100
  how to employ, 95–96
  use of comma in, 96, 217
Costume, custom, 147
Could have, not *could of,* 286
Could hardly, not *couldn't hardly,* 286
Could scarcely, not *couldn't scarcely,* 286
Cousins, Norman, "Sabines, Shoes, and
    Sanity," 306–307
Cubbedge, Robert, "Man and the
    Machine," 136–141
Custom, costume, 147

d

Danger words:
  as cause of fragments, 64–65
  used properly in subordination, 98
Dangling modifiers, 324–325
Dangling participles, 324–325
Dash, 228
Dates, use of commas in, 220

Decrease (and increase), vocabulary of, 89

Definition:
    constructing in an essay, 353–356
    in paragraph development, 39

Deliberate repetition of key words:
    to link paragraphs, 259–260
    to link sentences, 258–259

Desert, dessert, 148

Dessert, desert, 148

Details in a paragraph, ordering of, 42–44

Development, methods of paragraph, 20–22, 39–40

Diction, 282–296
    commonly confused verbs, 283–284
    comparisons, 282
    informal language, 294–296
    usage glossary, 285–286, 288

Dictionary, use of in spelling, 11

Different from, not different than, 286

Direct question, punctuation of, 227

Direct quotation, punctuation of, 229

Doubling, spelling rule, 341

Dropping the final *e*, spelling rule, 312–313

e

Each and *every:*
    agreement with pronouns, 128
    agreement with verbs, 122–123

Effect, affect, 147

Either and *neither:*
    agreement with pronouns, 128
    agreement with verbs, 123

Either, or:
    agreement with pronouns, 129
    agreement with verbs, 122

Either-or argument, 187

Emphasis words, informal and formal, 296

Errors to avoid in introductions and conclusions, 162–163

Essay pattern, 154

Essays:
    "Boy . . . Girl . . . Computer" by Gene Shalit, 2–7
    "Bull Connor's Birmingham" by

Essays (*cont.*)
    Martin Luther King, Jr., 28–30
    "Case for Drafting All Boys—And Girls, The" by Margaret Mead, 110–113
    "Celestial Crockery" by J. P. Chaplin, 80–85
    "Four Choices for Young People" by John Fischer, 200–204
    "Give Drugs to Addicts So We Can Be Safe" by Jonah J. Goldstein, 332–336
    "Love Is a Fallacy" by Max Shulman, 170–178
    "Man and the Machine" by Robert Cubbedge, 136–141
    "New Case for Chastity, The" by Dr. Ernest Gordon, 50–53
    "Sabines, Shoes, and Sanity" by Norman Cousins, 306–307
    "Who Cares?" by Leonard Gross, 240–244
    "Why, There's Not Enough Money Here for Prostitution . . ." by Ben Bagdikian, 270–274

Essay types:
    arguing an opinion, 363–365
    constructing a definition, 353–356
    explaining a process, 344–348

Essay writing, expository form, 152–154

Every one, everyone, 278

Everyone, everybody, everything:
    agreement with pronouns, 128
    agreement with verbs, 123

Everyone, every one, 278

Everyone-is-doing-it argument, 188

Evidence:
    adequate, 188
    relevant, 187

Examples, in paragraph development, 21

Except, accept, 147

Excessive coordination, 96, 100

Exclamation point, 227

Explaining a process, the essay, 344–348

Exposition, defined, 152

Expository essays:
    arguing an opinion, 363–365
    constructing a definition, 353–356
    explaining a process, 344–348
    general form of, 152–154

l

Later, latter, 148
Latter, former, 286
Latter, later, 148
Lay, lie, 283
Learn, teach, 284
Leave, let, 284
Less, fewer, 286
Let, leave, 284
Letters of alphabet, plurals of, 212
Lie, lay, 283
Like, as (as if), 288
Limiting the topic:
   of an essay, 152
   of a paragraph, 16–17
Linking expressions, 253–255
Literature, guides to, 211
Location, order of, in a paragraph, 44
Logic, 185–189
   adequate evidence, 188
   appropriate authority, 188
   attacking the man, 185
   circular reasoning, 189
   either-or argument, 187
   everyone-is-doing-it argument, 188
   false analogy, 189
   false cause, 187
   false comparison, 189
   feeding prejudices, 186
   generalization, 185
   guilt by association, 185
   hasty generalization, 188
   oversimplification, 186
   personal knowledge, 189
   qualifying positive statements, 188
   relevant evidence, 187
Logic, vocabulary of, 179–181
Logical relationship between a "set-off"
      section and the sentence to which
      it is attached, 324–325
Logical word placement for precise
      meaning, 321
Loose, lose, loss, 148
Lose, loose, loss, 148
Loss, lose, loose, 148
"Love Is a Fallacy" by Max Shulman,
   170–178

m

Machine in mass society, vocabulary of,
   143–144
Main body idea patterns, 154
Main body paragraphs:
   in definition essays, 356
   in process essays, 347
Main idea, in a paragraph, 15–16
Main ideas, in an essay:
   appropriateness, 153–154
   patterns, 154
"Man and the Machine" by Robert
      Cubbedge, 136–141
Man in mass society, vocabulary of, 145
Marks of punctuation, 216–220, 227–229
   (*See also* Punctuation)
Mass society:
   vocabulary of the machine in, 143–144
   vocabulary of man in, 145
May be, maybe, 278
Maybe, may be, 278
May, can, 286
Mead, Margaret, "The Case for Drafting
      All Boys—And Girls," 110–113
Methods to improve your spelling, 11–12
Might have, not *might of,* 286
Mind, words to describe the, 181–182
Misplaced modifiers, 321
Misplaced words, 321
Mnemonic devices:
   for commonly confused words, 148
   for sound-alikes, 37
   use in spelling, 12
Modifiers:
   dangling, 324–325
   misplaced, 321
Moral, morale, 148
Morale, moral, 148
Morality, words about, 55–56
Mythology, guides to, 211

n

Negative words, 34
Neither, nor:
   agreement with pronouns, 129
   agreement with verbs, 122

"New Case for Chastity, The" by Dr.
    Ernest Gordon, 50–53
Nobody, nothing:
    agreement with pronouns, 128
    agreement with verbs, 123
None, verb agreement with, 123
Nonrestrictive sections:
    formation of, 104–105
    use of commas with, 219–220
Nor, as coordinating conjunction, 95–96
Not only . . . but also, verb agreement
    with, 122
Noun combinations:
    formation of plurals, 249
    formation of possessives, 213
Nouns:
    collective, 124, 128
    defined, 128
Number, amount, 285
Numbers:
    compound, hyphen in, 279
    plurals of, 212
    when to use numerals; when to use
        words, 294

o

Opening of letter, punctuation of, 220
Opinion, arguing in an essay, 363–365
Or, as coordinating conjunction, 95–96
Ordering details in essays:
    in definition essays, 356
    in process essays, 347
Ordering details in a paragraph:
    order of importance, 42
    order of location, 44
    order of time, 43
Ought, not *had ought*, 288
Oversimplification, 186

p

Paragraph principles, applied to essay
    writing, 152–154
Paragraphs:
    arrangement of details in, 42–44
    coherence in, 253–260
    concluding, 161–162, 162–163

Paragraphs (*cont.*)
    development of, 20–22, 39–40
    introductory, 159–160, 162–163
    limiting topics of, 16–17
    methods of development, 20–22,
        39–40
        comparison and contrast, 40
        definition, 39
        examples, 21
        facts, 20
        incident, anecdote, or story, 21
    ordering details in, 42–44
    principles to essay writing, 152–154
    topic sentence in, 15–17
    unity in, 253–260
Parallelism, 315–317
Parentheses, 228
Parts of speech:
    adjective, 217
    coordinating conjunctions, 95–96
    noun, 128
    pronoun, 128, 213
    subordinating conjunctions, 98
    verb, 61
Passed, past, 35
Past, passed, 35
Patterns:
    main body idea, 154
    from paragraph to essay, 152
Peace, piece, 36
People:
    reference books about, 211
    words about, 8–10
Period, 227
Personal knowledge, 189
Piece, peace, 36
Planning an essay, guide for, 25
Plurals:
    formation of, 249–250
    of letters, numbers, symbols, etc., 212
    of possessives, 212–213
Pointers to remember:
    in a definition essay, 356
    in an opinion essay, 365
    in a process essay, 347
Positive form for comparisons, 282
Positive statements, need to qualify, 188
Possessive pronouns, 213

Possessives, formation of, 213
Poverty, vocabulary of, 275–276
Prefixes:
    hyphen with, 279
    list of, 375
Present participle, 61
Principal parts of verbs, 371–374
Principal, principle, 36
Principle, principal, 36
Process, explaining in an essay, 344–348
Pronoun:
    agreement with antecedent, 128–129
    defined, 128, 213
    possessive, 213
    relative, 64
Proofreading:
    for errors in sentence logic, 325
    for fragments, 65
    for grammar and punctuation, 93
    for spelling, 91–93
Punctuation:
    apostrophe, 212–213
    colon, 220, 228
    comma, 216–220
    dash, 228
    exclamation point, 227
    hyphen, 279
    interabang, 227
    parentheses, 228
    period, 227
    question mark, 227
    quotation marks, 229
    semicolon, 227

q

Qualifying positive statements, 188
Question mark, 227
Quiet, quite, 148
Quite, quiet, 148
Quotation marks, 229

r

Raise, rise, 284
Reasoning:
    circular, 189
    faulty, 185–189
Reason is that, not *reason is because,* 288

Reference, tracking down a, 209–211
Reference books:
    Bartlett's Familiar Quotations, 160
    Columbia Encyclopedia, 211
    Current Biography, 211
    Information Please Almanac, 211
    Mythology of All Races, 211
    *New Century Handbook of English
        Literature,* 211
    Who's Who, 211
    World Almanac, 211
References, guidelines for using, 211
Relative pronouns:
    as cause of fragments, 64–65
    list of, 64
Relevant evidence, 187
Repetition of key words:
    to link paragraphs, 259–260
    to link sentences, 258–259
Restrictive sections:
    formation of, 104–105
    no commas with, 219–220
Rise, raise, 284
Rules for spelling:
    changing *y* to *i,* 58
    doubling, 341
    dropping the final *e,* 312–313
    ie and *ei,* 183
Run-on sentence:
    correction of, 70
    identification of, 69–70
Run-together sentence, 69–70

s

"Sabines, Shoes, and Sanity" by Norman
        Cousins, 306–307
Salutation of letter, punctuation of, 220
Semicolon:
    basic uses, 227
    between coordinate sentences, 95
Sentence completeness, three-step test
        of, 61–65
Sentence fragment:
    correction of, 61, 63, 65
    identification of, 61–65
Sentences:
    commands, 62–63
    comma splice in, 69–70

Vocabulary building *(cont.)*
  vocabulary of increase and decrease, 89
  vocabulary of logic, 179–181
  vocabulary of the machine in mass
    society, 143–144
  vocabulary of man in mass society, 145
  vocabulary of poverty, 275–276
  vocabulary of social change, 114–116
  vocabulary of space travel, 86–88
  vocabulary of war, 309
  words about morality, 55–56
  words about people, 8–10
  words to describe the mind, 181–182
Vocabulary:
  of addiction, 337–339
  of apathy, 245–246
  of civil rights, 32
  of increase and decrease, 89
  of logic, 179–181
  of the machine in mass society,
    143–144
  of man in mass society, 145
  of poverty, 275–276
  of social change, 114–116
  of space travel, 86–88
  of war, 309

W

War, vocabulary of, 309
Ways of life, and attitudes, 205–206
Weather, whether, 36
Well, good, 286
Where is, where are, agreement of
    subject after, 123

Where, that, 288
Whether, weather, 36
Which:
  referring to things or places, 104
  for subordination, 104
Which sections, commas with, 219–220
Who:
  referring to people, 104
  for subordination, 104
"Who Cares?" by Leonard Gross, 240–
    244
Who's whose, 36
Whose, who's, 36
Who sections, commas with, 219–220
"Why, There's Not Enough Money Here
    for Prostitution . . ." by Ben
    Bagdikian, 270–274
Words to describe the mind, 181–182
Words of emphasis, informal and formal,
    296
Words about morality, 55–56
Words about people, 8–10
Words of transition, 253–255
Would have, not *would of,* 286

y

Y to *i,* spelling rule for changing, 58
Yardsticks of mature writing, 285–286,
    288
You:
  in a command, 62
  informal tone of, 294
Your, you're, 36
You're, your, 36